Mark Twain and the Art
of the Tall Tale

Mark Twain
and the Art
of the Tall Tale

HENRY B. WONHAM

New York   Oxford
OXFORD UNIVERSITY PRESS
1993

Oxford University Press

Oxford   New York   Toronto
Delhi   Bombay   Calcutta   Madras   Karachi
Kuala Lumpur   Singapore   Hong Kong   Tokyo
Nairobi   Dar es Salaam   Cape Town
Melbourne   Auckland   Madrid

and associated companies in
Berlin   Ibadan

Copyright © 1993 by Oxford University Press, Inc.

Published by Oxford University Press, Inc.,
200 Madison Avenue, New York, New York 10016

Oxford is a registered trademark of Oxford University Press

Library of Congress Cataloging-in-Publication Data
Wonham, Henry B., 1960–
Mark Twain and the art of the tall tale /
by Henry B. Wonham.
p.   cm.   Includes bibliographical references and index.
ISBN 0-19-507801-2
1. Twain, Mark, 1835–1910—Technique.
2. Tall tales—United States—History and criticism.
3. Oral tradition—United States.
4. Narration (Rhetoric)   5. Fiction—Technique.
I. Title.   PS1341.W65   1993
813'.4—dc20   92-14291

Chapter 6, "The Contest for Narrative Authority in *The Adventures of Tom Sawyer*,"
appears in *Critical Essays on "The Adventures of Tom Sawyer,"* edited by
Gary Scharnhorst. © 1993 by Gary Scharnhorst. Used by permission of
G. K. Hall & Co., an imprint of Macmillan Publishing Company.

2 4 6 8 9 7 5 3 1

Printed in the United States of America
on acid-free paper

For
Cornelia Quarles Wonham
and
Anna Emory Wonham

Acknowledgments

This book profited at every stage from the advice and encouragement of Harold H. Kolb, Jr., who first suggested the topic to me
in a graduate seminar at the University of Virginia in 1986 and
then directed its progress during the next five years. His unyielding
standards for clarity of prose and reliable scholarship inform every
page, even where I have failed to meet them. I would also like to
thank Mark Edmundson for his valuable counsel and friendship
during the final stages of the project. Alan Howard and Edward
Ayers also read the manuscript with care and offered useful suggestions for the final draft.

To undertake a book on Mark Twain is to encounter a community of scholars that must be unique in the profession of literary
studies for the sympathy and good humor with which it greets and
encourages newcomers to the field. There are far too many members of that community to acknowledge by name, but I would
especially like to thank Gary Scharnhorst for his constant support
of my work. James M. Cox, Susan K. Harris, and John Easterly
also commented extensively on the manuscript and thus helped me
avoid numerous missteps and redundancies. Other scholars whose
important suggestions on individual chapters helped shape the final
version include Gary Kulik, Camilla A. Collins, and Alan Gribben.

Portions of the book have appeared elsewhere in print, and I
would like to thank the publishers for their permission to reproduce this material. Early versions of Chapters 1 and 7 first appeared in *American Quarterly* and *American Literary Realism*, re-
spectively, and Chapter 6 was published in *Critical Essays on "The
Adventures of Tom Sawyer,"* ed. Gary Scharnhorst (Boston: Hall,
1993). I would also like to thank Elizabeth Maguire, Susan Chang,

and others at Oxford University Press who helped prepare the final manuscript.

My greatest debt is to my wife, whose love, patience, and friendship have sustained me throughout the years of research and composition that went into this book. Without her constant support and encouragement during an extended and unplanned "sabbatical" period, I could never have contemplated this project, much less seen it through to the end. To her and to our daughter, Emory, this book is lovingly dedicated.

Orlean, Va.   H.B.W.
May 1992

Contents

Mark Twain and the Art
of the Tall Tale

Introduction

"The World Is Grown Too Incredulous"

In 1774, as the American colonists geared up for rebellion, the London *Public Advertiser* printed a letter by "A Freeholder of Old Sarum."[1] Geography, according to the author, naturally "encourages a mutinous Disposition" among the Crown's vassals in North America. Living at such a remote distance from "the supreme Lords of their Persons and Property," the Americans quite predictably deny the authority of Britain—not out of political conviction but because, like all children, they possess a naughty streak, one that tends to become more pronounced as the colonial population increases. The most significant threat to imperial authority, therefore, according to the author, is the "amazingly prolific" American woman, whose ability to produce abundant offspring may, "in less than a Century," permit the rebels to "slip their necks out of the Collar." To prevent the colonists from becoming "very numerous," the writer proposes to send the royal army on a peaceful military campaign through "the several towns of North America." He continues:

Let a Company of Sow-gelders, consisting of 100 Men, accompany the Army. On their Arrival at any Town or Village, let Orders be given that on the blowing of the Horn all the Males be assembled in the Market Place. . . . There may be a Clause in the Bill to be left at the Discretion of the General, whose Powers ought to be very extensive, that the most notorious Offenders, such as Hancock, Adams, &c. who have been the Ringleaders in the Rebellion of our

3

Servants, should be shaved quite close. . . . In the Course of fifty
years it is probable we shall not have one rebellious subject in North
America. This will be laying the Axe to the Root of the Tree.

The writer goes on to point out that such a foreign policy would
produce a good supply of colonial operatic talent for the British
Empire, thus reducing the Crown's costly dependence on Italy for
tenor voices. As a final point, the Freeholder of Old Sarum argues
convincingly that his proposal would "put a Stop to the Emigra-
tions from this Country now grown so very fashionable."

Londoners who were old enough to remember Swift's *A Modest
Proposal* (1729), which offered a satiric recommendation for population control in Ireland, probably laughed at the *Advertiser's* satire
of domestic chauvinism, but Benjamin Franklin, the letter's author, bagged more than a few credulous readers with his impersonation of Old Sarum. The satirical ventriloquism of Swift's *Modest
Proposal* had been practiced in England at least since the appearance of Defoe's shocking pamphlet *The Shortest Way with the
Dissenters* (1702), but no one in the mother country expected this
kind of wit from an American. Indeed, Franklin's most outspoken
fellow colonists, especially in sober New England, were equally unprepared to engage in an ironic political dialogue, preferring as
they did a more straightforward defense of life and liberty. When
American literary revolutionaries such as Joel Barlow and John
Trumbull did resort to satire, their radical views emerged clearly
and often humorlessly, as in Barlow's unambiguously entitled
poem "The Conspiracy of Kings." Occasionally, American satirists
aped the enemy by speaking from behind a royalist mask, but the
mask tended to be perfectly transparent, as in Philip Freneau's
"George the Third's Soliloquy."[2] American political satire would
eventually acquire its own approach to ventriloquism in the writings of such characters as James Russell Lowell's Birdofredum
Sawin and David Ross Locke's Petroleum Vesuvius Nasby, but
those indigenous philosophers would not begin writing until the
middle of the nineteenth century.[3] Franklin alone among Revolutionary satirists had learned from Britain's most skillful dissenters
how to manipulate an audience by voicing its prejudices ironically
and with a straight face. As Lewis Leary explains, it was "under
Franklin's aegis" that "the ventriloquist writer invaded the new

world," speaking for the first time "from behind a pseudonymous mask, as Washington Irving and Samuel Clemens would speak."[4]

Samuel L. Clemens was indeed a ventriloquist of the first order, but the mask he named Mark Twain wears a slightly different expression than Old Sarum's, an expression that Clemens developed by cultivating native resources. In fact, at around the time of Old Sarum's appearance in the British press, another sort of ventriloquism was making its London debut — also under Franklin's aegis — to the delight of some British readers and the dismay of others. Franklin's letter to the *Public Advertiser* on May 22, 1765, demonstrates that, although he cultivated a Swiftian art in many of his best known satirical writings, the former printer's apprentice kept one ear open to laughter from the West, where a different sort of comic mask was emerging in the homespun folklore of America. In the *Advertiser's* May 15 issue, a man calling himself "The Spectator" — probably Franklin himself — had complained about "great Liberties" recently taken by members of the press in their zeal to report unfounded rumors concerning the progress of industry in America.[5] One week later, Franklin — this time calling himself "A Traveller" — responded to the Spectator's fictitious challenge, but not, as one might expect, by arguing for the accuracy of the press's coverage of colonial affairs.[6] Rather, the Traveller defends the practice of exaggerated reporting on the grounds that the truth is often uninteresting and apt to make men sullen: "Supposing, Sir, that the *We hears* they give us . . . were mere Inventions, yet they at least afford us an Amusement while we read. . . . Englishmen, Sir, are too apt to be silent when they have nothing to say; too apt to be sullen when they are silent." Having defended the practice of reportorial "Invention," the Traveller goes on to claim that his own information about colonial industry consists of "serious Truths," of which he offers several examples:

> Dear Sir, do not let us suffer ourselves to be amused with such groundless Objections. The very Tails of the American Sheep are so laden with Wool, that each has a Car or Waggon on four little Wheels to support and keep it from trailing on the Ground. . . . And yet all this is as certainly true as the Account, said to be from Quebec, in the Papers of last Week, that the Inhabitants of Canada are making Preparations for a Cod and Whale Fishery this Summer

in the Upper Lakes. Ignorant People may object that the Upper
Lakes are fresh, and that Cod and Whale are Salt-water Fish: but
let them know, Sir, that Cod, like other Fish, when attacked by
their Enemies, fly into any Water where they think they can be
safest; that Whales, when they have a Mind to eat Cod, pursue them
wherever they fly; and that the grand Leap of the Whale in that
Chase up the Fall of Niagara is esteemed by all who have seen it, as
one of the finest Spectacles in Nature! — Really, Sir, the World is
grown too incredulous.

It is difficult to imagine that many "superficial Readers" or other
"ignorant People" altered their low opinion of the North American
wool and cod industries in light of the Traveller's claims. Yet for
readers in London, Franklin's letter demonstrated the surprising via-
bility of another American commodity, tall humor, which would
become a popular British import within fifty years.[7] As Franklin's
readers were among the first to discover, the potent irony of Swiftian ventriloquism acquired a different flavor when the writer's
mask displayed the deadpan expression of an American yarn spinner, and the difference is revealing. Old Sarum, the pseudonymous
author of Franklin's 1774 letter, follows Swift's fictitious pamphle-
teer by initially withholding any indication that his opinions are to
be understood ironically. No reasonable first-time reader would
doubt that his condemnation of the mutinous colonies at the beginning of the letter is anything but straight invective. When America's
fecund women emerge as the source of political upheaval, the
reader perhaps becomes suspicious of the author's judgment and
intentions; and by the time Old Sarum has outlined his surgical
remedy, most readers have recognized that the mask is purely
ironic, that the meaning intended by the implied author is actually
the opposite of what the fictional author says.

The Traveller also wears a straight face, but his mock sincerity
works to produce a different set of responses. Whereas Old Sarum
initially stands in disguised opposition to the outlook of the implied
author, the Traveller speaks half sincerely and half ironically for
the figure behind the mask. His exaggerated claims do not encourage the reader to reverse an initial decision about the implied author's intentions, for the Traveller is not a mere foil. His letter
begins with a straightforward assertion that "mere Inventions"
(i.e., fictions that pose as fact) provide innocent "Amusement" and

are sometimes preferable to truthful stories when the truth is sullen or uninteresting. Yet neither is the Traveller entirely candid, for he immediately goes on to maintain that his own descriptions of colonial industry are not "mere Inventions . . . [but] serious Truths," a claim for which he offers the dubious "Faith of a Traveller" as security. Throughout the remainder of the letter, he continually slides in and out of alignment with the perspective of the implied author, often employing a straight statement (fish will seek safe water) as evidence for a questionable assertion (therefore, cod inhabit the Upper Lakes).

Moreover, the Traveller deliberately frustrates his reader's attempt to establish a clear distinction between plausible statements and outrageous assertions by drawing most of his information from actual press reports, such as news that agents for the king of Spain have purchased "1000 Pieces of Cannon" in Quebec and "25,000 Axes for their industrious Logwood-Cutters."[8] The impressive figures may indeed have been exaggerated when the *Advertiser* published them earlier that month, but these statements are at least plausible enough to be regarded as "serious Truths" in the letter writer's estimation. The ensuing claim about a cod and whale fishery wears the same plausible garb—it did actually appear in "the Papers of last Week"—but here that garb disguises a logical absurdity, which culminates in the image of whales swimming up Niagara Falls. Like Old Sarum, the Traveller maintains a straight-faced expression throughout, yet it is a straight face that remains uncommitted either to his strenuous truth claims or to his avowed fondness for invention. Unlike Old Sarum's purely ironic mask, which by the end of his letter encourages the reader to substitute an accurate reading for a misguided one, the Traveller's deadpan expression holds two attitudes in suspension, denying readers the opportunity to make a definitive interpretive choice. Moreover, the reader who refuses to endure the author's interpretive limbo becomes an object of the letter's humor, for the Traveller parodies an approach to interpretation as much as an attitude toward America. His letter closes with an appropriately ambiguous recommendation for readers:

Pendulum-like, [the world] is ever swinging from one Extream to another. Formerly every Thing printed was believed, because it was in Print: Now Things seem to be disbelieved for just the very same Reason. Wise Men wonder at the present Growth of Infidelity! They should have consider'd when they taught People to doubt the Authority of News-papers, and the Truth of Predictions in Almanacs, that the next Step might be a Disbelief in the well-vouch'd Accounts of Ghosts and Witches, and Doubts even of the Truth of the A — n Creed.

Little stands to be gained from a rigid generic distinction between Franklin's two styles of humorous ventriloquism, for the letters actually contain many more similarities than differences. Yet the Traveller's brand of irreverence, his disavowal of interpretive zealotry, betrays a cultural disposition that Franklin's readers in Boston and London were increasingly apt to recognize as American. By the early nineteenth century, this peculiar style of humorous storytelling was already well documented in the correspondence of European travellers in America, most of whom considered the native yarn spinner's knack for exaggerative description as evidence of moral depravity in the wayward former colonies. Whatever its psychological origin, the spirit that inspired Franklin's playful critique of interpretive overconfidence manifested itself at all levels of cultural life during the nineteenth century, becoming even more closely identified with the national character than America's harshest early critics could have predicted. By the second half of the century, scholars such as C. S. Peirce and Josiah Royce were founding a new school of philosophy by insisting, like their yarn-spinning counterparts, on an experiential and relative concept of truth, a concept of truth as what "works" rather than what "is." Observing the same cultural link, George Santayana placed William James beside the American humorists, praising both for their efforts to defy the facile idealism of the "genteel tradition."[9]

It is not likely that the pioneers of pragmatic philosophy were much influenced by local folklore, yet by 1850 literary yarn spinners such as James Kirke Paulding and Thomas Bangs Thorpe had already begun to express what Walter Benn Michaels calls a typically pragmatic "fear of subjectivity."[10] Peirce articulates this fear in his attack on Cartesian dualism, arguing that the self is always an interpretation, never a fixed and knowable point of reference, much as Franklin had described readers who swing "Pendulum-like . . . from one Extream to another."[11] What we take to be universal truths, according to both Peirce and the Traveller, are nothing more than interpretations that have been agreed on by a "community of knowers."[12] Truth, in this view, is a form of agreement, a negotiated settlement about what works effectively to accomplish our practical and conceptual needs.

Building on Peirce's notion of the self as a social and interpretive construct, Royce proceeded to challenge the validity of Christian faith and religious skepticism at once by claiming that neither perspective represents a legitimate interpretive posture.[13] If all human understanding is essentially a matter of interpretation, Royce argued, then both dogmatic faith and total skepticism require a denial of the individual's interpretive activity. The best that a good Christian can do, according to Royce, is not to offer faith blindly but to participate in the "community of interpretation," a collectivity that responds to the force of objections from skeptics while working to sustain a flexible agreement about fundamental principles.[14]

Royce's point, again much like the Traveller's, is that truth is accessible only through participation in a communal interpretive effort. In 1828 James Hall articulated such a pragmatic view of truth in a tall sketch that he included among his *Letters from the West*. As the scene opens, two characters are debating the validity of one's claim that he acted heroically when attacked by a nest of snakes. Hall asserts that the man was

> almost as valiant among these reptiles as Sampson among the Philistines. "I killed a hundred of them," he said, "in a few minutes, each one as large as my leg." "I do not dispute it," replied his friend, "but would be better satisfied if you would *fall a snake or two*." "There were *ninety*, I am sure." "Say fifty." "No, I can't; I am convinced there were *seventy-five*, and I'll not bate another snake to please any man."[15]

One can imagine that the champions of American pragmatism would have appreciated Hall's sketch, for the comic transaction conceives of truth as a tangible commodity, something like gold or silver, whose value is always subject to the pressures of the interpretive marketplace. It is important to recognize, however, that Hall's comic relativism, the notion of truth as commodity, is not simply reductive; in denying that truth can have an absolute value, the narrator of Hall's sketch does not suggest that the concept is altogether valueless. On the contrary, the two speakers agree on a fair price, and their agreement establishes a version of Peirce's community of knowers. Rather than an attribute of certain assertions in themselves, truth is understood in this view as a property conferred on assertions by a community through acts of interpretive negotiation. In much the same way, the tall tale always depicts truth as a relative commodity, for the participants in a yarn-spinning performance together set the price of confidence.

Although work on the tall tale in recent years has remained largely within the domain of folklore, theoretical issues raised by Hall's story and joined at the turn of the twentieth century by thinkers such as Royce and William James remain central to literary criticism in America. Versions of Peirce's community of knowers and of Royce's interpretive community have surfaced in the work of such different critics as Stanley Fish, Jonathan Culler, David Bleich, and Peter Rabinowitz, to name just a few. In their various efforts to locate determinate meaning somewhere between a purely autonomous text and a purely subjective reader, many contemporary theorists have appealed (often without acknowledgment) to Royce's notion of socially constituted norms of interpretation. Culler's phrase "interpretive competence," Stephen Mailloux's "interpretive conventions," and Fish's "interpretive communities" all mirror in some degree Royce's attempt to explain how individual interpreters arrive at — or, according to certain critics, create — meaning through some form of cooperative activity. James Hall and the literary yarn spinners who followed his example were, of course, primarily interested in the entertainment value of their early narrative experiments with tall humor, but even Hall's abbreviated account of an interpretive bartering session carries an intriguing set of theoretical implications. In the hands of writers like Hall, Paulding, and George Wilkins Kendall, the tall tale becomes a literary game in which contemporary theoretical notions of "competence," "cooperation," and "community" come to life as parts of an actual drama of interpretation.[16]

Mark Twain staged this drama in different ways and toward various ends throughout his career as a writer. In a letter to the New York *Sun*, he explained his vocation as a writer of fiction by asserting that his own narrative inventions, unlike other people's, were firmly grounded in what Franklin's Traveller would have called "serious Truths":

> I never yet told the truth that I was not accused of lying, and every time I lie someone believes it. So I have adopted the plan, when I want people to believe what I say, of putting it in the form of a lie. That is the difference between my fiction and other people's. Everybody knows mine is true.[17]

This statement is itself a tongue-in-cheek exaggeration, yet the test of credulity that pits character against character, or reader against writer, is essential to Mark Twain's conception of narrative performance. To present a story in writing or in person, Twain believed, is to initiate an encounter between rival interpreters, some of whom are privileged with inside knowledge, some of whom are filled with too much interpretive bravado, some of whom are merely incompetent to respond. This contest between innocent and experienced perspectives, as it takes shape in and through his fiction, is Mark Twain's greatest theme, and the tall tale offered him a means of dramatizing its endless permutations.

Belated as his self-described "call" to humorous literature was, Twain was unusually qualified to respond when it came in October 1865, for he already knew most of the tricks that earlier humorists had devised for the presentation of tall stories in writing.[18] His contributions to newspapers in California and Nevada Territory between 1862 and 1865 reveal his indebtedness both to an oral tradition of native yarn spinners, including fellow miners such as Jim Gillis, and to a parallel tradition of American literary humorists, men like Paulding, Thorpe, and Kendall, and the anthologists who undertook the first experimental steps toward assimilation of oral tall narrative to print. By 1865, when his story about a loaded jumping frog won him national recognition, Twain probably had not read either of W. T. Porter's important collections of backwoods humor, and his direct exposure to the work of other literary yarn spinners of the early nineteenth century is equally hard to document. He may have absorbed their significant contributions to American humor second hand through the writings and stage performances of contemporaries such as Artemus Ward. Nevertheless, by the time he left California to pursue a literary career in the East, Twain had inherited a rich tradition of mainly journalistic tall humor. With his earliest literary productions he began to carry this tradition in unexplored directions.

Explaining the purpose of his important anthology of American humor, *Tall Tales of the Southwest*, Franklin Meine offered the premise that "Twain's early writings marked the climax of a rich development, rather than the beginning of one."[19] Indeed, Twain's "The Jumping Frog" (1865) stands as a crowning literary achievement, "a kind of climax," as Bernard DeVoto also wrote, in the gradual emergence of "the anecdotal folk humor of the West."[20] In terms of the development of tall narrative as a significant component in American fiction, however, "The Jumping Frog" marks as much a beginning as an end. After 1865, as Twain's interest turned from newspaper sketches to the construction of longer narratives, the tall tale remained central to his imagination both as a source of anecdotal material and as an organizational device. As in the past, his humor still turned on sudden incongruities and a gift for deadpan narration, but Twain also found it increasingly necessary to think of the tall tale's rhetorical situation — the interpretive transaction between innocent and experienced perspectives — as a strategy for drawing his disparate comic material into extended and coherent narratives.

His initial efforts in this direction — *The Innocents Abroad* (1869), *Roughing It* (1872), and "Old Times on the Mississippi" (1875) — all revolve, with varying degrees of subtlety and consistency, around a generalized version of the classic tall-tale scenario: a tenderfooted narrator suffers embarrassment at the hands of more experienced characters because of his excessive credulity and stubborn romanticism. After repeated failures, the tenderfoot finally triumphs by successfully casting off illusions that were the products of his formerly sheltered environment. After 1872, Twain gradually began to purge his writing of the actual yarns that had produced, along with some priceless moments of humor, the digressive and episodic quality of *The Innocents Abroad* and *Roughing It*. Yet the rhetoric of the tall tale, the story of successive interpretive contests that culminate in a transforming education, continued to provide a structural and thematic pattern that he would return to throughout the rest of his career.

In turning from a series of mock-autobiographical works to *The Adventures of Tom Sawyer* (1876), a "phantasy of boyhood" as DeVoto called it, Twain took a first tentative step into decidedly unfamiliar terrain.[21] Recent scholarship has demonstrated that his exposure to nineteenth-century romantic fiction was far more extensive than he ever admitted, but even so the Wild Humorist of the Pacific Slope remained more comfortable with Bret Harte's brand of "condensed novels," of which Twain had written several in California, than with romantic fiction itself.[22] His disposition toward the wildcat adventures that passed for serious literature in Carson and Virginia City had surfaced in Chapter 51 of *Roughing It*, where he satirized the efforts of an ambitious literary club. Yet what Twain primarily rejected, as his essay on Cooper's literary offenses much later made clear, was not so much romantic fiction as the attitude of certain romancers toward the reader's interpretive predicament. Credulity, both actual and pretended, had performed an essential function in the comedy of Twain's early sketches and travel books, where voluntary suspension of disbelief always constitutes a problematic decision, and he never abandoned his early approach to storytelling long enough to feel entirely comfortable with the sort of writing that makes unreasonable demands on the reader's confidence. As a strategy of response, suspension of disbelief looked strangely like credulous overinvestment, a form of interpretive commitment that the yarn spinner invites only from his or her victims.

Nevertheless, rather than simply disparaging bad romances — although he continued to do that as well — Twain managed to give creative expression to his ambivalence about the problem of "investment" in romantic fiction by devising what might be called a conditional romance in *The Adventures of Tom Sawyer*. That is, he enacted a contest for narrative authority in the novel by pitting Tom's creative projects against the narrator's own, in effect destablizing the story's official rhetoric and initiating an important dialogue. Both storytellers are committed to a method of narration that involves heavy stylization and adornment of scenes and events, but Tom and his romantically inclined counterpart perform for different audiences, and their competing performances reflect very different attitudes toward the activity and intention of storytelling. Whereas the novel's official narrator, the architect of the idyll, seeks to elicit the reader's suspension of disbelief by describing the hero's adventures in conventionally picturesque diction, Tom simultaneously retells his adventures according to the tall tale's narrative and stylistic conventions. Expressing a yarn spinner's disdain for credulity, Tom "paints up" and "adorns" his account of the story's "facts," not — like the narrator — in order to win suspension of disbelief from his auditors, but to entertain cultural insiders with an imaginative rendering of events. Characters who make the mistake of buying into Tom's fictions with the reader's degree of romantic indulgence immediately become victims in a yarn-spinning game when their naiveté — which is generally grounded in vanity and hypocrisy — betrays itself to the rest of the community. The tall tale, as Tom's natural idiom, becomes Mark Twain's means of initiating a debate over narrative authority in a novel that manages to be a romantic adventure without committing itself to the assumptions endorsed by its romantic narrator.

By the 1880s, Twain's emerging vision of the "damned human race" had begun to erode his confidence both in the privileged status of the tall tale's community of knowers and in the oral genre's effectiveness as a social ritual capable of establishing and sustaining such a collectivity. Elite groups such as the "older citizens" of Virginia City or the pilots of "Old Times," groups knit together by their adherence to tall-tale conventions of performance and response, had emerged in his writings of the 1860s and 1870s as versions of a communal ideal. *Adventures of Huckleberry Finn* (1885) traces the breakdown of such communities in river towns along the Mississippi, the disintegration of a once powerful collusive relationship between the narrative performer and his audience. Huck and Jim suffer the consequences of Twain's loss of confidence, for although both characters possess the sort of narrative resourcefulness that might qualify them as cultural insiders, the tall tale as a social contract has become null and void in Huck's Mississippi Valley. Twain reconstitutes a version of *Roughing It*'s community of knowers in the imaginative space outside the text where readers negotiate with the implied author over the ironic significance of Huck's narration. But this interpretive inner circle is only an echo of the old yarn-spinning community, as Huck's perpetual isolation makes clear. The rhetoric of the tall tale had become for Twain less a strategy for communal affirmation than a subject for nostalgia.

Huckleberry Finn marks a sort of climax in the story of Mark Twain's creative assimilation of the yarn spinner's art, but not an ending. In *Pudd'nhead Wilson* (1894), Twain revives the tall tale's drama of performance and response in order to challenge the folk genre's central promise of communal affirmation. In hundreds of yarn-spinning episodes composed during the first thirty years of his career, Twain had expressed his belief that interpretation is essentially a communal affair, that individual interpreters can arrive at a workable compromise about what constitutes truth only by acting as a group. Indeed, the tall tale's game of challenge and response demonstrates above all that without compromise, interpretation becomes a purely idiosyncratic process. The yarn spinners of Twain's fiction delight in exposing the naiveté of their victims because every idiosyncratic response affirms the privileged outlook of the interpretive community and ensures its continued power over the individual. That community fails to provide a refuge for Twain's beleaguered hero in *Huckleberry Finn*, yet membership in a folk collectivity where performance and response are communal projects at least remains an ideal for Huck, one that he never quite attains. In *Pudd'nhead Wilson*, Twain takes a decisive step beyond the tall tale, for in that novel he employs the genre's familiar rhetoric in order to disavow the interpretive privilege of the yarn-spinning community. The novel's cultural insiders, including Pudd'nhead and the reader, are invited to delude themselves into assuming that tacit collaboration with the implied author will entail detachment from the story's implicating ironies, as was the case in *Huckleberry Finn*. Yet the novel finally demonstrates through a series of inversions that all interpretations are equally motivated by self-interest, that no interpretive posture can avoid complicity in crimes committed by the citizens of Dawson's Landing. The novel ultimately rejects the tall tale's assumption of communal authority by revealing, as Evan Carton puts it, "the consubstantiality of its characters with its author and readers."[23]

After *Pudd'nhead Wilson*, elements of tall humor continue to surface in Twain's writing, but the rhetoric of the tall tale no longer serves as the informing principle of interaction between narrative performance and audience response. The heroes of his late fiction are transcendent figures, otherworldly redeemers who arrive on earth equipped with privileged insight into the condition of a perpetually tenderfooted human race. Throughout most of Twain's career, however, the yarn spinner had been the figure who, for him, wielded the power to unify and redeem a community through his control of language. In exploring the limits of that control, Twain extended and transformed a national tradition of literary tall humor that reaches back to late-eighteenth-century America. Behind his 1865 story of a barroom confrontation between Simon Wheeler and a pedantic stranger, according to Bernard DeVoto, lay "a whole generation of newspaper humorists, wholly forgotten now, who delighted in the vigor of Western life."[24] Many of those humorists, no longer wholly forgotten, fashioned an appropriately vigorous prose out of their experiments with tall narrative, experiments that helped to shape Twain's attitude toward the enterprise of literary storytelling.

1

The Emergence of Tall
Narrative in American Writing

Benjamin Franklin may have been among the first patriots to challenge foreign readers with an example of tall humor, yet by the end of the eighteenth century Americans were already notorious for their seemingly irrational and depraved love of exaggeration, and no account of travel through the western and southern settlements was complete without some anecdote intended to illustrate this idiosyncrasy of the national character. Some of the more credulous early visitors to America inadvertently provided evidence of the nation's passion for yarn spinning by including information gleaned from native sources in their notes on the geography, history, institutions, and people of the new country. Travelling across western Maryland and Virginia shortly after the Revolution, for example, Isaac Weld witnessed several typical narrative performances by settlers who must have detected in Weld's harsh opinion of American culture an opportunity to practice their own peculiar brand of satire. The gentleman writes that he encountered "four or five" invalids whose testicles — so he was told — had been torn off in combat with barbarous neighbors. Deaf to the laughter his hosts must have been sharing behind his back, Weld goes on to report: "I have been credibly assured that [in the Carolinas and Georgia] the people are still more depraved . . . and that in some particular parts of these states, every third or fourth man appears with one eye."[1]

Weld was neither the first nor the last unsuspecting visitor to accept the seemingly credible assurances of his American hosts too hastily, for citizens of the New World were just as apt to parody foreign opinion by exaggerating their own depravity as they were to brag about the productivity of the native sheep. In both cases, the exaggerated response sought to deflate European criticism without actually confronting its charges. Travellers who had been exposed beforehand to baseless myths about the New World had no trouble believing in the unspeakable barbarity of its people or in the most unheard-of wonders of nature, provided that the news came from an honest-looking American or a reputable newspaper. Uninformed critics of the young republic hungered for fantastic news, and native yarn spinners acquired a reassuring measure of superiority by furnishing enough of it to keep their guests well fed.

Tall humor grew up both in response to Europe's uninformed critique of life on the frontier and in response to the frontier itself. Settlers in the American wilderness from Jamestown to California consoled themselves by piling stories of hardship and loss on one another until the representation of life became laughably absurd. Walter Blair and Hamlin Hill quote a survivor of Jamestown's tragic winter of 1609, who reflected solemnly that one man murdered his wife, "powdered" (i.e., salted) her, and "had eaten part of her before it was known; for which he was executed, as he well deserved. Now whether she was better roasted, boiled, or carbonado'd [broiled] I know not; but such a dish as powdered wife I never heard of."[2] By exaggerating the conditions that made life virtually unbearable, inhabitants of the frontier were at the same time expressing their defiance and taking refuge in laughter. Tall humor has always flourished at the fringes of settlement, where people who have endured nature's hardships encounter others who will accept a stranger's account of what the experience was like. For the group that shares the yarn spinner's privileged point of view, the inflated story of cruelty and suffering—by making those things laughable—may signal a dual victory over both condescending outsiders and the very conditions of life that inspire the tale.

One particularly insightful British commentator recognized that the "tallness" of the humor that arrived from America during the first half of the nineteenth century did not account for its effectiveness *as* humor. Writing in 1838, "H. W." explained to his countrymen that their former subjects exaggerated compulsively not because the Americans bore a congenital aversion to sincerity, as was often maintained by less sympathetic critics, but because exaggeration generates humorous incongruities:

> The curiosity of the public regarding the peculiar nature of American humour seems to have been very easily satisfied with the application of the all-sufficing word exaggeration. . . . Extravagance is a characteristic of American humour, though very far from being a peculiarity of it. . . . The man who put his umbrella into bed and stood himself up in the corner, and the man who was so tall that he required to go up a ladder to shave himself, with all their bretheren, are not humorous and ludicrous because their peculiarities are exaggerated, but because the umbrella and the man change places, and because a man by reason of his tallness is supposed too short to reach himself.[3]

Exaggeration itself, as H. W. observes, is neither particularly American nor particularly humorous until the exaggerated image engenders an incongruous picture. "No old-time cowboy," according) Mody Boatright, "would expect to amuse you by saying that the outfit for which he worked owned a billion acres of land, as gross an overstatement as this would be." Instead, "he would say that they used the state of Arizona for a cow pasture; that it took three days to ride from the yard gate to the front gallery; that the range reached so far that the sun set between headquarters and the west line camp."[4] H. W. quotes a Kentucky steamboat captain whose proud description of his ship further illustrates the technique: "She trots off like a horse — all boiler-full pressure — it's hard to hold her in at the wharfs and landings. *I could run her up a cataract*. She draws eight inches of water — goes at three knots a minute — and jumps all the snags and sand-banks."[5] The captain's initial claim that his ship "trots off like a horse," full of power and spirit, involves an exaggeration that is neither humorous nor original. As he extends the image, however, attributing more and more equine qualities to his vessel, the metaphor becomes increasingly incongruous. The exaggeration, which at first is really no more than a figurative description, generates a plausible absurdity as the steamboat begins to act literally, instead of figuratively, like a spirited horse, jumping sandbanks as a horse jumps rail fences and pulling at the reins when it is tied to the wharf.

H. W.'s analysis of the technique of American tall humor was uncharacteristically acute, although even such a thoughtful critic could not explain why a widespread appreciation for incongruous exaggeration had emerged among a democratic people, "a people," as he described them,

> without poor; without rich; with a "far-west" behind them; so situated as to be in no danger of aggression from without; . . . with no established church; with no endowments for the support of a learned class; . . . who never had feudalism on their soil; and who, instead of having the manners of society determined by a royal court in all essentials imitative to the present hour of that of Louis the Fourteenth of France, had them formed, more or less, by the stern influences of Puritanism.[6]

If democracy, in short, is the great leveller of traditional societal differences, whatever that implies for the future stability of the nation, why is American humor a humor of radical discrepancies and incongruities? One answer is that the magnificence of the land itself inspired a tendency toward what Tocqueville called "giganticism" in the American imagination.[7] Perhaps a more satisfying answer, one that at least responds directly to H. W.'s query, is that America was indeed founded on grand promises and high ideals rather than on existing institutions, and its humor emerged very early as a commentary on the discrepancy between those ideals and the reality they brought into being. Louis D. Rubin, Jr., locates the basic American humorous situation, or "the great American joke," in "the gap between the cultural ideal and the everyday fact, with the ideal shown to be somewhat hollow and hypocritical, and the fact crude and disgusting."[8] Tall humor was especially capable of inflating America's promises to such an extent — a democratic sheep, after all, needed a wagon to support its tail — that an inevitable contrast with real conditions suggested itself in the minds of those who knew enough not to be taken in by the promise. If a credulous stranger swallowed the exaggeration whole, that only added to the pleasure of privileged listeners, whose laughter at the image of a native supersheep constituted a tacit acceptance of real conditions obscured by the joke. Tall humor is American not because it is incongruous — all humor is that — but because it articulates incongruities that are embedded in the American experience.

A country founded, settled, and closely observed by men and women with extraordinary expectations, both exalted and depraved, could not help but appreciate the distance that separated the ideal from the real, the "language of culture" from the "language of sweat," the democratic dream from the social and economic reality of the early American republic.[9]

Speculation aside, the tall tale as a form of oral narrative flourished in North America as it had nowhere else. Whether out of affection for a language as immense as the continent itself, or as an ironic comment on their own inflated dreams, Americans adopted tall talk as a national idiom and the tall tale as a national form of humorous storytelling. Actually, the form is far from indigenous. Tall-tale variants exist in the lore and popular literature of cultures throughout the world, and folklorists trace its origins to ancient times. Certain tales that perhaps seem to express a uniquely American spirit in fact belong to an identifiable intercultural tradition, such as a popular story about words that freeze and cannot be heard until they are thawed. Carolyn Brown has established an unlikely sequence by uncovering the tale in Plutarch's *Moralia*, in Castiglione's *Book of the Courtier*, and in an American yarn by "J. O. Lobb of Nebraska," published in a volume entitled *Shingling the Fog and Other Plain Lies*.[10] An eighteenth-century German, R. E. Raspe, produced what remains the most widely circulated collection of tall tales in writing, *Baron Munchausen's Narrative of His Marvellous Travels and Campaigns in Russia* (1786), which by 1800 had been translated into five languages.

Although the form is undeniably international and belongs to no single period, the tall tale did find a special home in the American imagination during the eighteenth and nineteenth centuries. Of the 3,871 humorous types and motifs collected by folklorists in America and later compiled by Ernest Baughman, 3,710 were tall tales. By comparison, Baughman's *Type and Motif-Index of the Folktales of England and North America* records only 29 tall tales out of 3,966 types and motifs collected in England, lowland Scotland, Wales, and Ireland combined.[11] The author concludes, somewhat gratuitously, that "the tall tale . . . is an overwhelmingly American form," a statement that Raspe and his heirs would have appreciated, as American readers pushed *Munchausen* through twenty-four editions during its first fifty years.[12]

Perhaps as a way of celebrating the seemingly limitless potential of the land, perhaps as an ironic response to their own substantial hardships, many Americans embraced the tall tale as a comic ritual capable of affirming their collective experience, often at the expense of cultural outsiders.[13] Not surprisingly, writers in genres from travelogue to short fiction recognized the national obsession with yarn spinning as an important opportunity, and by 1830 some had begun experimenting with hybrid versions of the oral tall tale in print. In 1848, for example, two experienced storytellers squared off in the pages of William T. Porter's newspaper *The Spirit of the Times* when the pseudonymous author, a Major Bunkum, was accosted one night in his riverside camp by a stranger who wanted to know how the major had forded the roaring Trinity River:

> "Oh," say I, "mighty easy, you see, stranger, I'm powerful on a perogue, and so I waited until I see a big log driften' near the shore, when I fastened it, sot my critter astraddle on it, got in the saddle, paddled over with the saddle bags, and steered with the mare's tail!"
> "Yer didn't tho' by Ned!" says he, "did yer?"
> "Mighty apt to," say I, "but arter you've sucked in all that, and got yer breath agin', let's know how *yer* crossed."
> "Oh," says he, (settin' his pig eyes on me), "I've been ridin' all day with a consarned ager on, awful dry; and afeared to drink at the perara water holes, so when I got to the river, I went in for a big drink, swallowed half a mile of water, and come over dry shod."
> "Stranger," says I, "you're jest one huckleberry above my persimmon; light and take some red-eye, I thought yer looked green, but I was barkin' up the wrong tree."[14]

By challenging the stranger to defend himself in an interpretive showdown, Major Bunkum initiates a game of imagination that has important social consequences. With his men gathered around him, the major acts as spokesman for a community, and his yarn about crossing the river on horseback intends to reinforce that community's exclusivity by drawing on inside knowledge. The major's men, who make up one segment of his audience, have presumably crossed the river with him and are therefore competent to measure the distance that separates fact from fiction in his tale. Their interpretive work is done in silent collusion with the yarn spinner, whose deadpan expression invites several possible misreadings from the stranger. If the stranger buys into the yarn at face value, he reveals himself as a fool. If he objects that such a crossing is impossible, he just as surely marks himself as an outsider. It turns out, however, that the major's antagonist is himself an unexpectedly competent interpreter, for he responds with a plausible absurdity that immediately wins the group's approval. The tall tale's oppositional game becomes a collaborative game when the stranger's yarn-spinning prowess earns him assimilation into the group.

This sort of invitation for collusive agreement between a narrative performer and privileged members of his or her audience is by no means unique to the tall tale, but it does provide a basis for distinguishing the form from more common speech acts. Describing the rules that govern normal conversation, H. P. Grice posits the existence of a "cooperative principle," which holds that within a speech community, individual linguistic repertoires overlap like circles in a Venn diagram.[15] The "cooperative principle" is a form of tacit agreement among speakers who, in the interest of effective communication, consent to restrict their discourse to the area mutually covered by the linguistic repertoires of the participants engaged in conversation. The tall tale may be understood as a speech act that exploits the complacency of listeners who invest too much confidence in the teller's apparent compliance with the "cooperative principle." While Bunkum feigns sincerity with his deadpan presentation, he intends to "cooperate" in Grice's sense with only part of his audience. His seemingly plausible narrative is designed to fool the green-looking stranger into assuming that the performance occurs within a shared linguistic space, a shaded area in the Venn diagram. Yet the trappings of plausibility that might encourage an inexperienced listener to interpret the story as true conceal a more secretive cooperation that occurs between the teller and cultural insiders. For these interpretive partners, Grice's "cooperative principle" defines an elite community that includes only those listeners who are competent to receive in the spirit of fiction a narrative that is told as fact. The stranger triumphs by demonstrating, to everyone's surprise, that he already belongs within the yarn's community of knowers.

One of the functions of a yarn-spinning performance is to reinforce the identity of this elite group, to define the shaded area in the Venn diagram where tacit cooperation among culturally aligned individuals does take place. Carolyn Brown explains that a skillful yarn spinner elicits the participation of his or her inside audience by drawing the substance of the tale from out of a "deep cultural matrix," a fund of specialized and often exclusive knowledge that constitutes the group's common experience.[16] This is why tall tales are frequently based on weather conditions, the habits of animals, or the hardships of life that are peculiar to a given region. An artful narrator's elaborate exaggeration of those conditions of everyday life is likely to fool a naive traveller, but the credulity of outsiders only adds to the enjoyment of the privileged inside audience and its spokesman. Wayne Booth makes a related point when he asserts that successful irony depends on at least three kinds of agreement between the author and reader: agreement on a common language, a common cultural experience, and a common experience of genres.[17] The yarn spinner's ploy is to feign agreement where none exists, to invite interpretive commitment from listeners who lack either cultural experience or experience of the genre, or both. Moreover, it is important to realize that the teller's effort to transform the group's special knowledge into fantastic representation is not a denial of experience; rather, the yarn spinner's exaggerated imagery promotes a renewed acknowledgment of actual conditions that inspired the tale, knowledge of which binds and perpetuates the group. Davy Crockett's assertion that sunrise was delayed one especially cold morning, for example, exaggerates weather conditions to a ridiculous extent, but the very extravagance of the representation affirms, in a backhanded way, that it really is cold at sunrise in the Tennessee mountains: "One January morning it was so all screwen cold that the forest trees were stiff and they couldn't shake, and the very daybreak froze fast as it was trying to dawn."[18] The teller's absurdities serve to reinforce the identity of a cultural elite by celebrating through fantasy a knowledge that is the product of experience.

Booth's conditions for ironic engagement between an author and a reader neatly parallel the terms of Brown's "cultural matrix," but the analogy between written and oral modes of engagement is not perfect. This is because, as Bunkum's tale illustrates, the yarn spinner's performance contains a variety of potential meanings that wait to be realized in the spontaneous activity of listeners. The members of Bunkum's audience participate in the narrative event by adopting interpretive strategies that help to determine the significance of his performance. This transactive model of performance and response may bear figurative relevance for the kind of engagement that usually occurs between writers and readers, but the situation is in fact quite different when a reader encounters an author's verbal meaning. Reflecting on the dynamics of the reading situation, Wolfgang Iser describes an "arena" in which the reader confronts an author in "a game of the imagination," but this figurative game occurs literally in isolation, apart from any collectivity and without spontaneous interpretive cooperation from other readers.[19] Walter Slatoff explains that "one can explore works in seminars and discussion groups, one can attend to and make use of the experiences and observations of others, and gain new insights and ways of responding, but a reading . . . can occur only in an individual consciousness."[20] Walter Ong pursues the same point by noting that the term "audience" is literally inappropriate to describe the relation of a writer to his or her readers:

> The oral narrator has before him an audience which is a true audience, a collectivity. "Audience" is a collective noun. There is no such collective noun for readers, nor, so far as I am able to puzzle out, can there be. "Readers" is a plural. Readers do not form a collectivity, acting here and now on one another and on the speaker as members of an audience do.[21]

The problem that faced the early assimilators of oral tall humor is simply stated: readers cannot experience a text collectively, yet the tall tale is largely defined in terms of a collectivity that includes both the narrator and members of his or her inside or "true audience." Individual readers can compare experiences and interpretations and thereby arrive at an agreement about what a narrative amounts to, but their immediate experience always takes place in the solitary presence of the text. Shared tastes among individuals and clever marketing by publishers may contribute to the formation of a "readership," but that term is really an abstraction that masks the activity of individual readers without designating a true collectivity. The point is emphasized by Ong's scenario of a speaker addressing an audience that is equipped with texts:

At one point, the speaker asks the members of the audience all to read silently a paragraph out of the text. The audience immediately fragments. It is no longer a unit. Each individual retires into his own microcosm. When the readers look up again, the speaker has to gather them into a collectivity once more. This is true even if he is the author of the text they are reading.[22]

Mark Twain was similarly aware that the author who reads his work to a living audience is something of "an artifice," a superfluous character who tells his narrator's story second hand.[23] As an accomplished lecturer, Twain recognized that only by addressing members of the listening audience directly, responding to their spontaneous gestures and gesturing in return, can the yarn spinner enact the tall tale's process of interpretive transaction, for that process requires a literal "arena" and an actual community of interpretation. The author of a written tale, as Twain often pointed out, regardless of his or her sincerity in transcribing the words of a gifted yarn spinner, is limited by the fact that he or she is never present to participate in the reader's experience.

Some early yarn spinners worked to overcome such obstacles to literary assimilation, but most accepted the reader's disfranchisement as a natural condition. As Major Bunkum's brief yarn demonstrates, the tall tale's interpretive game can be oppositional, collaborative, or both, depending on the spontaneous activity of individual listeners, who declare their relationship to the yarn spinner's inner circle by responding with an interpretation. Readers of the sketch, on the other hand, receive the major's account in the past tense, as a reported event. Their capacity to participate as interested members of Bunkum's audience has been precluded both by the exigencies of the reading situation and by the author's intentional management of their perspective. A writer who intended to enact the tall tale's flexible game of initiation or exclusion, instead of simply representing its rhetoric in action, had to do more than describe the scene of performance accurately. To encourage the convergence of text and reader, America's literary humorists had to develop new ways of understanding and playing the game of the tall tale. As part of that project, writers such as George Wilkins Kendall, Thomas Bangs Thorpe, and William Hawes of New York composed yarns that consciously intend to make the reader into what Stanley Fish has called "an actively mediating presence" in literature.[24] Together with a few contemporaries, and with varying results, they sought to locate readers within the imaginative arena defined by the oral tall tale, to play a yarn spinner's game according to the old rules but in a new setting. Although they produced little truly exceptional literature of their own, the nation's early literary yarn spinners did foster tendencies in American writing that would eventually come to define what David S. Reynolds has called an "indigenous *ecriture*," an "American Subversive Style" character-ized by formlessness, extravagance, and unbridled wildness – a style that would reach maturity in some of Mark Twain's greatest fiction.[25]

Writing in the 1830s, Tocqueville predicted the qualities of that style when he asserted that "the literature of democracy will never exhibit the order, regularity, skill, and art characteristic of aristo-cratic literature. . . . The [democratic] style will often be strange, incorrect, overburdened, and loose, and almost always strong and bold."[26] Many American writers sought to prove Tocqueville wrong by adopting "aristocratic" models; others, like James Hall and James Kirke Paulding, discovered something intriguing and poten-tially quite useful in the verbal ingenuity of their yarn-spinning countrymen, whose vernacular style was certainly "strange" and usually "strong and bold" as well. In reproducing that style, how-ever, the literary pioneers of nineteenth-century American humor meant initially to be anything but subversive.

In its oral setting, as we have seen, the performance of a tall tale functions as a communal assault against idiosyncratic interpreta-tion. A yarn spinner who shares a basic set of experiences with cultural insiders in the audience distorts his representation of the world in order to bait outsiders into adopting an interpretation that diverges, perhaps widely, from the communally accepted one, and the outsider's failure to conform ensures members of the group a measure of cultural superiority. The meaning of a tall tale, in this oral scenario, is indistinguishable from the event of performance; significance is the product of a transactive process that occurs in the rhetorical space between narrative presentation and response.[27] Many of the writers who first experimented with literary assimila-tion of tall narrative, however, were inclined to view the yarn spin-ner's vernacular performance, for all its strength and boldness, as itself a form of narrative idiosyncrasy. Instead of spokesmen for a folk community and its values, yarn spinners of early literary tall humor tend to be idiosyncratic operators, who perform their narrative trickery in defiance of interpretive norms that are defined by a literary tradition. Even in the hands of the most sympathetic writers, the literary tall tale thus becomes something quite unlike its oral counterpart, a sort of stylistic curiosity rather than a communal repudiation of alien points of view.

This perhaps inevitable transformation of the oral genre into a very different literary beast might not be worth noticing except that the tall tale's communal function, its ability to articulate and affirm a community's values, tended to get lost in the process of literary assimilation. Walter Blair observed that "if an author merely set down the golden words of a fine storyteller, a funny thing happened on the way to the printer: they turned to dross."[28] Writers approached the problem of literary assimilation in different ways, yet what most frequently got lost on the way to the printer was the social or rhetorical dimension of the yarn-spinning performance, the game of initiation and exclusion in which participants vie for power by aligning themselves with one interpretive outlook or another. Without this game, the tall tale is interesting only to the extent that it fails to conform to narrative and stylistic conventions of the literary culture that patronizingly assimilates it. To enact the game of performance and response, American writers had to reconceive the tall tale's subversive quality, to think of the form less as evidence of idiosyncrasy than as a communal response to idiosyncrasy.

The difficulty of this subtle maneuvering toward full assimilation of the form can be measured by the confusion expressed among readers of the earliest literary yarns. By 1781, sixteen years after Franklin's report on the colonial wool and silk industries had appeared in London, Americans already possessed a considerable reputation for disingenuousness, and many prided themselves on that reputation. Yet American readers were largely unprepared to recognize their own favorite species of humorous narrative when it appeared in print. Readers such as Timothy Dwight, a leader of the Hartford Wits and a man who had travelled extensively in North America, were baffled and outraged that year by the appearance of a curious volume entitled *The General History of Connecti-*

cut by the Anglican clergyman Samuel Peters. In what at first appears to be a perfectly straightforward record of colonial history, readers discovered what Dwight called "a mass of folly and falsehood,"[29] such as the following account of an incident that occurred near Windham:

> One night in July, 1758, the frogs of an artificial pond, three miles square, and about five miles from Windham, finding the water dried up, left the place in a body, and marched, or rather hopped, towards Winnomantic River. They were under the necessity of taking the road and going through the town, which they entered about midnight. The bull-frogs were the leaders, and the pipers followed without number. They filled the roads forty yards wide, for four miles in length, and were for several hours in passing through the town unusually clamorous.
>
> The inhabitants were equally perplexed and frightened: some expected to find an army of French and Indians; others feared an earthquake, and dissolution of Nature. The consternation was universal. Old and young, male and female, fled naked from their beds, with worse shriekings than those of the frogs. The event was fatal to several women. The men, after a flight of several miles, in which they met with many broken shins, finding no enemies in pursuit of them, made a halt, and summoned resolution enough to venture back to their wives and children.[30]

Windham may indeed have been remarkable among New England towns for the clamor made on summer nights by its amphibious neighbors, but the author of this history has stretched his facts considerably. As a loyal Anglican who had been forced to leave his wealthy estate and his native America behind at the outbreak of revolution, Peters was motivated by more than a documentary interest in his account of the character, habits, and history of the pious colony of Connecticut. It is therefore not altogether surprising that his description of the invasion of Windham by "an army of thirsty frogs" reveals a deficiency in the colonial character without actually naming it. Yet although the author was surely motivated at least in part by disdain, his tale shares as much with the art of Baron Munchausen as with that of Swift. Like a skillful backwoods yarn spinner, he presents his history of Connecticut as though it were purely digestible fact, never indicating his awareness that such unusual events contain elements either of comedy or of satire. His book begins with a laboriously detailed and meticulously documented account of the conflicting claims of settlers in the new colony, a tactic commonly used by yarn spinners to prepare a disarming context for ensuing flights of fantasy. When he later asserts that the Connecticut River narrows are so swift that a crowbar will float downstream, that realistic context becomes stretched to the point of breaking.[31]

Like Franklin's description of whales that leap up Niagara Falls, the account of a floating crowbar functions as an invitation for either credulous overinvestment or cynical underinvestment from the reader. The Traveller's warning against interpretations that swing "Pendulum-like . . . from one Extream to another" is relevant here, for Peters's satire of American shortcomings is at the same time a yarn spinner's parody of interpretive extremism on both sides of the Atlantic. Many readers in London, "whose gullets," according to one Englishman, "are known to be the largest, the widest, and the most elastic in the world," swallowed his history whole, considering it further justification for their opinion of Yankee cowardice and religious fanaticism.[32] New Englanders like Timothy Dwight considered the book a purely slanderous affront to their colonial past, and they denied its authenticity with a fervor that probably gave the author great satisfaction. As late as 1876, nearly a hundred years after what was then the only printing of the *General History*, James Hammond Trumbull of Connecticut produced a refutation that focused especially on Peters's undocumented account of atrocities committed under the infamous blue laws.[33] And in 1877, the debate continued with the republication by a descendant of Peters of the original manuscript, together with an appended defense of its accuracy as historical writing.[34] There is no evidence to suggest that anyone read the strange collection of yarns as something other than either truth or lie—as perhaps a blend of the two and a parody of both.

Although the heated debate over Peters's *General History* now seems more comical than the book itself, the century-long interpretive controversy is instructive, for contemporary literary critics and folklorists alike tend to repeat the error that Timothy Dwight originally committed when he identified Peters's volume as a mere collection of lies. Contrary to this popular tendency, the tall tale is not in any rigorous sense a lie, which may be understood as a false utterance presented with the intention that it should be interpreted only as true. E. D. Hirsch, Jr., explains that a lie does not contain as part of its "verbal meaning" a contradictory will to tell the truth, for "if part of the verbal meaning of a lie were that it is false, then there would really be no such thing as a lie."[35] We do not say, Hirsch points out, "that someone has misunderstood a lie when he is taken in by it." On the contrary, "he has understood it only too well; the liar's verbal meaning has been successfully communicated." An inept or a confused liar might be torn by contradictory impulses, of course, and his divided will might compromise his ability to deceive an audience, but the verbal utterance, the lie itself, would still not in this case contain two meanings at once. The liar may proceed to contradict his intention to deceive by betraying himself, but even then the verbal meaning of the lie does not contain a contradictory meaning.

The tall tale is a very different form of deception, for it does contain more than one potential meaning—it does express a will to lie and a contradictory will to tell the truth at the same time. The yarn spinner is not, however, like the inept liar, divided by two wills; rather, he projects multiple verbal meanings at once by addressing at least two audiences, and his utterance is calculated to mean something different to each. Readers in New England, in other words, were no more wrong for interpreting Samuel Peters's tales as "mere Inventions" than Londoners were for thinking them "serious Truths," for the tall tale is a narrative form that accommodates contradictory authorial impulses within a single utterance. The best interpretation of Peters's *General History*, as Benjamin Franklin might have explained, calls for a careful balancing of potential meanings rather than the discovery of a single one. Indeed, Franklin's manifesto had described the tall tale's ideal interpreter as a cultural insider who tacitly engages in a process of negotiation or synthesis, carefully refraining from overinvestment in any of the yarn spinner's apparent verbal meanings.

The fact that so few readers went on record as adopting Franklin's interpretive strategy might be explained in several ways. First, it is impossible to say what percentage of Peters's readership laughed quietly with the author at the public outrage his book inspired. The most outspoken response to a yarn always comes from its victims, while culturally privileged members of the audience tend to mirror the teller's deadpan expression. A second explanation is that written tall humor was uncommon in 1781, and readers in Hartford were no more expecting to meet a yarn spinner between the covers of Peters's book than were their counterparts in London. A third explanation attributes the confusion to Peters's own narrative methods and to the authorial intentions that led him to the tall tale in the first place. In fact, except for the account of a floating crowbar and a few similar absurdities, the *General History* contains very little "information" that could have been intended to alert even knowledgeable readers that the book's title invites a genre mistake. As a result, Peters's volume fudges the distinction between the tall tale and its near cousin, the hoax, a distinction that is worth emphasizing because it helps explain the *General History*'s confused reception and because the same confusion persists in much contemporary writing about tall tales in American literature.

Literary hoaxes are as old as writing itself, although the form enjoyed a fairly sustained vogue in nineteenth-century America, especially during the 1830s, when the newspaper hoax burst on the public with an irreverence that outraged readers and boosted paper sales at the same time. A typical instance occurred in 1835, when Benjamin Day's New York *Sun* provided the city with a fascinating series of articles, allegedly reprinted from the Edinburgh *Journal of Science*, concerning Sir John Herschel's recent discovery of life on the moon. The author described lunar vegetation, oceans, bison, pelicans, and other wonders that had become visible through an advanced new telescope, located at the Cape of Good Hope. The fourth installment, on August 28, shook the *Sun*'s already astonished readership with the news that furry, winged men had been sighted on the moon's surface:

> We counted three parties of these creatures, of twelve, nine, and fifteen in each, walking erect toward a small wood. . . . About half of the first party had passed beyond our canvas; but of all the others we had a perfectly distinct and deliberate view. They averaged four feet in height, were covered, except on the face, with short and glossy copper-colored hair, and had wings composed of a thin membrane, without hair, lying snugly upon their backs from the top of the shoulders to the calves of the legs.[36]

The author of the hoax, Richard Adams Locke, confessed to his crime only after the *Sun* received inquiring letters from Yale University and from numerous scientific journals interested in contacting Sir John. One of the most enthusiastic responses came from a Springfield, Massachusetts, missionary society, which inquired of Sir John "whether science affords any prospects of a method of conveying the Gospel to the residents of the moon." Once the joke had been revealed, Edgar Allan Poe reportedly stopped work on the second part of "The Strange Adventures of Hans Pfaall" because he felt he had been outdone in the performance of a plausible absurdity.[37]

With its relentless parody of credulous expectations, the newspaper hoax emerged during the 1830s as the most sensational literary variant of tall humor, but the hoax remained explicitly a variant, and in terms of rhetorical effect the two forms could not have been more different. That is because by thoroughly concealing its fictional nature behind the guise of realistic presentation, the hoax treats its entire audience in the same way that the tall tale treats only its naive victim. Another way of putting the difference would be to suggest that the tall tale is a highly exclusive narrative genre, one that incorporates the misinterpretations of incompetent listeners into its structure, whereas the hoax is less a genre than a genre mistake waiting to happen. Richard Adams Locke and Samuel Peters knew that the perpetration of a hoax occurs at the expense, rather than for the entertainment, of its audience. Neither writer envisioned his audience as consisting of distinct groups of interpreters—that is, of cultural insiders and outsiders. Their exaggerated representations make special interpretive demands on no one cultural group in particular, and neither writer provides the sort of clues that would indicate an intention to share the joke with a specific class of readers. Some particularly skeptical portion of Locke's audience may have derived pleasure from listening to others express their naive astonishment, but there was no communal affirmation in this cooperative activity, no culturally binding force in this form of inside knowledge.

This is not to suggest that Peters and Locke failed in their effort to reproduce a written version of the oral tall tale, nor should it be assumed that they bore some obligation to try. The point is simply that the tall tale had not yet fully emerged as a literary form in

possession of the qualities that distinguish the genre in oral performance. Early experiments with written tall narrative tended to
blend lie, hoax, and tall story in a rhetorically complex, often
confused, mixture of narrative intentions, and this confusion persists today in efforts to define the tall tale as an independent genre.
With a few notable exceptions, most scholars interested in the im-
pact of traditional oral humor on the development of American
literature have accepted Franklin Meine's and Bernard DeVoto's
decision to subsume the genre under the more general rubric of the
"frontier anecdote."[38] Norris W. Yates has improved somewhat on
this effort at classification by identifying the tall tale as "a fantastic
yarn rendered temporarily plausible by the supporting evidence of
realistic detail."[39] Yates's definition is a useful starting point because of its focus on the realistic underpinning of what is outwardly
a form of narrative fantasy. Several critics have made the important observation that tall tales frequently originate in actual facts
that, only after embellished retelling, become molded into material
for humor. One can safely go further and assert that the tall tale
always makes fact, or plausible invention, its point of departure.
Whereas many oral narrative forms, like fable and fairy tale, traditionally begin with an indication that what follows is to be taken as
fiction ("Once upon a time," for example), the tall tale often begins
with an elaborately factual description or a claim for the absolute
accuracy of the ensuing report. The explicitness of the claim, of
course, serves as a warning that the yarn's appearance of sincerity
is just that — appearance. As Yates implies, the narrator will frequently adopt a deadpan attitude of grave seriousness and clothe
his story in realistic images before revealing its fantastic or illogical
substance to select members of the audience.

What Yates's definition overlooks in its use of the phrase "temporarily plausible," however, is that although the storyteller takes
his listeners to an exaggerated limit of credulity, he never entirely
transcends that limit. The realistic images through which he conveys his fantastic tale have the effect of grounding his absurdities
in a perpetual rather than a temporary sense of plausibility that is
crucial to the humorous effect of the story. James E. Caron explains that the terms "fantastic" and "marvelous" generate more
confusion than insight when applied to tall humor, for whereas
fantasy "implies the supernatural," "the tall tale very often does

not breach natural law; rather, it pushes the known to an outer limit."[40] Thus even the most outrageous yarns frequently end with a reassertion of the opening claim to sincerity or an absurd "proof" that implausible events described in the tale really did occur. Henry James understood the narrative strategy when he described Christopher Newman's days in the West, sitting around cast-iron stoves, watching "'tall' stories grow taller without toppling over."[41] Such stories do topple over for listeners who are unwilling to follow the yarn spinner to an outer limit of plausibility. For Newman, however, whom James conceives as a cultural insider, tall stories simply grow taller, and the enjoyment comes in watching them teeter as they grow.

None of this is to suggest that the narrative's thin claims to sincerity should be accepted at face value. James M. Cox has aptly explained that the tall tale derives its humor from the constant discrepancy between communally accepted images of reality and the representation of reality created through the teller's flights of exaggeration.[42] Put another way, a tall narrative is neither purely factual nor purely fantastic, but depends for its effect on the ability of cultural insiders to perceive its relation to both fact and fantasy. If the connection in the listener's mind between reality and representation is at any point broken by the storyteller's excessive fantasy, then the narrative's humorous effect is lost. Competent members of the audience are never "sold" by the teller's exaggerations, yet neither are they purely cynical. Their response places them in a rhetorical middle ground, suspended between knowledge of the tale's distortion and appreciation for the teller's dexterity in stretching the limits of plausibility.

Harold H. Kolb, Jr., who, like Cox, has explored the characteristic interplay of fact and fantasy in tall tales, formulates the same point in an intriguingly different way. With explicit reference to its nature as oral performance, Kolb calls the tall tale a story told as truth but heard as fiction, with the comic effect depending on the competent listener's ability to perceive the difference.[43] The importance of this formulation lies in its recognition of the unique agreement that is tacitly made between the teller and certain members of the audience. The listener's part in a tall-tale encounter begins, as does every interpretive act, with a generic conception, and competent listeners will recognize cues in the yarn spinner's delivery that call for a particular approach to interpretation. If the audience includes potential victims, the narrator's culturally privileged listeners will frequently abet the performance by keeping to themselves so that the yarn spinner can insist on a better price for the confidence of his naive listeners. The object of such cooperation, of course, is to encourage a generic mistake on the part of listeners who are unable or unwilling to occupy the tall tale's rhetorical middle ground. This disadvantaged class of listeners makes the mistake of either flatly accepting or rejecting the narrative's truth claims, of interpreting as either truth or lie an exaggerated narrative that stands somewhere between the two.

Authors of the earliest written tall humor to surface in North America typically committed this mistake, although they could hardly have adopted a more sympathetic attitude toward what they considered a disreputable practice. Europeans and New Englanders travelling in America at the turn of the century were often treated to an impromptu display of native wit, yet they naturally performed the role of the gullible or resentful cultural outsider in the tall-tale performance. Not only Mrs. Trollope and Captain Marryat, two of the most illustrious victims of tall deception by shrewd Americans, but travellers of every sort were challenged by native yarn spinners, and their often resentful accounts of such confrontations include some of the earliest recorded tall tales.[44] One traveller, Estwick Evans, expressed more naive amazement than outrage when in 1818 he faithfully reported the astonishing fact, supplied by a reliable inhabitant of the region, that thornbrushes near Vevay, Indiana, produced spikes that could be used in place of nails.[45] Intended victims were sometimes less credulous, but they saw no humor in such unfriendly treatment of strangers, and many proceeded to record the eccentricity of native storytellers as evidence of the moral depravity of backwoodsmen in general. Much of the voluminous western travel literature of the period echoed Isaac Weld's scathing indictment of frontier immorality, an indictment based, in part, on what he and other travellers saw as a chronic and offensive aversion to sincerity among Westerners.

Even more sympathetic portrayals of the backwoods character, such as Timothy Flint's *Recollections of the Last Ten Years* (1826), tended to acknowledge a cultural penchant for yarn spinning while completely ignoring the humorous interest of tall narrative. Flint's readers were told of a Kentucky flatboatman who entertained his family with "a great fund of interesting narrative" and many pleasant stories about the "ingenious knavery" of Yankees, but Flint saw little entertainment value for his readers in such narratives and so omitted them from the text.[46] James Beckworth, Christian Schultz, and other sympathetic writers provided vivid contemporary portraits of native yarn spinners such as the legendary Black Harris, frequently describing their stories as notoriously tall, but neither Beckworth nor Schultz related the substance of the tales themselves.[47] The chroniclers of frontier life around 1810 sought to maintain credibility in the eyes of eastern and European readers, and so they diplomatically avoided indulging in the sort of narrative that thrives on the incredible. They generally accepted James Hall's opinion that although tall humor reflected a fascinating peculiarity of the American character, travellers possessed no right "to mislead the world by putting the creations of their fancy into print."[48]

Although they were in the minority, some writers of the period perceived the tall tale less as an indication of moral deficiency than as a narrative form worth pursuing for its value as humorous entertainment. After Samuel Peters's unreliable *General History of Connecticut*, James Kirke Paulding's *Letters from the South* (1817) is probably the second collection of humorous tall tales in America and the first to connect the genre with native character types, such as the hunter and the boatman. The book recounts Paulding's trip through Virginia, including remote communities in the Blue Ridge Mountains, where he encountered storytellers who claimed to have experienced outrageous adventures. Like earlier travellers, Paulding related these adventures indirectly to the reader as anecdotes picked up from local tradition rather than as curious incidents befalling the author himself. Yet the yarns in *Letters from the South* clearly hold some narrative interest for the author, who does not, like so many earlier travelling correspondents, depict the yarn spinner's art as a pointless breach of confidence. Instead, tall-tale performances in Paulding's book enact a somewhat clumsy game of interpretation in which the author finds his credulity tested. A friendly tanner and "honest man," for example, told Paulding a snake story that occurred in a remote mountain valley renowned throughout the region for the size and number of its snakes:

A gentleman on a visit to the springs once hired him [the tanner] and another person, a hunter, to accompany him to this valley, in order to ascertain whether the stories he had heard, but disbelieved, about it, were true. They descended it, but without seeing a single snake; and the gentleman began to banter the hunter, who told him to stamp hard upon the flat stone where he was standing. He did so, and presently a good dozen rattlesnakes came out, to see who knocked at the door, I suppose. Alarmed at the sight of the strangers, the snakes began to sound their rattles like so many Philadelphia watchmen waked from a sound sleep, and thereupon came forth several thousands of these reptiles, who rattled and hissed at such an execrable rate, that they were glad enough to retreat out of the valley with all convenient expedition. . . . [The tanner said that] there was a great smell of cucumbers, and that for his part he did not much mind the rattlers, being used to them, but he could not reconcile himself to the looks of a rascally fellow, the like of which he had never seen before, who carried a great fin on his back, was shaped like a sunfish, and hissed ten times louder than his neighbors.[49]

In conclusion, Paulding offers a modified truth claim with his comment that "the existence of a valley somewhere in this part of the world, containing a vast number of rattlesnakes, is believed by many well informed people; but as to the little fellow with the fin, his being must remain a matter of doubt for the present."

The author's indirect narration of the tanner's yarn dilutes its effectiveness as entertainment, but Paulding's presentation introduced a new dimension to the literary tall tale. Whereas Peters had employed a yarn spinner's technique to parody the interpretive assumptions of his readers, Paulding incorporates the test of credulity at a number of levels within the narrative itself. The "gentleman" in the tale, for example, has heard several unusual stories that he claims to disbelieve, although his decision to hire the tanner as a way of confirming his doubt suggests that he may have been a victim himself in some prior storytelling event. Paulding assumes the gentleman's former role as auditor, listening with partial credulity to the tanner's version of the snake story. At one more remove from the original yarn-spinning event, the reader at last receives essentially the same outrageous tale from Paulding, who revives the gentleman's assertion of partial uncertainty with his final comment about the doubtful existence of "the little fellow with the fin." The structure of perpetual narrations is cumbersome, but Paulding is straining to depict the yarn-spinning event as something rhetorically more complex than a mere narrative deception, as perhaps a game of credulity in which the reader indirectly maintains a competitive interest. In Peters's version of the literary tall tale, the game of credulity had been strictly oppositional, almost in the manner of a hoax; Paulding comes closer to the oral genre by figuring the tall tale as a collaborative encounter over the price of confidence.

For all its clumsiness as a storytelling technique, Paulding's method of indirect narration allowed him to represent the snake tale less as a fixed "text" than as a "pretext" for rhetorical confrontation between characters with different interpretive outlooks. By 1831 he had discovered a more effective method for initiating this form of encounter by staging the yarn spinner's performance as a sort of play within a play. In a typical scene from his influential comedy of manners, *The Lion of the West* (1831), Paulding's most celebrated backwoods character, Nimrod Wildfire, interrupts the course of events by digressing into a fishing story. While back in Kentucky, the hero was one day fishing for catfish, which he calls lawyers, "'case you see they're all head, and the head's all mouth."

> Why, I'll tell you. I was fishing for lawyers, and knowing what whappers some of um are, I tied my line in a hard knot right around my middle — for fear the devils might twitch it out of my hands afore I know'd it. . . . Well, what do you think if a varmint as big as an alligator didn't lay hold and jerk me plumb head foremost into the river — I wish I may be struck into a split log for a wedge! There was I, twisted about like a chip in a whirlpool! Well, how to get away from the varmint I was sort of "jubus," when all of a sudden, I grabb'd him by the gills and we had a fight — he pulled and flounced — I held fast and swore at him! Aha, says I, you may be a screamer, but perhaps I'm a horse! The catfish roll'd his eyes clean round till he squinted — when snap went the line, crack went his gills, and off he bounced like a wild Ingen.[50]

The idea of swearing at a fish is not absurd, as any fisherman will admit, but few anglers have seen a catfish roll its eyes and squint. Details that go just a bit too far in the direction of fantasy without wholly abandoning reality place the narrative in that interpretive middle zone that is the tale teller's domain, and the willingness of Wildfire's auditors to occupy that zone with him becomes a defining character trait in the play. The first character to swallow the yarn spinner's inflated accounts of his home state is the British tourist Mrs. Wallope, a caricature of America's favorite symbol of credulity, Frances Trollope. The hero's American relatives, the Freemans, are more guarded in their appreciation for Wildfire's narrative ingenuity, and Paulding thus implicitly enacts a satirical confrontation in which British attitudes about America are not so much directly repudiated as tacitly parodied.

Although Paulding was among the first literary yarn spinners to focus attention on the interplay of narrative performance and response in a tall tale, his attitude toward Wildfire's potentially subversive style betrayed a typically genteel bias. Yarn-spinning events in the play determine the triumph of American wit over British credulity, but Wildfire himself emerges more as a caricature than as an effective representative of the vernacular values that seem at times to prevail in the play. In fact, although the hero's digressive yarns effectively exploit European assumptions, his assaults against verisimilitude never serve to establish a parallel to the interpretive community that develops on the banks of the Trinity River in Major Bunkum's tale. Even to his most sympathetic listeners, Wildfire's ability to embellish the truth is a charmingly forgivable idiosyncrasy, dangerous to philistines and simpletons but in no way challenging to the stilted morality and etiquette of his genteel American relatives. Indeed, Mr. Freeman endures Wildfire's performances with only a little more patience and condescension than Mrs. Wallope. He apologizes repeatedly during the play for his nephew's exuberance, attributing it to Nimrod's upbringing a thousand miles from good society, and Wildfire himself regrets his lack of a "genteel education" in the play's final speech.[51] Paulding counted on the novelty and energy of tall humor in *The Lion of the West* as no author had done before, but he did not intend his hero's stories to engage other characters in the play, much less members of the theater audience, as participants in a rhetorical game that might have claimed other victims than the defenseless Mrs. Wallope. Members of the audience were invited to witness a yarn-spinning performance and to recognize its somewhat diluted partisan significance, but their actual participation in a rhetorical partnership with the yarn-spinning hero never became a serious possibility.

The literary forms of travelogue and dramatic farce offered natural advantages for assimilation of the oral tall tale, as Paulding's innovative work in both genres demonstrates. Travelogue included a built-in encounter between a traveller and local people who might conspire to perpetrate a narrative deception, while the farce made it possible for writers to dramatize a narrative performance, to avoid indirect narration, and to focus attention on the dynamics of performance and response. Nevertheless, the most fruitful experimentation with tall narrative in writing occurred in the form of short fiction. Literary yarn spinners, most of them professional journalists, experimented freely with point of view, presenting tall humor from a variety of perspectives in order to explore its potential as both entertainment and social commentary. Editors such as George Wilkins Kendall of the New Orleans *Picayune* and Asa Greene of the short-lived New York *Constellation* were quick to recognize the marketability of such experiments, and they made their papers important early outlets for what was still among readers in 1830 an unorthodox brand of comedy. Together with Joseph M. Field's St. Louis *Reveille*, the Louisville *Journal*, the New Orleans *Delta*, and others, these newspapers provided a broad readership with original native humor in the form of short fiction, and their material frequently reached a larger national audience after it was picked up by William T. Porter's *Spirit of the Times*.

Porter was undoubtedly the most important advocate for what he called this "new vein of literature," and the national scope of his *Spirit* made him an effective spokesman.[52] He invited a wide range of humor, not all of which was tall, and supported stylistic innovations that sought to represent the "strange language and habitudes, and the peculiar and sometimes fearful characteristics of the squatters and early settlers."[53] The writers who dared to move into this terrain employed various narrative strategies, but Porter was able to generalize about the *Spirit*'s brand of humor by describing it as a blend of realism and condescension, remarking of his authors that most are gentlemen, not only highly educated, but endowed with a keen sense of whatever is ludicrous or pathetic, with a quick perception of character, and a knowledge of men and the world; more than all, they possess to an eminent degree the power of transferring to paper the most faithful and striking pictures with equal originality and effect.[54]

Many *Spirit* tales employ the "box-like structure" described by Walter Blair, in which an eloquent narrator introduces a vernacular yarn spinner, whereas other stories assume the form of a mock epistle, after the fashion of Seba Smith's Jack Downing letters.[55] Still other tales recorded in the *Spirit* and elsewhere dramatize a storytelling scene in which the narrator interacts directly with a fictional audience, without the interference of a refined gentleman in their midst. These different approaches to presentation, and the many permutations that were achieved by combining them, allowed contributors to explore a wide range of literary effects, some of which suggest interesting solutions to the problem of audience involvement in a written tale. As Porter's comment implies, however, most of the *Spirit*'s tall narratives reflect an educated author's condescension toward a vernacular storyteller whose tale the writer has stooped to report. This prevailing attitude served to thwart the reader's identification with the storyteller, thus limiting the reader's participation in the tale's rhetorical contest. For the most part, as Norris Yates has shown, the *Spirit*'s yarns invite no identification with the figure of the yarn spinner, whose style as a raconteur tends to emphasize a "propensity to poverty, vice, improvidence, dishonesty, and low cunning."[56] Writers generally sought to enact the tall tale's drama of performance and response as a way of repudiating the yarn spinner and his values, while at the same time affirming interpretive norms derived from a literary, as distinguished from a vernacular, tradition.[57]

The predominant attitude of *Spirit* contributors toward the art of exaggeration emerges clearly in a series of framed tales that stretch the limits of plausibility to describe the outrageous poverty and hardship of life on the frontier. One cultivated gentleman describes the horror he experienced during a visit to one of the poorest regions of Arkansas, where he was told by the local inhabitants of hogs so undernourished that they could not eat corn because the kernels fell right through the pores on their shrunken skin. The geese in the area were so lean that they would not fall to the ground after having been shot, but had to be pulled down from the sky with a stick.[58] In another *Spirit* article, an eloquent writer called "Esperance" relates his visit to a squatter's cabin in Tennessee, where the host tells of his son's suffering from violent attacks of fever and ague. On one occasion, the boy actually shook himself out of his britches, and on another he shook so violently that he ended up in the fire. The doctor "fout the varmint his darndest all day but he couldn't face him — he was whipped certain." The uncontrollable shaking continued to disrupt the squatter's household until the old man tried his own remedy. The father lured his son outside and switched the shakes out of him, "and he ain't been troubled with the shakes since."[59]

Tales that represent the "ludicrous" and "pathetic" conditions of life on the frontier were among the *Spirit*'s most popular contributions. They are undeniably tall, but such tales deploy the yarn spinner's art as a means of disparaging, rather than affirming, the vernacular community whose values are at stake in the narrative performance. In its oral setting, as a yarn exchanged among equally destitute neighbors, the paradoxical image of geese that are lighter than air might be explained as an attempt to transform hardship into a fortifying source of communal laughter. In the *Spirit*'s version, however, the storyteller's narrative ingenuity has lost its power to redeem the suffering of a community, for the writer's elevated tone and perspective encourage readers to appreciate the image as evidence of perpetual physical depravity. *Spirit* writers produced hundreds of such tales, usually playing on the radical discrepancy between the elevated perspective of a writer such as Esperance and the exaggeratedly mean outlook of his vernacular characters. It is a brand of humor that employs the art of the tall tale in creating a comic contrast, but one that ignores the basic social impulse behind the oral yarn spinner's use of exaggeration as a narrative device.

Another class of tales, most of them unframed epistles, includes tall accounts of the prosperity of miners in California. As in the stories about crude squatters, these tales usually employ wild exaggeration as a means of ridiculing the gold fever that was threatening eastern industry and agriculture with the lure of migration.

Writing from the vicinity of "Californy's Mokaleme Diggings," one correspondent tells of mountains of gold, produced by volcanic eruption, from which streams of precious metal flow down the sides. Sweet potatoes grown near these mountains reach three feet in length, and profits from the diggings average $30 million per hour. The writer, "Peter Zigzag," proposes to spend a portion of his earnings to dig a tunnel from St. Louis to San Francisco, which would house a railroad and a ship canal.[60]

Nimrod Wildfire had exaggerated the virtues of his home state of Kentucky in a similar vein, remarking that "if you but plant a crowbar over night *perhaps* it will sprout tenpenny nails afore morning," and Paulding hoped that audiences would laugh with his hero at Mrs. Wallope's wide-eyed acceptance of such boasts.[61] The writers who submitted sketches to Porter's *Spirit* claiming to be California correspondents, on the other hand, meant to ridicule the idealism of gold seekers by employing elements of tall narrative as a debunking device.[62] Peter Zigzag is not a California miner speaking to potential interpretive cohorts, men who share a cultural experience and a familiarity with yarn-spinning techniques. Rather, he is a writer's satirical portrait of a fortune-hunting Californian, whose yarn-spinning acumen is only one more indication of a shifty and disreputable personality. As with many of the *Spirit*'s yarns, the California tales are really literary satires in which a gift for yarn spinning distinguishes a character as, in Yates's words, someone prone to "poverty, vice, improvidence, . . . and low cunning."

Whether he surfaced within a narrative frame, in a mock epistle, or beside the evening campfire, the artful storyteller usually emerged as a disreputable type whose chronic habit of exaggeration never threatened to involve members of the literary audience in a rhetorical contest of wits. Readers in 1840 might have enjoyed the performance of a yarn before a group of rustics, but the author's condescending attitude effectively disqualified them from vicariously participating in that collectivity. In most of the *Spirit*'s yarns, the vernacular storyteller's distorted representations never really challenge the rational standard implied by the writer himself, a point that Pascal Covici makes in describing the similarity of American southwestern humor with that of Henry Fielding's eighteenth-century England:

> For the reader who aligns himself with the rational author, the world is no mystery. . . . The refined reader is encouraged to trust his sense of ethics as well as his sense of what is real. The behavior of the fictional characters is held up against an implicit standard accessible to all men of reason.[63]

The *Spirit*'s tall narrators routinely ply their art as an expression of vanity or hypocrisy, and their flights of exaggeration therefore tend to appear "Ridiculous," in Fielding's sense of the word. The yarn spinner's narrative performances provide no unifying social function for the community that attends them. Instead, such performances represent a humorous failure on the part of lower-class characters "to adhere to the standards of a cultivated civilization, a failure," as Covici puts it, "to recognize and to accept one's inferior position in society."[64] In a sense, such humor did serve to unify a society, albeit an aristocratic rather than a folk one; but it accomplished this feat by disavowing rather than affirming the tall tale's interpretive community. A refined gentleman reading the *Spirit* in 1852 could laugh at the exaggerated depiction of life in rural Tennessee because Esperance's presentation of the yarn enabled him to stand outside the tall tale's rhetorical encounter. The author's use of a yarn-spinning technique intends to persuade the reader that his own life is indeed governed by reason, that interpretation need not be subject to negotiation, and that the reader's own judgment and morality are somehow less ludicrous and pathetic than the squatter's.

A minority of writers in the *Spirit* and elsewhere achieved very different literary effects by adopting a less condescending attitude toward the yarn spinner and his art. Their tales employ the same basic structural devices—the narrative frame, the mock epistle, the dramatized performance—but they cast the yarn spinner in another light, and this subtle shift in perspective bears important consequences for the presentation of tall humor. In a brief framed tale by George Kendall of the *Picayune*, a Texas ranger named Bill Dean explains to a group of newcomers how he avoided starvation on the Texas prairie by living off the meat of a dead pack horse. Cooking the meat in the desert proved to be a real challenge for the resourceful ranger, because the brittle prairie grass burned like gun powder. A greenhorn asks Bill how he managed, and the following tale ensues:

> Why, the fire caught in the high grass close by, and the wind carried the flames streakin' across the prairie. I followed up the fire, holding my chunk of meat directly over the blaze, and the way we went it was a caution to anything short of a locomotive doin's. Once in a while a little flurry of wind would come along, and the fire would get a few yards the start; but I'd brush upon her, lap her with my chunk, and then we'd have it again, nip and chuck. You never seed such a tight race — it was beautiful.
>
> We've not doubt . . . but did you cook your meat in the end?
>
> Not bad, I did'nt. I chased that d——d fire a mile and a half, the almightiest hardest race you ever heer'd tell on, and never give it up until I run her right plumb into a wet marsh: there the fire and chunk of horse meat come out even — a dead heat, especially the meat.
>
> But wasn't it cooked?
>
> Cooked! — no! — just crusted over a little. You don't cook broken-down horse-flesh very easy, no how; but when it comes to chasing up a prairie fire with a chunk of it, I don't know which is the toughest, the meat or the job.[65]

In his introduction to the tale, Kendall refers to Dean as a roguish "wag," but the story clearly portrays the ranger's narrative, not to mention culinary, resourcefulness in a positive light. Moreover, the author has made an effort to locate the tale within a context of performance in which the tale serves as a point of encounter between characters with different interpretive skills and expectations. Dean's understated climax works so well because it is unanticipated by his overeager listeners, the greenhorns who paradoxically add momentum to the storyteller's flight of imagination by interrupting with their facile questions. Kendall invites his readers to align themselves with Dean by identifying the yarn spinner's fictional audience as a collection of newcomers to the prairie, potential victims for the teller and his interpretive cohorts. It is they, Dean's fictional victims, who emerge as "ridiculous" and "pathetic," not because they are prone toward improvidence and vice, but because they are too eager to be fooled.

One way to explain what Kendall achieved in the Bill Dean sketch is to invoke Henry James's celebrated assertion that a writer must "make his reader very much as he makes his characters," for the narrator's attention to the context of performance is really an attempt to coax his reader into adopting an insider's perspective.[66] Although in terms of cultural experience Kendall's readers probably had more in common with Bill Dean's fictional listeners than with the yarn spinner himself, Kendall in effect warns against identifying with the greenhorns in Dean's audience. Moreover, the author offers nothing in the way of a rational standard that might implicitly disparage Dean's abuse of logic and verisimilitude. Unlike many other *Spirit* contributors, Kendall achieves a delicate balance of authorial restraint and intervention in his effort to establish a context of performance through which the yarn spinner emerges as spokesman for an interpretive community, one that openly invites the reader's identification.

Tales that offer the reader an insider's perspective were not common, but it is a testament to Porter's enthusiasm for all forms of backwoods humor that so many do appear in the columns of the *Spirit*. One writer, William P. Hawes, who wrote under the pseudonym "Cypress, Jr.," went further than most of his contemporaries toward re-creating the situation of an oral performance in order to convey a sense of the tall tale as a narrative event. In "A Bear Story," which Hawes originally published in 1842, Cypress plays a minor role as witness to a storytelling session among experienced yarn spinners. George Washington Harris would use this modified version of the framing device to great effect in his Sut Lovingood yarns, but Hawes was one of the first to experiment with the effect, beginning in the late 1830s. The narrative begins abruptly, almost as though the reader were entering unnoticed into a room where old friends are swapping gigantic stories:

"What an infernal lie," growled Daniel.
"Have my doubts," suggested the somnolent Peter Probasco. . . .
"Ha! ha! ha! Ha! ha! ha!" roared all the rest of the boys together.
"Is he done?" asked Raynor Rock.
"How many shirks was there?" cried Long John, putting in his usual lingual oar.

"That story puts me in mind," said Venus Raynor, "about what
I've heerd tell on Ebenezer Smith, at the time he went down to the
North Pole on a walen' voyage."

"Now look out for a screamer," laughed out Raynor Rock, refill-
ing his pipe. "Stand by, Mr. Cypress, to let the sheet go."[67]

By means of this elaborate preparation, Hawes literally makes
"his reader very much as he makes his characters." James may
have envisioned the writer's invention of his audience more as a
theoretical and imaginative process than as a literal exercise in
characterization, but Hawes is not a novelist, and his decision to
begin the tale by dramatizing typical audience responses creates an
important effect. The cynical but encouraging comments of
Raynor Rock and Peter Probasco serve a didactic function much
like Benjamin Franklin's warning to readers who swing "Pendulum-like . . . from one Extream to another." Similarly, Daniel's
objection to the previous yarn, that it was "an infernal lie," serves
less as a rationalist's demand for verisimilitude than as a cultural
insider's demand for more ingenuity from the yarn spinner, who
must satisfy his listeners by bending the limits of plausibility. In
effect, Hawes dramatizes the event of performance in order to
encourage his reader to participate in Venus's narration by occupy-
ing—together with Raynor, Peter, and Cypress—that rhetorically
neutral zone between truth and lie.

Venus's yarn describes a ship captain's hunting adventure in po-
lar bear country. The captain spots a bear on a broad ice pack and
follows him across its fragile surface. After a brief chase, the bear
turns on the hunter and charges. With his rifle ready, the hunter
shows great patience and courage by waiting until the enraged bear
has advanced to within ten feet of his kneeling position before
firing. Unfortunately, the bullet strikes the bear on the shoulder,
stunning him for a moment without effecting a mortal wound. As
the bear lies on the ice in pain and surprise, the hunter prepares to
finish the job with his knife, but he discovers to his dismay that his
lower half, which had become wet during the chase, has frozen
solid while he kneeled motionlessly. The bear gradually raises his
body in order to continue his charge but discovers that his lower
limbs have also frozen. As the two antagonists snarl helplessly at

each other, the ice pack begins to break up, and the two float off into the North Atlantic together on a single floe, still snarling.

One of the listeners at this point objects: "By jolly! that was rather a critical predicament, Venus . . . I should have thought that the Captain's nose and ears and hands would have been frozen too." Venus replies plausibly enough: "That's quite naytr'l to suppose, sir, but you see the bear kept him warm in the upper parts, by being so cloast to him, and breathed hard and hot on the old man whenever he growled at him." The ice pack floats for three weeks southward through the North Atlantic, and in so doing prompts another objection from the audience.

> "But, Venus, stop: tell us in the name of wonder, how did the captain contrive to support life all this time?"
>
> "Why, sir, to be sure, it was a hard kind o' life to support, but a hardy man will get used to almost — "
>
> "No, no: what did he eat? What did he feed on?"
>
> "O — O — I'd liked to've skipped that crc. Why, sir, I've heard different accounts as to that. Uncle Obe Verity told me he reckoned the Captain cut off one of the bear's paws, when he lay stretched out asleep, one day, with his jack-knife, and sucked that for fodder."

Venus prefers a different version of the story, in which an unsuspecting seal climbs onto the ice floe one day, and the two wanderers share a prodigious feast of raw meat. The former antagonists grow to be close comrades, and their separation at the end of the story is unexpectedly moving. In the warmer water of the South, the floe breaks in two, and the bear, in a parting gesture of kindness, throws the largest remaining piece of seal meat onto the captain's fragment. They float in different directions and never meet again.

Venus's decision to alter the ending emphasizes the mutability of the tale, which seems to evolve spontaneously before the reader in the manner of oral rather than written narrative. Raynor Rock and Peter Probasco do not receive the yarn passively, and Venus is forced to respond to their commonsense objections in order to locate and sustain his tale in that nebulous region between fantasy and probability. His success is acknowledged by "the boys," whose sneering approval is intended to guide the reader's own response to the story. Perhaps most significantly, Hawes betrays no hint of condescension or irony toward the yarn spinner, whose fabrications never seem like the marks of an inferior intellect or satirical jibes at his substandard morality. Instead, Venus's embellishments are an essential part of a uniquely engaging narrative transaction.

Hawes's approach to the incongruous concept of a reading audience anticipated the methods of later writers, who persisted in his attempt to re-create the "soul" of oral performance, as Twain once called it, by carefully producing an illusion of the tall tale's spontaneous drama of performance and response.[68] Hawes believed that readers could best appreciate the humor of a tall tale from the point of view of its inside audience. He and a few other *Spirit* contributors recognized that no reader can actually participate in that collectivity, but a skillful literary yarn spinner might at least offer a sense of vicarious participation. To that end, he focused his attention on the context of performance, the exchange of comments that can imply subtle shifts of alliance among the participants in a yarn-spinning event. By 1850, several writers had learned that the tall tale names a form of social ritual as much as it names a style of narration, that to present a tall tale is to describe an interpretive game with important social consequences for its participants. It remained for later writers, such as Mark Twain, to enact that game in an even more unlikely setting by introducing the tall tale's transactive rhetoric to the American novel.

2

Mark Twain's Development as a Literary Yarn Spinner

In 1847, the year Sam Clemens entered the newspaper trade as a printer's devil, the Hannibal, Missouri, *Journal* reported on the exceptional durability of some local homespun. After explaining how he inadvertently uprooted a nine-foot-wide tree stump with the seat of his pants, the correspondent declared proudly: "My wife made the cloth for them pantaloons, and I han't worn any other kind since."[1] In a similar spirit, Orion Clemens, editor of the Hannibal *Western Union*, comforted local farmers in August 1851 with a report that the soil in Maine is so poor that before planting, the down-easters must "look for crivices in the rocks, and shoot the grains in with a musket." Conditions in one Virginia county were even more desperate that year, according to the *Western Union*, which reported that horses there "are so thin that it takes twelve of them to make a shadow, and when they kill a beef they have to *hold him up to knock him down.*"[2]

Sam Clemens had joined his brother's paper early in 1851, and he may have embarked on a long career of literary yarn spinning by setting the *Western Union* items into print. Such pieces were useful as occasional filler for empty newspaper space, and Hannibal readers probably appreciated the somewhat crude inversion of expectations, whereby Esperance's brand of exaggerated condescension focuses on the depravity of eastern, rather than western, agriculture and industry. Sam Clemens would soon become an expert at such calculated inversions, yet his apprenticeship as a humorist led him to better models than Esperance, and even the earliest examples of his work reveal a more sophisticated approach to literary yarn spinning. Like a number of his contemporaries, including Bret Harte and Joel Chandler Harris, Clemens understood the importance of contextualization in a written yarn—the importance, as Walter Blair might put it, of transmitting not just "the golden words of a fine storyteller," but the sense of a rhetorical situation as well.[3] After a few false starts, Hannibal's most promising young humorist learned to appreciate that a yarn, abstracted from its context of performance, becomes little more than a joke, and as Mark Twain later pointed out on numerous occasions, the tall tale is never a very good joke because it lacks a punch line.[4]

Clemens probably never read tales by George Kendall or William Hawes, yet throughout the 1850s and 1860s he read widely in newspapers from New York, Boston, and Philadelphia that were printing the latest work of other humorists, many of whom had learned their craft from the *Spirit*'s pioneering columns. By 1860, a second generation of literary yarn spinners had begun to achieve national recognition, men like J. Ross Browne, Artemus Ward, and Petroleum V. Nasby, and they exerted a more direct influence over Clemens than did any of the *Spirit*'s original contributors.[5] With an inscrutable deadpan style that worked equally well on the lecture platform, Ward and his fellow literary comedians removed some of the gentlemanly prudishness that had characterized earlier efforts to represent the yarn spinner's art in print. Most important for Clemens, the "phunny phellows," as they were sometimes called, showed that a literary yarn spinner could dramatize his own part in the event of narrative performance by manipulating a comic persona. Following Ward's lead and drawing on a long tradition of literary tall humor, Clemens reached his stride as a humorist when he discovered such a persona, one that enabled him to participate actively in the tall tale's interpretive contest.[6] It is at this point that Sam Clemens's humor begins to offer the reader what Mark Twain later called "the spontaneity of a personal relation [with the storyteller], which contains the very essence of interest."[7] Such a personal relation does indeed occur in the humorist's best early work, where reader and writer find themselves engaged in an uncertain negotiation over the "authority" of authorship.

Clemens's earliest literary experiments with tall humor were notably more ambitious than the brief tales he and Orion occasionally lifted from popular almanacs to fill empty newspaper space. In a widely reprinted letter to Annie Taylor, composed in May 1856, he adopted the part of a literary yarn spinner for the first time, foreshadowing future performances by such narrators as Simon Wheeler and Jim Baker. The letter's humor stems from the limitless extension of a simple figurative description of insects in terms that are appropriate to human beings. The writer begins:

> Night before last I stood at the little press until nearly two o'clock, and the flaring gas light over my head attracted all the varieties of bugs which are to be found in natural history, and they all had the same praiseworthy recklessness about flying into the fire. They at first came in little social crowds of a dozen or so, but soon increased in numbers until a religious meeting of several millions was assembled on the board before me, presided over by a venerable beetle, who occupied the most prominent lock of my hair as his chair of state.

As in a tall tale, fantasy invades the narration almost imperceptibly as soon as the narrator begins to confuse figurative with literal description:

> The big "president" beetle . . . rose and ducked his head and, crossing his arms over his shoulders, stroked them down to the tip of his nose several times, and after thus disposing the perspiration, stuck his hands under his wings, propped his back against a lock of hair, and then, bobbing his head at the congregation, remarked, "B-u-z-z!" . . . [A]fter a moment's silence the whole congregation burst into a grand anthem, three dignified daddy longlegs, perched near the gas burner, beating quadruple time during the performance.[8]

As his literary performance draws to a close, the writer warns that "it would take a ream of paper to give all the ceremonies of this great mass meeting," and one senses that Clemens relished his perverse trope almost enough to try. Despite its straining for humor, however, the sketch contains a number of effects that are characteristic of the more successful tall narratives of Mark Twain's later career. One is the use of compelling visual detail as a method of counterpoising the author's flights of absurdity. The writer be-

gins by describing his visitors in figurative terms that express the
basic joke, but are notably lacking in particulars: "little social
crowds," "a religious meeting of several millions," "the vast assem-
blage," "a venerable beetle," "innumerable lesser dignitaries," "a
great bug jubilee." As the sketch progresses, these figurative or
metaphorical expressions become the basis for a fantasy in which
bugs literally think and behave like human beings. The elaboration
of such a modest idea is at least partially effective because, like a
good storyteller, Clemens balances the mounting absurdity of his
letter with a heightened attention to detail, so that the generalized
metaphorical language of the first part is followed by increasingly
detailed imagery in the second, as in the description of "three digni-
fied daddy longlegs, perched near the gas burner, beating quadru-
ple time during the performance." Similarly, the generalized movements of the first paragraph, like "flying into the fire," become
meticulously observed, hence absurd, gestures in the second: "The
big 'president' beetle . . . rose and ducked his head and, crossing
his arms over his shoulders, stroked them down to the tip of his
nose several times." By way of conclusion, Sam tells Annie that he
combed precisely 976 beetles out of his hair the next morning,
"every one of whose throats was stretched wide open, for their
gentle spirits had passed away while yet they sung."

The coordination of realistic detail with absurdity of content is
central to the technique of the tall tale, as it is to virtually all forms
of fantastic narrative, but a plausible standoff between the two
never quite materializes in Sam Clemens's early letter.[9] Instead of
blurring the line between plausible and outrageous events like a
yarn spinner, the letter writer deliberately calls his reader's attention to what Samuel Johnson would have called the "perverseness
of industry" that inspires "combinations of confused magnificence."[10] A tall tale, even something as simple as Jim Townsend's
account of a lake so buoyant that "boys paddle about on granite
boulders," derives its humor from a perverse combination of
ideas.[11] But Townsend's straight-faced delivery of the yarn intends
to disguise or understate the sense of perversity that so infuriated
Samuel Johnson when he encountered it in metaphysical poetry.
An effective yarn spinner does not — like Donne, Cowley, or the
young Sam Clemens — flaunt the ingenuity that inspires him to produce "combinations of confused magnificence." Instead, his dead-

pan expression and attention to detail allow him to blend elements of fantasy with elements of realism in a combination that is entertaining to culturally initiated interpreters and potentially embarrassing to outsiders. Clemens's entomological conceit is no more outrageous than Townsend's story about young boys floating about on granite boulders, but in 1856 the letter writer had not yet discovered the value of a literary straight face.

Later in the same year, the twenty-year-old printer began publishing a series of letters that occasionally make more effective use of the elements of tall humor. The Thomas Jefferson Snodgrass letters to the Keokuk *Post* contain a variety of tall devices, most of which echo Esperance's exaggerated condescension toward the crudity and violence of frontier life. Yet the letters occasionally indulge in a more complex play of exaggeration, as in Snodgrass's account of his arrival at the Quincy train station. The backcountry narrator has heard of the magnificent "iron horse," but he has neither seen nor ridden on a locomotive. As he records his initial reaction to this formidable creature of modern technology, self-parody momentarily yields to a powerful descriptive impulse.

> Thunderation. It wasn't no more like a hoss than a meetin house. If I was going to describe the animule, I'd say it looked like — derned if I know *what* it looked like, unless it was a regular old he-devil, snortin fire and brimstone out of his nostrils, and puffin out black smoke all around, and pantin, and heavin, and swellin, and a chawin up red hot coals like they was good. A feller stood in a little house like, feedin him all the time, but the more he got the more he wanted, and the more he blowed and snorted. After a spell the feller catched him by the tail, and great Jericho, he set up a yell that split the ground more'n a mile and a half.[12]

This passage comes closer to the style of *Huckleberry Finn* than anything the author had written before 1856. The reason lies not only in the metered repetition of "and," the long sentences made up of short descriptive phrases, and the careful selection of visually compelling verbs, such as "snortin," "puffin," "pantin," "heavin," "swellin," and "chawin." What makes the passage really effective is the fact that Snodgrass, in his naiveté, truly pictures the engine as a kind of living creature. This is not an eloquent narrator employing exaggerated language in order to produce a witty comparison between an engine and an animal. Instead, Snodgrass really expects to see an iron horse at the station, and his amazed description is the most appropriate one he can devise for what *he* sees. His use of exaggeration is not a virtuoso performance of metaphysical wit, but a compelling disclosure of character and perception. Part of the beauty of Huck Finn's language lies similarly in his casual use of incredible images that, for all their unexpectedness, are perfectly appropriate to the mind that creates them, as when Huck describes the oncoming steamboat as "a black cloud with rows of glow-worms around it."[13]

Snodgrass's exaggerative humor occasionally takes on a life of its own, yet the persona was never really suited to the task of assimilating oral tall narrative to print. Edgar Marquess Branch has explained that the Snodgrass letters belong to the tradition of aristocratic humor of the Old Southwest, in which an educated writer customarily entertains his sophisticated readers with the antics of lower-class, "gullible and self-defeating" characters.[14] Snodgrass's obvious social ineptitude, as when he enthusiastically joins in with the orchestra during an opera, is intended to play on this implied discrepancy between his crudity and the reader's detached sophistication.[15] His language occasionally becomes something more than "self-defeating," as when he employs equine terms in a peculiarly animated description of a locomotive, but the persona will not sustain such ingenuity for more than a few sentences at a time. Snodgrass's verbal gift remains somehow just another by-product of his ignorance, a damning signal of vernacular tendencies toward improvidence and vice, the humorous appreciation of which requires more detachment than identification from his readers.

If the Snodgrass letters seem to reproduce the *Spirit*'s condescending attitude toward "ludicrous and pathetic" lower-class characters, it was not long before Clemens began to experiment with other uses for tall humor. In the character of Sergeant Fathom, he for the first time treated a vernacular figure less as the butt of humor than as the creative impulse behind the performance of a humorous yarn, and this alteration marks an early turning point in Sam Clemens's development as a writer. "River Intelligence" appeared in the New Orleans *Crescent* on May 17, 1859, after the former typesetter had spent two years training as a river pilot. Having received his license in April, Clemens wasted no time in selecting the most venerable and experienced of his new colleagues, Captain Isaiah Sellers, as the target of his first published prose burlesque. Sellers was famous among pilots not only for his skill and knowledge of the river, but for the "brief paragraphs of plain practical information about the river" that he occasionally submitted to the New Orleans papers.[16] One such paragraph had appeared in the *True Delta* on May 7:

> Our friend, Capt. Sellers, one of the oldest pilots on the river, and now on the Wm. M. Morrison, sends us a rather bad account concerning the state of the river. Capt. Sellers is a man of experience, and though we do not coincide in his view of the matter, we give his note a place in our columns, only hoping that his prophecy will not be verified in this instance:

> > Steamer Wm. M. Morrison
> > Vicksburg, May 4, 1859.

> The river from your city up to this port is higher than it has been since the high water of 1815, and my opinion is that *the water will be in Canal street* before the 1st day of June. Mrs. Turner's plantation, which has not been affected by the river since 1815, is now under water.

> > Yours, &c.,
> > Isaiah Sellers.[17]

Sam Clemens's parody of the *True Delta* item appeared in the *Crescent* ten days later. The pretended editor introduces his correspondent as "Our friend Sergeant Fathom, one of the oldest cub pilots on the river," at first mimicking the language of the *True Delta* article, and then diverging into a series of tongue-in-cheek homages to the cub, whose reports, according to the editor, "are always read with the deepest interest by high and low, rich and poor, from 'Kiho' to Kamschatka, for be it known that his fame exceeds to the uttermost parts of the earth."[18] The sergeant's report itself begins with the familiar phrasing of Sellers's May 7 column:

> The river from New Orleans up to Natchez is higher than it has been since the niggers were executed, (which was in the fall of 1813) and my opinion is, that if the rise continues at this rate *the water will be*

on the roof of the St. Charles Hotel before the middle of January. The point at Cairo, which has not even been moistened by the river since 1813, is now entirely under water.

Up to this point, the sketch is purely satirical. Its humor rests on the contrast between Sellers's arrogant style of offering advice and Sergeant Fathom's similar but exaggerated presentation. Fathom does not, like the editor, speak with tongue in cheek; he takes himself quite as seriously as does his prototype. Completely oblivious that his remarks might be taken in some other spirit than total seriousness, he plays the fool by extending the captain's arrogance to new limits.

Straightforward as its method seems, the sketch at this point suddenly undergoes a subtle but significant change of direction. After advising his readers not to be concerned with the data presented above, the sergeant begins a lengthy story that is intended as justification for his advice. Although his narrative style continues to parody that of Sellers, the sergeant's role in the sketch changes dramatically, for he ceases to play the fool and instead becomes an apparently experienced yarn spinner, fully aware that his statements are invented for the entertainment of his readers. Fathom's story begins:

> In the summer of 1763 I came down the river on the old *first* "Jubilee." She was new, then, however; a singular sort of single-engine boat, with a Chinese captain and a Choctaw crew, forecastle on her stern, wheels in the center, and the jackstaff "no where," for I steered her with a window shutter.

It would be ridiculous to suggest that the sergeant, who is writing in 1859, naively believes in what he is saying any more. He may still want to convince his readers, and his air of self-importance persists, but the sergeant is no longer an arrogant fool who simply misses the humor implied by his narration. The naiveté that contributed to the satire of the editor's introduction and to the sergeant's first paragraph has become a deadpan expression: it looks the same, but its wearer is not nearly as serious as he was a few sentences earlier, when he observed that the river had reached its highest point since 1813. As the story progresses, it becomes apparent that the satire against Sellers has yielded to a different style of humor in which the narrator, who is still supposedly a parody of the old captain, emerges as both clever and entertaining.

> Well, sir, we wooded off the top of the big bluff above Selma — the only dry land visible — and waited there three weeks. . . . Finally, it [the river] fell about a hundred feet, and we went on. One day we rounded to, and I got in a horse-trough . . . and went down to sound around No. 8, and while I was gone my partner got aground on the hills at Hickman.

The tale concludes with the sergeant's explanation for his claim that, despite occasional flooding of the river, "the time is approaching when it will cease to rise altogether."

> In conclusion, sir, I will condescend to *hint* at the foundation of these arguments: When me and DeSoto discovered the Mississippi, I could stand at Bolivar Landing (several miles above "Roaring Waters Bar") and pitch a biscuit to the main shore on the other side, and in low water we waded across at Donaldsville. The gradual *widening* and *deepening* of the river is the whole secret of the matter.

"River Intelligence" begins in much the same manner as the letters of Thomas Jefferson Snodgrass, by portraying the vernacular speaker as an outsider, a fool who misses the humor implied by his own exaggerated language. The satire against Isaiah Sellers, which provided the impetus for the sketch and which delighted Bill Bowen and the other pilots, features Sergeant Fathom as a foolishly arrogant extension of the old captain, and Clemens sustains this satire for as long as he is mimicking Sellers's actual writing style. Once the literal parody of the *True Delta*'s May 7 report has ended, however, Clemens alters the character of the sergeant's reflections, stringing out his "fantastics," as Mark Twain later called them, to sublime levels of absurdity.[19] Isaiah Sellers's air of omniscience persists as Fathom's central personality trait, but Clemens's handling of that trait shifts when the humor of parody begins to blend with the humor of fantasy. In the opening section, the sergeant's omniscience makes him seem ludicrous; by the end, it has become the necessary imaginative faculty of a talented yarn spinner. His performance is really a hybrid blend of satire and tall tale rather than a fully articulated yarn-spinning event, yet the reader who considers the piece explicitly satirical probably wonders why, by the end, he or she is laughing with rather than at the rustic story-teller.

Sergeant Fathom's sudden transformation in the second part of "River Intelligence" signaled an important discovery for Sam Clemens. Throughout his juvenilia of the 1850s, the young humorist's impressive gift for hyperbole had virtually always focused on some target, like "Abner Gilstrap" of the Bloomington *Republican*, whose habits or eccentricities could be made to seem laughable by means of parody.[20] The parodic impulse came to Clemens naturally and often, yet many of the early pieces that seem most characteristic of the later Mark Twain, pieces such as "River Intelligence," are what might be called problem parodies. Mikhail Bakhtin has explained that "in parody two languages are crossed with each other, as well as two styles, two linguistic points of view, and in the final analysis two speaking subjects."[21] Only one of those languages, the one being parodied, is "present in its own right," according to Bakhtin; the other is present "invisibly, as an actualizing background for creating and perceiving." Clemens often managed to sustain such a balanced conflict of implicit and explicit "linguistic points of view," but some of the most exciting moments in his early work occur when the parodic structure breaks down—that is, when the parodied voice begins to speak with its own authority, as in Snodgrass's description of the "iron horse" at Quincy. At such moments, the parodied voice almost overwhelms the normative and "actualizing background" against which both Snodgrass and Fathom ought to appear consistently ludicrous. It is as though the writer at some point discovered in the exaggerated verbal eccentricity of his intended victim a potent and unexpected creativity, which he then found impossible to contain. The result is an even more contentious brand of parody than Bakhtin describes, for in "River Intelligence" the conflict between two linguistic points of view, between the mock editor's satiric authority and the sergeant's omniscient authority, moves toward an uncertain resolution. Foreground and background become indistinguishable as the writer and his intended victim struggle to determine who, finally, will parody whom.

Clemens had not yet considered dramatizing this contentious play of "crossed" languages, yet on his arrival in Nevada Territory in 1861 — a land as vast as it was unpredictable — the former printer and pilot received precisely the encouragement he needed. His bent toward satire and comic invective, two of his favorite literary postures, remained strong, but Clemens became enchanted by the apparently aimless, "rambling and amorphous" stories he heard in the mining country of Nevada and California.[22] In his 1907 eulogy for Jim Gillis, a favorite practitioner of the yarn spinner's art, Mark Twain described the meandering quality that he frequently sought to reproduce in his own prose style through a premeditated attention to the writer's craft.

> He had a bright and smart imagination and it was of the kind that turns out impromptu work and does it well, does it with easy facility and without previous preparation, just builds a story as it goes along, careless of whither it is proceeding, enjoying each fresh fancy as it flashes from the brain and caring not at all whether the story shall ever end brilliantly and satisfactorily or shan't end at all.[23]

By 1861, Sam Clemens had begun to suspect that, in fact, "it takes a heap of sense to write good nonsense."[24] During his years in Nevada, he acquired a profound respect for men like Jim Gillis, as well as much of the "sense" — or, more appropriately, the craft — that would enable him to adapt Gillis's yarn-spinning style to literature.

To that end, Clemens began to refine his humorous technique in a number of ways immediately after his arrival in the West. In a series of letters to the Keokuk *Gate City*, composed during his first winter in Nevada, for example, he introduced a fictive audience in order to give his meandering yarns a performative quality. As Franklin Rogers has explained, all three letters in the 1861 series are addressed to a character whom the narrator calls "Mother," but who bears only a distant resemblance to Jane L. Clemens. In fact, the "Mother" of the letters is a romantic fool whose attitudes are intended to place the narrator's deflating humor in high relief. Rogers uncovered the personal letter on which the first installment of the published correspondence was based, and his analysis of Clemens's revision offers rare insight into the young author's increasingly sophisticated methods as a humorist. In the opening paragraph of the personal version, Clemens quotes his mother as writing: "tell everything as it is—no better, and no worse." The first Keokuk letter begins: "You ask me in your last to tell you about the country—tell everything just as it is—no better and no worse—and *do* let nonsense alone."[25] As Rogers points out, the additional warning against "nonsense" conveys an important hint about the "waywardness" of the narrator, preparing the reader for an extended juxtaposition of two radically different ways of seeing and describing the world.[26] The implied relationship between the romantically inclined mother and her wayward son allowed Clemens to locate the humor of the letters within a fixed rhetorical context. In Walter Blair's words, borrowed from another context, Clemens had succeeded for the first time in "so representing his listener and his storyteller as to relate them to the story."[27]

In the second letter from Nevada, the author tells his mother about a pack trip to the Humboldt region. The episode forms the basis for Chapters 26 to 33 of *Roughing It*, but the most memorable character in the letter does not appear in Twain's 1872 account of the journey.[28]

At first, Billy drove, and we pushed behind the wagon. Not because we were fond of it, ma—Oh, no—but on Bunker's account. Bunker was the "near" horse, on the larboard side. Named after the Attorney General of this Territory. My horse—you are acquainted with him, by reputation, already—and I am sorry you don't know him personally, ma, for I feel toward him, sometimes, as if he were a blood relation of our family—he is so infernally lazy, you know— my horse, I was going to say—was the "off" horse on the starboard side. But it was on Bunker's account, principally, that we pushed behind the wagon. For whenever we came to a hard piece of road, that poor, lean, infatuated cuss would fall into a deep reverie about something or other, and stop perfectly still, and it would generally take a vast amount of back-snaking and shoving and profanity to get him started again; and as soon as he was fairly under way, he would take up the thread of his reflections where he left off, and go on thinking, and pondering, and getting himself more and more mixed up and tangled in his subject, until he would get regularly stuck again, and stop to review the question. . . . [W]hen I departed, I saw him standing, solitary and alone, away up on the highest peak of a mountain, where no horse ever ventured before, with his pensive figure darkly defined against the sky — still thinking about it.[29]

The Bunker sketch generates humor by portraying animal behavior in terms that are appropriate to rational human beings, just as the image of a "religious meeting" among bugs — taken literally instead of figuratively — involves a perverse association of ideas.[30] Yet rather than openly relishing his incongruous imagery, the narrator of Clemens's Nevada letter adopts a deadpan expression that invests his portrait of an intellectual horse with another sort of interest. Like the ideal yarn spinner described in "How to Tell a Story," this narrator describes Bunker's human personality traits "gravely," careful to appear "innocently unaware that they are absurdities."[31] His seriousness cannot be interpreted as actual naiveté, as was the case with Snodgrass, yet he half conceals his ingenuity by seeming to believe in his own words, consciously locating his yarn somewhere between the extremes of metaphysical wit and naive error. Clemens was becoming increasingly aware that a narrator's attitude toward his material plays an important role in determining the nature and effectiveness of the performance as a whole. In sharpening the image of his narrator, the author was actually involved in creating his most important fictional character, a character whose appearance in the Keokuk letters, Franklin Rogers agrees, marks the "first known instance in which Samuel L. Clemens adopted for the purposes of narration that guise or persona which he named 'Mark Twain' early in 1863."[32] He had not yet discovered the name, but the expression of deadpan sincerity that would become his hallmark on the lecture platform five years later was already emerging as an effective literary posture.

In the fall of 1862, the former printer, pilot, and miner embarked on yet another career. According to Albert Bigelow Paine, Joe Goodman of the Virginia City *Territorial Enterprise* hired Clemens as a local reporter on the strength of a boast that might easily have come from Nimrod Wildfire or Mike Fink: "I was sired by the Great American Eagle and foaled by a continental dam."[33] Almost immediately on his arrival in the *Enterprise* office, Clemens began demonstrating his sharpened powers of exaggeration for the benefit of Washoe readers, wasting no time in acting on his belief that "stirring news . . . was what a paper needed" and that, in the absence of actual excitement, he himself was "peculiarly endowed with the ability to furnish it."[34] By stretching the facts without neglecting details, a reporter could make news out of almost anything, as Mark Twain recalled in *Roughing It*.

> I . . . found one wretched old hay-truck dragging in from the country. But I made affluent use of it. I multiplied it by sixteen, brought it into town from sixteen different directions, made sixteen separate items of it, and got up such another sweat about hay as Virginia City had never seen in the world before.[35]

Frontier newspaper work of the sort that Joe Goodman demanded from his reporters provided a natural setting for tall humor, and the *Enterprise* office soon became a proving ground for the literary yarn spinner in Sam Clemens. When Goodman cautioned his new local correspondent never to write "'We learn' so-and-so, or 'It is reported,'" but "say 'It *is* so-and-so,'" he might as well have been coaching the yarn spinner on how to maintain a deadpan expression.[36] Clemens succeeded all too well at simulating an authoritative tone in the two famous hoaxes of his reporting career, the "Petrified Man" and "A Massacre near Carson," which together earned a wide and notorious reputation for Mark Twain, the pseudonym he began to employ regularly in January 1863.[37]

Occasionally, Mark Twain abandoned both the newspaper hoax and the simple "hay-wagon" variety of exaggerated reporting in favor of a more complex story structure. In "Over the Mountains," an 1863 item for the *Enterprise*, he depicted a storytelling encounter in which, for the first time, the character Mark Twain adopts the listener's role in a yarn-spinning performance, while a talkative driver of the "Pioneer" stagecoach plays the storyteller.[38] In an effort to keep his sleepy companion awake, the stage driver begins cheerfully to relate anecdotes about other passengers who have yielded to sleep at his side, only to end up sprawled on the roadside, "all jammed and bloody and quivering in death's agony." As with the fictive mother–son relationship of the Keokuk letters, Twain prepares a dramatic context for the ensuing yarn by exaggerating not only the driver's roughness, but the reporter's refinement and eloquence as well. In a sentence designed specifically to exploit the contrast of narrative styles, the driver begins:

> "Now," he said, after urging his team at a furious speed down the grade for awhile, plunging into deep bends in the road brimming with a thick darkness almost palpable to the touch, and darting out again and again on the verge of what instinct told me was a precipice, "Now, I seen a poor cuss—but you're asleep again, you know, and you've rammed your head agin' my side-pocket and busted a bottle of nasty rotten medicine that I'm taken to the folks at the Thirty-five Mile House."

The driver soon resumes with a narrative that is intended to startle the reporter out of his drowsiness:

> "As I was saying, I see a poor cuss tumble off along here one night— he was monstrous drowsy, and went to sleep when I'd took my eye off him for a moment—and he fetched up agin a boulder, and in a second there wasn't anything left of him but a promiscus pile of hash! It was moonlight, and when I got down and looked at him he was quivering like jelly, and sorter moaning to himself, like, and the bones of his legs was sticking out through his pantaloons every which way, like that." (Here the driver mixed his fingers up after the manner of a stack of muskets, and illuminated them with the ghostly light of his cigar.) "He warn't in misery long though. In a minute and a half he was deader'n a smelt—Bob! I say I'll cut that horse's throat if he stays on this route another week."

In framing the driver's rough vernacular performance with his own purple prose, the reporter deploys a favorite technique of the southwestern humorists, but his intention is not to revert to an older, more gentlemanly style of humor. The narrative frame had served writers like Esperance as a means of insulating their efforts at vernacular performance, enabling writers to indulge in low comedy without challenging standards of decorum. In Twain's sketch, on the other hand, the narrative frame works to bring characters with different styles and assumptions *into* rhetorical conflict. The reporter's prose style suggests a stark contrast with the driver's oral delivery, but that contrast neither isolates the vernacular storyteller nor marks his performance as substandard. Instead, the framing technique serves to emphasize differences over which the two characters will collide in a rhetorical encounter that seems to defy the very integrity of the frame.

The driver's yarn may be more an exercise in hyperbole than in imaginative storytelling, but Twain's management of perspective in the scene points out the direction he would follow two years later in "The Jumping Frog" and other more ambitious attempts at literary yarn spinning. During his years with the *Enterprise*, he learned that an exaggerated narrative in writing, however outrageous, is itself of limited interest unless behind the narration there exists a rhetorical contest of wits. In an 1881 letter to Joel Chandler Harris, he articulated this point after Harris had disclaimed the originality of his "Uncle Remus" tales. Twain's letter explained that the primary interest of the tales lay elsewhere than in the material Harris had borrowed from oral storytellers:

> You can argue *yourself* into the delusion that the principle of life is in the stories themselves and not in their setting but you will save labor by stopping with that solitary convert, for he is the only intelligent one you will bag. In reality the stories are only alligator pears. One merely eats them for the sake of the salad dressing.[39]

In 1881, Twain understood clearly that the writer of a tall tale, unlike the oral narrator from whom he perhaps learns his material, must depict the relationship of the teller to his audience. He must, as Walter Blair and Hamlin Hill have suggested, "clarify such matters as why one listens to a long-winded monologue and why the other gives it the substance and form he does."[40] In the Keokuk letters from Nevada, a young Sam Clemens had begun to employ tall stories as points of interpretive confrontation between partially developed fictional characters. In "Over the Mountains," the narrative frame had provided another means of juxtaposing characters with different approaches to narrative performance and response. To a large extent, the literary device that made rhetorical drama possible was "Mark Twain," a character flexible enough to play the cultural insider or the fool with equal facility. And it is this drama, as Sydney J. Krause and other critics have endeavored to show, that invests "Jim Smiley and His Jumping Frog" with its powerful interest.[41]

Bret Harte recalled having heard Twain perform the frog story in San Francisco, shortly after his return from Jackass Hill and Angel's Camp:

> He said the men did nothing all day but sit around the bar-room stove, spit, and "swap lies." . . . He went on to tell one of those extravagant stories, and half unconsciously dropped into the lazy tone and manner of the original narrator. . . . The story was "The Jumping Frog of Calaveras."[42]

Twain could imitate to perfection the manner of a seasoned professional like Ben Coon or Jim Gillis, but the task of transferring that manner to the printed page finally required at least three drafts and a great deal more than half-unconscious attention to questions of style and structure. The pattern of his revisions indicates that those questions involved principally the attitude of the writer toward the vernacular narrator from whom he receives the tale. In the earliest surviving version, "The Only Reliable Account of the Celebrated Jumping Frog of Calaveras County," Simon Wheeler is "a venerable rural historian" who lives in "unostentatious privacy," and from whom the author has received a "just and true account."[43] In this version, Mark Twain plays the part of a naive and reverential listener, fully absorbed by the rustic's inventive narrative.

Perhaps Clemens found this attitude too implausible, for he soon began a second version, "Angel's Camp Constable," in which a more urbane Mark Twain adopts an ironic attitude of bemused condescension toward the vernacular yarn spinner: "I was told that if I would mention any of the venerable Simon Wheeler's pet heroes, he would be sure to tell me about them, but that I must not laugh during the recital, as he would think I was making fun of them, and it would give him mortal offense."[44] Whereas the first version makes the character of the author contemptible by exaggerating his naiveté, the second invites the reader to enjoy a ridiculous folk story from the detached perspective of an educated and self-assured writer. Neither version depicts a fair contest in which the event of performance might provide a setting for genuine and engaging conflict between fictional characters.

In the third version, as it appeared in the New York *Saturday Press* on November 18, 1865, Mark Twain has been tricked into a rhetorical corner where he must endure Wheeler's "infernal reminiscence" of the "infamous" Jim Smiley.[45] According to Joseph Twichell, Twain pigeonholed the first two drafts because he found them "poor and flat."[46] He preferred the third because in it the relationship between the garrulous Simon Wheeler and his impatient, unappreciative auditor locates the tale within a specific context of performance. His revision added nothing either to the substance of Wheeler's tale or to the yarn spinner's easygoing narrative style. What Twain sought after two false starts was a plausible and realistic drama of performance through which to relate the fictional storyteller to his fictional listener in such a way that the reader enjoys "the spontaneity of a personal relation, which is the very essence of interest."

Twain's early development of methods for effectively conveying oral yarns in print involved no magical breakthrough, and he would likely have been the first to point out that his early success as a literary yarn spinner owed a great deal to the methods of previous humorists. But the jumping frog story was unprecedented in its manner of blending the concreteness of a storytelling performance, as described by the pedantic realist Mark Twain, with the fantastic imagery and illogic of a very different kind of narrative creator, Simon Wheeler. It is the drama that unfolds between these two competing imaginations, and the contrast between their chosen media, that fuels the sketch with interest and ignites its satire. Bernard DeVoto made a similar point when he described the essential method of Mark Twain's humor by pointing to the interplay of fantasy and reality in "Jim Baker's Blue-Jay Yarn." Baker's winged friends, with their unexpectedly refined qualities of intellect and emotion, are the "monstrous fabrications" of Baker's active imagination. Yet the old miner himself, according to DeVoto, "is a creation from the world of reality. He lives, and no fantasy has gone into his creation, but only the sharp perception of an individual." "Fantasy," DeVoto concludes, "is thus an instrument of realism and the humor of Mark Twain merges into the fiction that is his highest reach."[47]

DeVoto might just as easily have explained that realism becomes an instrument of fantasy, for in Twain's most important early writing neither imaginative impulse finally subsumes the other. By "dramatizing a part of himself," as Everett Emerson has put it, often assuming the role of an incompetent listener, Twain compromised his own claims to narrative authority and set in motion a rhetorical contest between the competing voices of his imagination.[48] His "failure" to resolve that contest, to relocate narrative authority in some stable place, has traditionally frustrated readers such as George Santayana, who praised Twain for challenging the "genteel tradition," but then complained that the American humorists, and Twain in particular, devised "nothing solid to put in its place."[49] Santayana was right to notice that Twain affirmed nothing solid; what he affirmed instead was an unending process of dialogue and interpretation, of performance and response. In his most promising early experiments as a writer, Twain barely managed to control the proliferating voices of his humor, each of which makes its own claim to the writer's unstable creative authority. The tall tale, with its mutable form and its rhetorical pattern of interpretive challenge and response, offered him a means of dramatizing the interaction of voices without pretending to have resolved them into a single, unified voice.

3

Joyous Heresy:
Travelling with the
Innocent Abroad

Americans expended considerable energy attempting to answer criticism from European travellers in the New World during the late eighteenth and early nineteenth centuries. In their defense, writers such as Royall Tyler were understandably prone to grasp at whatever advantage they could claim, with the result that many of the earliest responses to European criticism probably provoked more amusement than respect on the other side of the Atlantic. As one of the first and best known patriots to brandish a pen in the nation's defense, Tyler helped to initiate a tradition of American response to European censure by producing his own observations of travel in England, published anonymously in 1808 as *The Yankey in London*. In a typical passage, the American writer condemns what he considers the pernicious habit among members of the most polite British society of polluting their language with "evanescent vulgarisms of fashionable colloquy," or slang. He goes on to object that "there are a number of words now familiar, not merely in transient converse, but even in English fine writing, which are of vulgar origin and illegitimate descent, which . . . degrade their finest modern compositions by a grotesque air of pert vivacity."[1]

The Yankee is especially rankled by the word "clever," which the British frequently employ to mean "skillful" or "adroit." He observes that

Englishmen, from the peer to the peasant, cannot converse ten minutes without introducing this pert adjunct. The English do not, however, use it in the same sense we do in New England, where we apply
it to personal grace, and call a trim, well-built young man, clever—
which signification is sanctioned by Bailey's and the elder English
dictionaries.

Had America's cultural sovereignty depended on the effectiveness
of such attacks, it might have been a much longer and ultimately
less successful struggle. Not surprisingly, a proposed second volume of Tyler's travel observations never appeared in print, possibly
indicating that his strategy for out-Britishing the British was not
terribly effective at bolstering the national pride.

Fortunately for America, more resourceful writers fashioned
other weapons with which to answer the charge of cultural depravity in the New World. If the former colonists could not speak
more correctly than their European critics, at least they could speak
differently, in fact so differently that no degree of Old World
refinement and polish could decipher the full meaning of an American's idiom. Hence when a character named Jonathan Peabody
made a fictional journey to London as part of James Kirke Paulding's 1813 production of *The Bucktails; or Americans in England*,
he was full of unmistakably native pride, whistling "Yankee Doo-
dle" and bragging in defiance of his foreign critics: "I'm half horse,
half alligator, and a little bit of the Ingen, I guess."[2] Paulding's
foppish British characters were thoroughly subdued by such figurative boasting, and they seemed equally befuddled by the American
gift for spinning out formulations like "I guess," "I reckon," and
"I calculate." Royall Tyler would have been embarrassed to hear
his fictitious countryman Sam Slick brag in a similar vein of his
peculiar advantage over the British in Thomas Chandler Haliburton's *The Attaché; or Sam Slick in England* (1843). Sam admits he
may be inferior to his English hosts in manners and refinement,
but he knows "a leetle, jist a leetle, grain more, p'r'aps," about the
British "than they [know] of the Yankees."[3] More specifically, Sam
finds that "they're considerable large print are the Bull family,"
"you can read 'em by moonlight," whereas the narrator warns of
Sam himself that "it was not always easy to decide whether his
stories were facts or fictions."[4] After "shampooing the English" in

one episode, the champion of Yankee slang exclaims, "Oh dear! how John Bull swallows this soft sawder, don't he?"[5]

Paulding, as usual, played an important role in establishing the yarn spinner's art as a national trait capable of asserting American democratic values against criticism from Europe. His *John Bull in America; or, The New Munchausen* (1825) satirized Britain's thirst for confirmation of its already firm belief that the liberated colonies were populated by wild animals and even wilder humans. The mock editor of this purportedly unfinished manuscript explains that, despite the title he has chosen, readers should be prepared to enjoy "a work of incomparable veracity."[6] The manuscript's author, according to the editor, was an Englishman, probably a staff writer for London's *Quarterly Review*, a journal famous for its denunciations of America. While gathering observations of American life, the author disappeared without a trace, leaving only a tattered notebook behind. Finding the mysterious Englishman's work to be "of severe and inflexible truth," despite its author's occasional willingness to "stretch his belief into the regions of the marvellous," the editor has decided to publish the unclaimed manuscript. Predictably, the new Munchausen's narrative often verges on the fantastic, although in his eagerness to confirm a cultural bias, the Englishman is the last to suspect that his accounts of American brutality and vice are even partially exaggerated.

> The Governor told me a story of a man, who tied his black servant naked to a stake, in one of the neighboring canebrakes, near the city, which abound with a race of moschetoes that bite through a boot. He was left one night, in the month of December, which is a spring month in this climate, and the next morning was found stone dead, without a drop of blood in his body. I asked if this brutal tyrant was not brought to justice? The Governor shrugged his shoulders and replied, that he was now a member of Congress![7]

Paulding's caricature of the hopelessly credulous Englishman proved a far more convincing response to British attitudes than had Royall Tyler's haughty critique of London slang.[8] The tall tale was readily available as a weapon that could be used against unsuspecting European travellers in America, and it was not long before American globe-trotters like J. Ross Browne, Samuel Fiske, and Mark Twain were arriving in foreign lands, armed with this slender superiority. In their dispatches to readers at home, America's travelling humorists declared their independence from traditional romantic and associationist approaches to descriptive writing about foreign cultures.[9] Browne, for example, warned in *Yusef* (1853) that readers would find his account of experiences in Palestine more cheerful and less profound than other books on the Holy Land: "it will be seen that I have not felt it to be my duty to make a desponding pilgrimage through the Holy Land; for upon a careful perusal of the Scriptures, I can find nothing said against a cheerful frame of mind."[10] Samuel Fiske, another popular dissenter from the "desponding" school of travel correspondence, published a memoir of his journey through Europe, North Africa, and the Holy Land in 1857 under the title *Mr. Dunn Browne's Experiences in Foreign Parts.* A typical passage tended to demystify European experience for American readers by adopting a yarn spinner's figurative and hyperbolic language:

> A German bed is a sort of coffin about five feet long and two wide, into which a body squeezes himself and passes the night completely buried in feathers, and digs himself out in the morning. . . . I never endured the thing but one night, during which I dreamed of undergoing no less than four distinct deaths, one by an anaconda necklace, one by a hempen ditto, one by the embrace of a grizzly bear, and a fourth by the press of a cider-mill.[11]

Fiske's humor may have been less than overpowering, but his focus on sordid details rather than historical panoramas marked an important coming of age in the American interpretation of its past. His prefatory remarks, echoing Browne's disclaimer in *Yusef*, signaled an intention to describe foreign lands as they might have appeared to the eye of an unromantic American:

> I shall endeavor . . . to keep wide open my eye financial, agricultural, commercial, architectural, legal, critical, metaphysical, and quizzical. I shall also take a bird's eye view of the feathered tribes, cast a sheep's eye at the flocks and herds, and obtain dissolving views of the beet sugar crop and salt mines. . . . No rouge will be laid on the face of the old lady, and no artificial helps resorted to, to improve her beauty; no milliner's fripperies, trinkets, and jewels,

but a simple dress. Mine shall be a "plain, unvarnished tale:" no quips and quiddities, sly innuendoes and oddities of language to disturb the digestion of an after dinner reader.[12]

In June 1867, ten years after the publication of Fiske's book, Mark Twain boarded the *Quaker City* and followed an almost identical route toward the East, determined, like his predecessors, to dispense with the conventional picturesque mode and to report his experience in a language and from a perspective that Americans could understand. Like Paulding's Jonathan Peabody and Haliburton's Sam Slick before him, Mark Twain's narrator arrives in the Old World with only a yarn spinner's shrewdness to compensate for an abundance of ignorance. But that small advantage is decisive in establishing the perspective of Twain's American innocent abroad. The narrator is aware that many experiences escape his unrefined appreciation, yet he neither apologizes for his rough humor nor makes pretenses toward understanding what is alien to his sensibility. He recognizes himself as a greenhorn in matters involving European standards of taste and sophistication, yet he is always ready to strike back by exploiting the credulity of foreigners. His intention, like Fiske's, is "to suggest to the reader how *he* would be likely to see Europe and the East if he looked at them with his own eyes instead of the eyes of those who traveled in those countries before him."[13]

Albert Bigelow Paine noted that Twain's correspondence from Europe and the Holy Land "preached heresy—the heresy of viewing revered landmarks and relics joyously, rather than lugubriously."[14] In fact, the author's favorite strategy in the series of letters he sent to the *Daily Alta California* and to two New York newspapers between 1867 and 1868 was to view his subject matter both lugubriously and joyously, so that his humor tended to operate in the contrast between competing points of view.[15] In a typical passage from the original series of letters, the narrator presents an exaggeratedly luxuriant image of Lake Como, explicitly mimicking the picturesque mode of landscape description: "Last night the scenery was striking and picturesque. On the other side crags and trees, and snowy houses were pictured in the glassy lake with a wonderful distinctness, and streams of light from a distant window shot far abroad over the still waters."[16] After several more lines of indulgent scene painting, the narrator declares, "but enough of description is sufficient, I judge." Feeling he has perhaps gone too far in his praise of Lake Como, he shifts his focus to America with a digressive comment on the "wonderful translucence of Lake Tahoe," and a different sort of scene painting ensues:

> I speak of the north shore of Tahoe, where one can count the scales on a trout at a depth of a hundred and eighty feet. I have tried to get this statement off at par here, but with no success; so I have been obliged to negotiate it at fifty per cent. discount. At this rate I find some takers, perhaps you may as well receive it on the same terms — ninety feet instead of a hundred and eighty.

The narrator's juxtaposition of these two images is significant, for his sudden willingness to negotiate the claim about Tahoe's translucence punctures the romantic picture of Como as well. Moving rapidly from lugubrious description to joyous heresy, as Paine might have put it, the narrator establishes an ongoing contrast between different ways of assessing and reporting experience. Twain employs essentially the same joke in a later episode, again echoing James Hall's 1828 account of an interpretive bartering session in which competing storytellers figure truth as a relative commodity. After a lengthy account of his ascent of Mount Vesuvius, the narrator proposes an interpretive joint venture as the only hope of affording a local legend whose extravagance is too dear:

> It is said that during one of the grand eruptions of Vesuvius it discharged massy rocks weighing many tons a thousand feet into the air, its vast jets of smoke and steam ascended thirty miles toward the firmament, and clouds of its ashes were wafted abroad and fell upon the decks of ships seven hundred and fifty miles at sea! I will take the ashes at a moderate discount, if any one will take the thirty miles of smoke, but I do not feel able to take a commanding interest in the whole story by myself.[17]

Each of America's early yarn-spinning ambassadors, from Peabody to Dunn Browne, had played some version of this game, mingling wide-eyed reverence with a native genius for subversive, irreverent talk. Fiske was particularly adept at juxtaposing panoramic descriptions with sordid particulars, a tactic already standard in more "serious" travel correspondence dating from the first part of the nineteenth century.[18] Nevertheless, familiar as many of its comic devices must have seemed in 1869, readers greeted *The Innocents Abroad* with unprecedented enthusiasm. Other writers knew all too well how to employ the Vesuvius brand of understatement as a way of qualifying their exaggeratedly luxurious descriptions; what separated *Innocents* from its prototypes was Mark Twain's refusal to stop at the sort of contrast suggested by mere understatement — his insistence, in other words, on dramatic confrontation in favor of verbal contrast.

Twain had learned from "The Jumping Frog" and other early pieces that the narrative interest of tall humor stems primarily from the interpretive drama that surrounds the performance of a tale. Thus on his return to America in 1868, he began revising his *Alta* letters in an effort to dramatize the often static comedy of the original correspondence. It was a step that other humorists, J. Ross Browne most notably, had omitted, yet one that proved decisive as a means of organizing what Bruce Michaelson has called Twain's "pleasure tour through modes of narration."[19] Like earlier humorous correspondents, the narrator of *The Innocents Abroad* moves rapidly and unexpectedly from one voice to another — from sentimentalism to parody, from patriotism to anti-Americanism, from silliness to sober observation. Yet in each of his guises, the narrator remains a player in the tall tale's interpretive game, and Twain's ability to give that game dramatic expression lends the book a measure of coherence that is lacking in Browne's *Yusef* and other comic travelogues of the period. Michaelson aptly describes *Innocents* as "a stylistic experiment with the principle of improvisatory play."[20] Insofar as all improvisation is to some extent governed, the rules of that play are the rules of the tall tale's rhetorical drama, which Twain's revisions enact at every opportunity as a way of steering his "pleasure tour" toward its appointed destination.

The Vesuvius and Tahoe passages survived Twain's reworking of the *Alta* letters, yet many of the changes he undertook in preparing a manuscript for book publication reflect a conscious effort to dramatize his humorous material. The most important single change involved a shift in the narrative situation. The third in his series of fifty letters to the *Alta*, for example, begins with a description of the Moroccan port of Tangier, which the author praises with faint damnation: "This is jolly! This is altogether the infernalest place I have ever come across yet. Let those who went up through Spain make much of it — these dominions of the Emperor of Morocco suit me well enough."[21] When he revised the passage for book publication early in 1868, Twain made only minor changes: "This is royal! Let those who went up through Spain make the best of it — these dominions of the Emperor of Morocco suit our little party well enough" (57). The substitution of "royal" for "jolly," and the omission of the slang "infernalest," may be understood simply as part of the author's stated attempt to "weed [the letters] of their . . . inelegancies of expression" as a concession to eastern readers.[22] With the more significant insertion of "our little party," on the other hand, Twain intended to prepare a dramatic context for ensuing episodes. Much like the fictive mother of the 1861 letters from Nevada, "our little party" functions throughout *The Innocents Abroad* as a portable audience, a travelling yarn-spinning community whose exchange of yarns and interpretations allows Twain to locate his narrator's verbal pranks in a situational context. The doctor, Dan, Jack, and the Youth, together with the narrator and occasional others, perform yarns, pranks, and deceptions for the entertainment of the group, and they respond as a "community of knowers" to the sanctified fictions they encounter in Europe and the Holy Land. The "I" that reports its impressions of Tangier in the *Alta* letter becomes one of "the boys" in *The Innocents Abroad*, and while the revision has little effect on the descriptive quality of the passage, its effect on subsequent episodes is significant. With Twain as its spokesman, this small community of experienced raconteurs assesses the validity of traditional European fictions with standards imported from America.

Twain was deliberate about replacing the *Alta* narrator's individual perspective with the group perspective of the book, even when such revisions contributed nothing to the humor or elegance of a passage. A sentence in the New York *Tribune* letter of November 9, 1867, for example, originally read: "The real name of this place is Cesarea Phillippi, but I call it Baldwinsville because it sounds better and I can recollect it easier."[23] In his revision, Twain transferred the joke a few miles to the east, attributing the wisecrack to "our little party" instead of to himself: "We rested and lunched, and came on to this place, Ain Mellahah (the boys call it Baldwinsville)" (347). The author's justification for inserting "the boys" here and in similarly curious revisions throughout the book emerges only in the longer episodes, where "our little party" comes to life and significantly alters the direction of Mark Twain's humor. In the *Alta* letter of September 22, 1867, for example, the narrator offers the following description:

> Speaking of barbers reminds me that in Europe they do not have any barber-shops. The barbers come to your room and skin you. (I use that term because it is more correctly descriptive than shave.) They have a few trifling barber-shops in Paris, but the heaviest establishment of the kind only boasted three barbers. There, as everywhere else in Europe, as far as our experience goes, they put a bowl under your chin and slop your face with water, and then rub it with a cake of soap, (except at Gibraltar, where they spit on the soap and use no bowl, because it is handier;) then they begin to shave, and you begin to swear; if you have got a good head of profanity on, you see the infliction through; but if you run out of blasphemy, there is nothing for it but to shut down on the operation until you recuperate.[24]

This is Mr. Twain of the *Alta* letters at his best, skillfully employing understatement and metaphor in a good-natured attack on the quality of European services. The narrator of *The Innocents Abroad* describes two shaving episodes, both of which focus more intensely on an actual event. The second episode, which takes place in Venice, is particularly worthy of comparison with the *Alta* version:

> The boys sent for a barber. . . . I said, "Not any for me, if you please."
> I wrote on. The barber began on the doctor. I heard him say:
> "Dan, this is the easiest shave I have had since we left the ship."
> He said again, presently:
> "Why, Dan, a man could go to sleep with this man shaving him."
> Dan took the chair. Then he said:
> "Why, this is Titian. This is one of the old masters."
> I wrote on. Directly Dan said:
> "Doctor, it is perfect luxury. The ship's barber isn't anything to him."

> My rough beard was distressing me beyond measure. The barber
> was rolling up his apparatus. The temptation was too strong. I said:
> "Hold on, please. Shave me also."
> I sat down in the chair and closed my eyes. The barber soaped my
> face and then took his razor and gave me a rake that well-nigh threw
> me into convulsions. I jumped out of the chair: Dan and the doctor
> were both wiping blood off their faces and laughing.
> I said it was a mean, disgraceful fraud. (173)

Whereas the humor of the *Alta* letter is generated by Mr. Twain's versatility as a descriptive narrator, capable of working up "a good head of profanity," the book relies for its effect on a game of credulity involving several characters. In *The Innocents Abroad*, the shaving experience has become less a subject for comic description than the pretense for narrating a brief encounter between gullible and conspiring members of "our little party." As in an earlier story, which pitted the experienced Simon Wheeler against a naive and indignant Mark Twain, it is the relationship between antagonists that generates the humor of the episode.

The difference between the comic method of the letters and that of the book is even more pronounced in the scenes that describe the harassment of Italian guides. In the sixth *Alta* letter, dated July 16, 1867, Twain relates his experience with a Genoan guide who claims to be one of only three citizens of that city who can speak and understand English. The guide leads his patron to the birthplace of Christopher Columbus, where Twain spends fifteen minutes "in silent awe before this inspiring shrine."[25] Only later does the guide mention that it was not exactly Columbus but Columbus's grandmother who was born there. The purported linguist then conducts the narrator to the municipal palace, where three of the explorer's letters are displayed. When asked if Columbus wrote them himself, the guide answers, "Oh, no." The narrator becomes frustrated:

> I began to suspect that this fellow's English was shaky, and I thought
> I would test the matter. He showed us a fine bust of Columbus on a
> pedestal, and I said, "Is this the first time this person, this Colum-
> bus, was ever on a bust?" and he innocently answered, "Oh, no." I
> began to think, then, that when he didn't understand a question, he
> just answered, "Oh, no," at a risk and took the chances. So I said,

"This Columbus you talk so much about—is he dead?" And the villain said quietly, "Oh, no!" I tested him further. I said, "This palace of the Dorias which you say is so old—is it fifty years old?" "Oh, no." "Is it five hundred?" "Oh, no." "It's a thousand, though, ain't it?" "Oh, yes." So his plan was to answer, "Oh, no," twice, always, and then, "Oh, yes," by way of a change. All the information we got out of that guide we shall be able to carry along with us, I think.[26]

The guide's method of concealing his ignorance of English wins a few laughs in this passage, yet when Twain revised the episode for *The Innocents Abroad*, he again shifted the emphasis of his humor from language to drama. As Leon T. Dickinson has remarked in his important study of the book, the humor of the revised version no longer focuses on the guide's ignorance of English, "but rather [on] his consternation in the face of the questions put to him" by the boys.[27] The chief inquisitor is not Mark Twain but the doctor, a consummate yarn spinner and grave humorist who, like the ideal teller described in "How to Tell a Story," "does his best to conceal the fact that he even dimly suspects that there is anything funny" about his statements.[28] The doctor's skill is indeed considerable, according to the narrator's account, for he "can keep his countenance, and look more like an inspired idiot, and throw more imbecility into the tone of his voice than any man that lives" (209–10). Thus the episode with the Genoan guide becomes something more like a tall-tale encounter than a game of words and misunderstanding when the doctor decides to entertain his friends by fooling the unsuspecting European with his deadpan sincerity. Intending to exploit the same American fascination with Columbus that had cost Mark Twain fifteen minutes of wasted awe in the *Alta* letter, the guide leads the boys on a relic hunt:

"Come wis me, genteelmen! Come! I show you ze letter-writing by Christopher Columbo! Write it himself! Write it wis his own hand! Come!" . . .

We looked indifferent—unconcerned. The doctor examined the document very deliberately, during a painful pause. Then he said, without any show of interest:

"Ah—Ferguson—what—what did you say was the name of the party who wrote this?"

"Christopher Columbo! Ze great Christopher Columbo!"
Another deliberate examination.
"Ah — did he write it himself or — or how?"
"He write it himself! Christopher Columbo! His own handwriting, write by himself!"
Then the doctor laid the document down and said:
"Why, I have seen boys in America only fourteen years old that could write better than that."
"But zis is ze great Christo — "
"I don't care who it is! It's the worst writing I ever saw. Now you mustn't think you can impose on us because we are strangers." (210)

The irony of the doctor's last statement lies in the fact that the guide is actually the stranger in this encounter, and his failure to recognize the doctor's deadpan attitude provides entertainment for the boys, who are cultural insiders despite the fact that they are on foreign soil. The humor of the episode results not from the guide's poor English, as in the letter, but from the dramatic consequences of his failure to understand the doctor's tone. As in the shaving scene, the revised version places the original verbal comedy in a situational context that is patterned after a tall-tale performance. The credulity of cultural outsiders like the Genoan guide and, later, the American Pilgrims aboard the ship becomes a rallying point for the boys throughout the book. They repeatedly challenge outsiders with the doctor's brand of veiled absurdity, and those "tests," as the narrator calls them, allow Twain to dramatize the encounter between Old and New World perspectives as he had not done in the original correspondence.

In his addition of new episodes to the book, Twain pursued the same priority of dramatization over description, and again the tall tale provided a rough dramatic principle. In several scenes, including one that did not appear in the letters, the narrator parodies his own credulity, which is rooted in an inherited assumption of European superiority in matters of taste and refinement. In his effort to appear sophisticated by European standards, the narrator falls victim to a shop girl's straight-faced flattery:

It seemed a stylish thing to go to the theatre in kid gloves, and we acted upon the hint. A very handsome young lady in the store offered me a pair of blue gloves. I did not want blue, but she said they would look very pretty on a hand like mine. The remark touched me tenderly. I glanced furtively at my hand, and somehow it did seem rather a comely member. I tried a glove on my left hand and blushed a little. Manifestly the size was too small for me. But I felt gratified when she said:

"Oh, it is just right!" . . . "Ah! I see *you* are accustomed to wearing kid gloves—but some gentlemen are *so* awkward about putting them on."

It was the last compliment I had expected. I only understand putting on the buckskin article perfectly. . . . She kept up her compliments, and I kept up my determination to deserve them or die.

"Ah, you have had experience! [A rip down the back of the hand.] They are just right for you—your hand is very small—if they tear you need not pay for them. [A rent across the middle.] . . ."

I was too much flattered to make an exposure and throw the merchandise on the angel's hands. I was hot, vexed, confused, but still happy; but I hated the other boys for taking such an absorbing interest in the proceedings. (55–56)

The girl's flattery is not a tall tale, but rhetorically it works the same way. The narrator's vanity and credulity cause him to misinterpret her affected sincerity, and again the performance offers priceless entertainment for the boys. As before, they play the part of cultural insiders, although it later turns out that the inside knowledge that allows them to appreciate the ruse has been won at a cost. After Dan and the doctor soliloquize about the importance of refinement and experience in a gentleman, the narrator learns that the boys have already attempted to buy kid gloves and that they, too, have suffered humiliation as a result of their vanity. In the end, their mutual victimization draws the members of the "little party" closer together and helps to define their peculiarly American values against those of Europe: "We threw all the purchases away this morning. They were coarse, unsubstantial, freckled all over with broad yellow splotches, and could neither stand wear nor public exhibition. We had entertained an angel unawares, but we did not take her in. She did that for us" (57).

Actually, the boys perform a twofold function in the book. Together with enabling the author to dramatize the verbal humor of the letters, they implicitly supply the reader with a consistent perspective toward that humor In his preface to *The Innocents*

Abroad, Twain declares that his reflections of travel intend "to suggest to the reader how *he* would be likely to see Europe and the East if he looked at them with his own eyes" (15). James M. Cox has pointed out that Twain's comment expresses the veiled assumption that "as long as the narrator is honest, there is no real distinction between the narrator and the reader. The narrator's feelings and vision stand for the reader's own."[29] In fact, however, the narrator's gullibility and romanticism frequently inject ironic distance between his perspective and that of the reader. Thus when Mark Twain suddenly adopts the role of naive victim, as in the kid-glove scene, the reader shares a laugh with the boys at his expense. "Our little party" functions throughout the book as an ideal inside audience, capable of inviting and sustaining the reader's sympathy whether Twain's narrator is playing the role of spokesman or victim in the group's entertainment.

Elaborating on this question of the narrator's flexible role, Forrest G. Robinson voices a traditional concern about the book when he writes of Twain's narrator that "sudden shifts of tone betray a marked ambivalence about America, and a conspicuous incapacity to sustain a tone of humorous impersonation."[30] Robinson is right to observe a conspicuous lack of stability in the narrator's tone, for *The Innocents Abroad* is indeed a "pleasure tour through modes of narration," and Twain seems just as comfortable playing the innocent as the old timer. Yet the tall tale effectively structures this conspicuous instability by establishing, instead of a consistent narrative tone, a stable rhetorical game in which the narrator consistently participates. Whether the mode of narration is innocent or experienced, sentimental or parodic, the game unfolds among its players in essentially the same way.

The narrator's "marked ambivalence about America" also operates within the larger consistency of the tall tale's rhetorical encounter. Robert Regan has written that it was only toward the end of the journey, in September 1867, that Twain finally discovered "the theme that was to constitute the bedrock of *The Innocents Abroad*."[31] In his thirty-seventh letter to the *Alta*, according to Regan, in which the correspondent describes the hypocritical piety of the *Quaker City*'s pilgrims, "Mark Twain for the first time winnows chaff from wheat, separates 'pilgrims' from 'sinners,'" and thus settles on "the theme of his first great work." "Without foreshadowing," Regan continues, "a dramatic antagonism made its appearance." Whereas guides were easy prey because they failed to understand "our little party's" sense of humor, the *Quaker City*'s American pilgrims came to represent a more formidable opposition to the attitudes expressed by the narrator and his friends. The pilgrims not only fail to appreciate the narrator's humor; they reject it with a self-righteousness that he never observes in even the most repellent foreigners. Their narrow and inflexible vision of truth leads them on more than one occasion to "commit a sin against the spirit of religious law in order that they might preserve the letter of it." Citing scriptural authority, the pious tourists cruelly misuse their horses rather than risk breaking the Sabbath, and later they desecrate sacred shrines in order to collect reminders of their journey through the Holy Land (323). Zealously determined to parade their piety before the world, they embody the hypocrisy of what Twain elsewhere deemed "the most malignant form of Presbyterianism, — that sort which considers the saving of one's own paltry soul the first and supreme end and object of life."[32]

As he revised the *Alta* correspondence for publication, Twain sought to project his new theme by juxtaposing the interpretive assumptions of the pilgrims against those of "our little party," a plan that required some important changes. In the original letters, for example, a character named Mr. Blucher had served as the vernacular foil for Mr. Twain's romantic and picturesque idiom.[33] Blucher appears frequently in the *Alta* correspondence, where he characteristically interrupts the narrator's ornate descriptions with a contradictory horse-sense comment or a deflating observation, much as the crude Mr. Brown repeatedly interrupts the romantic Mr. Twain in the author's Hawaiian letters. Yet as the revision began to take shape, Twain recognized the possibility of incorporating a larger theme by dissolving the Twain–Blucher character axis, and as a result Mr. Blucher is almost entirely absent from the text of *The Innocents Abroad*. Blucher's irreverence and the narrator's original romanticism converge in the perpetually shifting attitudes of the boys, who encounter a new kind of foil in the sanctimonious pilgrims. While "our little party" engages in hard interpretive bargaining over the plausibility of every secondhand report of experience, the *Quaker City*'s pilgrims cannot make sense of the narrator's willingness to negotiate over belief, for they deny the existence of any gray area between truth and lie. Franklin Rogers points out that the confrontation between the self-proclaimed sinners and their pious antagonists is only partially dramatized, yet the nascent conflict represents Twain's first extended treatment of what would become his greatest theme: the pragmatic and commonsense values of a vernacular community, whose natural idiom is the tall tale, confront the rigid beliefs of a society that sanctions conventional myths with the stamp of absolute truth.[34]

The contest between rival approaches to interpretation and experience is waged with exemplary valor by both parties on the banks of the Jordan River. The pilgrims are determined that their experience of the sacred river conform strictly to the expectations they have transported all the way from America. Hence after a cold night in the bushes at the river's edge, they strip naked and wade into the freezing water, singing hymns. Mr. Blucher's cynical idiom is audible in the narrator's account of the adventure.

> But they did not sing long. The water was so fearfully cold that they were obliged to stop singing and scamper out again. Then they stood on the bank shivering, and so chagrined and so grieved that they merited honest compassion. Because another dream, another cherished hope, had failed. They had promised themselves all along that they would cross the Jordan where the Israelites crossed it when they entered Canaan. . . . While they did it they would picture to themselves that vast army of pilgrims marching through the cloven waters, bearing the hallowed Ark of the Covenant and shouting hosannahs and singing songs of thanksgiving and praise. (430)

Finally, to the narrator's evident disappointment, Jack rescues the shattered hopes of the party by leading the way across the river "with that engaging recklessness of consequences which is so natural to youth" (433). The narrator observes that, henceforth, the real danger will issue less from the rushing Jordan than from the current of sanctimonious rhetoric that is likely to flow from the lips of the victorious pilgrims. They succeed in experiencing the Jordan River according to the clichéd expectations with which they came, and it is the cliché rather than the experience that they will carry home to America.

The narrator, of course, arrives in the Holy Land with similarly unrealistic expectations, although unlike the pilgrims he does not regard them as inviolable. His description of the same river combines a pilot's interest in detail and a yarn spinner's knack for hyperbole:

> When I was a boy I somehow got the impression that the River Jordan was four thousand miles long and thirty-five miles wide. It is only ninety miles long, and so crooked that a man does not know which side of it he is on half the time. In going ninety miles it does not get over more than fifty miles of ground. (433)

The narrator repeatedly laments the fact that "travel and experience mar the grandest pictures and rob us of the most cherished traditions of our boyhood," but his lament is insincere (433). He actually revels in a process of sudden displacement, whereby expectations vie with experience in an unending series of inversions. His allegiance lies neither with "the most cherished traditions of . . . boyhood" nor with the reality that undermines them; rather, his interest is in a perpetual sequence of contrasts that he guarantees by exaggerating both the memory and the experience in his narration.

In the book's first shaving scene in Paris, for example, the narrator elaborately describes the expectations instilled in his mind by secondhand reports about the luxury of Parisian barber shops.

> From earliest infancy it had been a cherished dream of mine to be shaved some day in a palatial barber shop in Paris. I wished to recline at full length in a cushioned invalid chair, with pictures about me and sumptuous furniture. . . . At the end of an hour I would wake up regretfully and find my face as smooth and as soft as an infant's. Departing, I would lift my hand above that barber's head and say, "Heaven bless you, my son!" (84)

This illusion is promptly deflated by the "reality" of a Parisian shave, although the narrator's description of the event is no less extravagant than the false expectations it displaces.

> I sat bolt upright, silent, sad, and solemn. One of the wig-making villains lathered my face for ten terrible minutes and finished by plastering a mass of suds into my mouth. I expelled the nasty stuff with a strong English expletive and said, "Foreigner, beware!" Then

this outlaw strapped his razor on his boot, hovered over me ominously for six fearful seconds, and then swooped down upon me like the genius of destruction. The first rake of his razor loosened the very hide from my face and lifted me out of the chair. (85)

As James M. Cox has explained, "the 'reality' which deflates the expectation is clearly not actuality, but an extravagant invention which, poised against the clichés, displaces them."[35] The narrator's "old dream of bliss," like the other misconceptions he and the boys carry to Europe, turns out to have been a fraud, and his description of a razor-wielding "genius of destruction" thus supplies a preferable, although no less outrageous, fiction. It is a preferable fiction because, like a yarn, the narrator's account of his Parisian shave disparages illusion in favor of self-conscious fantasy. Whereas the pilgrims successfully blind themselves to experience by sanctifying false expectations, Twain's narrator acknowledges the Parisian fraud for what it is and answers with an aggressive invention of his own.

As the shaving episode makes clear, Twain's narrator is committed to a series of exaggerated poses, and his unpredictable movement from one to another generates much of the book's comedy. Forrest Robinson describes this "spastic lurching" between states of innocence and experience as a symptom of Twain's profound ambivalence, noting that the narrator of *The Innocents Abroad* possesses "a consciousness irremediably at odds with itself, moving at great speeds between mental states, struggling quite in vain to find a comfortable point of vantage on a deeply unsettling experience."[36] Robinson continues: "The failure to achieve this equipose between opposites and incompatibles registers in the book's characteristically nervous, at times even frantic rhythm, and in its gathering inclination to locate the source of its painful frustration not in experience but in consciousness itself." Robinson's psychoanalytic insight is acute, but his assumption that Twain's unstable narrator must be in search of "equipose" turns the book's humorous strategy into a symptom of mental unrest. Twain was quite as capable as Robinson of finding a "comfortable point of vantage" from which to describe his unsettling experience in a Parisian barber's chair, but such a description would have been far short of humorous. In his narration of the event, he chose to exaggerate both the expectation and the experience because effective humor always moves "at great speeds between mental states," and it does so precisely in order to prevent the reader from settling upon a "comfortable point of vantage." The "painful frustration" that Robinson observes in the text may in fact issue more from the critic than from the humorist, for Twain's game of juxtaposition *requires* a "divided consciousness" and a "frantic rhythm" for its effect.

Robinson and many other readers are right to notice that Twain's incessant movement between different narrative poses compromises the book's unity and coherence. At his best, however, Twain organizes the sometimes "spastic" interplay of voices in *The Innocents Abroad* by enacting the tall tale as a dramatic and rhetorical principle. In his revision of the *Alta* letters, he invented characters and episodes that enabled him to embed the verbal juxtapositions of the letters in a series of situational contexts based on the tall tale's pattern of interpretive challenge and response. Members of the narrator's "little party" gallop through foreign lands delighting in "splendid lies" and disparaging "disgraceful frauds" as they go, bargaining over the relative truth of every report and accepting the visible world as the only reliable standard. The tall tale did not resolve the contradictions inherent to the narrator's game of exaggerated contrasts, but it gave his many poses a coherent dramatic principle, a way of connecting with one another. The narrative consciousness of *The Innocents Abroad* is indeed divided, as the book's readers have always understood, but the tall tale's interpretive game allowed Twain to enact those divisions, enabling him to convert them into a form of play.

4

The Tall Tale as Theme and Structure in *Roughing It*

Frustrated with his urban existence in New York, Charles Stanley, the young hero of Emerson Bennett's *The Trapper's Bride* (1848), contemplates life on the western frontier. Like the tenderfooted narrator of Mark Twain's *Roughing It*, Charles derives his initial impressions of western life from an exceedingly safe distance.

> He delighted to read and ponder over the wild tales of the pioneers in the *West*, and the extravagant tales of border life were eagerly listened to, and carefully remembered by him. Cooper's tales of the Indians were his favorite volumes; and often while alone in the woods would he revolve in his mind the character of the old scout of Cooper's writings, and plan for himself a career which should rival that in romance and chivalry.[1]

Like many a literary greenhorn before and after him, Charles later discovers that his Cooperesque impressions fail to correspond precisely with frontier experience. In his case, however, the discovery occurs when expectations prove too tame and conservative, for Bennett's West holds more wild adventure and romantic intrigue than Natty Bumppo ever enjoyed. After demonstrating an uncanny, although previously latent, knack for trapping and hunting, Charles becomes infatuated with the fair-skinned and radiant "Valley Flower," a member of that idealized race of lordly savages that Mark Twain and his burlesquing contemporaries loved to mock.[2] When a band of renegade Indians kidnaps his intended bride, Charles performs feats of bravery that would have inspired even

Natty's awe and respect. The hero finally subdues the novel's principal bad Indian and carries away the good one.

With Cooper's Leatherstocking novels as a formidable precedent, writers of western romance endeavored to satisfy an avid eastern readership by describing ever more incredible tales of adventure. Moral qualities and physical prowess, like the landscape itself, seemed naturally to acquire Gothic proportions as soon as characters left the settlements and ventured into the remote western territories. Novels like Bennett's *The Prairie Flower*, Charles Murray's *The Prairie Bird*, D. W. Belisle's *The American Family Robinson*, and numerous others by such writers as Pierce Egan, Mrs. M. E. Braddon, Mrs. Henry Wood, and Ned Buntline tantalized eastern readers by projecting the frontier through increasingly heavy doses of what Twain called "the mellow moonshine of romance."[3] Bookish and cosmopolitan characters such as Charles Stanley, or the equally resourceful hero of R. Richards's *The California Crusoe*, discovered a western reality that exceeded even their most naive dreams of adventure. Few readers complained when Bennett and his contemporaries described the same buffalo hunts and hairbreadth escapes over and over in novel after novel; if the clichéd rescue of the immaculate maiden from the clutches of some unregenerate villain could be made more shocking than before, it served its purpose.

During the 1850s, inspired by the truly sublime extravagance of many western romancers, a complementary burlesque tradition began to acquire recognition on both sides of the Divide by mocking the outrageous impressions of western life that had become residual in the American imagination. In 1853, under the pseudonym "Old Block," Alonzo Delano published a series of sketches that *would* have adhered to romantic conventions of narration and description, except that the author's incorrigible pen knife repeatedly interrupts at chosen moments to insert a deflating comment. Old Block takes considerable pains to create a picturesque scene, only to be thwarted by his talkative utensil, much as the brusque Mr. Brown would thirteen years later interrupt Mr. Twain's picturesque rendering of the Sandwich Islands:

It was at the close of a sultry day, in the latter part of October, 1850, that a solitary traveller might be seen . . . emerging from the foothills of the Sierra Nevada . . . while the dusty and toil worn garments, and the slow pace of his weary steed [Pen Knife: Pshaw! why don't you say mule—it was a mule of the meanest kind] . . . confound it, you destroy all the romance of the thing.[4]

When they appeared in 1853, Delano's *Pen Knife Sketches* helped to popularize a style of humor that came to be associated with California and the West, a style that hinged on the contrast between exaggeratedly romantic images of western life and equally exaggerated accounts of abject poverty and hardship on the frontier. Old Block's tale "The Greenhorn" described the arrival in California of a zealous young fortune hunter from the East, full of the same dreams of opportunity and adventure that lure Charles Stanley away from New York. In Delano's version, however, the greenhorn discovers that the occupational hardships of a miner's life tend to become more tangible as one experiences them. After much comical suffering and very little mining, the young man finally becomes richer only in his knowledge that "all is not gold that glitters."[5]

Delano's sketches of mining life and John Phoenix's popular collection of tales and sketches, *Phoenixiana* (1855), helped to breed an entire generation of humorists that included such personalities as Artemus Ward, Petroleum V. Nasby, Orpheus C. Kerr, Bill Arp, and Josh Billings, to name only the most prominent.[6] Their styles of composition and stage performance were diverse, but the "literary comedians" as a group relied heavily on Delano's brand of tall humor, playing images against expectations in a cycle of inflation and deflation. Eastern perceptions of the West were so conditioned by rumor and romance that an adept yarn spinner like Artemus Ward could describe a plausible frontier scene drawing entirely on conventional mythology and cliché. Ward would then explode the perception with one of his characteristically sudden turns of expression, delivered with a look of perfect innocence and bewilderment. One spectator recalled that he would deliver his jokes "with an air of profound unconsciousness," his eyes beseeching patience from the audience, "as if he were above all things trying to get his thoughts really disentangled this time."[7] Occasionally, the strategy involved a full-fledged yarn, although in general the narrative element in the humor of the literary comedians received less emphasis than the interplay of exaggerated images and expectations.

Ward and his colleagues practiced their burlesque technique mainly in short sketches, condensed novels, and platform appearances. Their comedy of defeated expectations fed on the romantic indulgence of novelists such as Cooper and Emerson Bennett, but the western humorists generally refrained from attempting novel-length projects of their own until J. Ross Browne began to assimilate the burlesque strategy to longer works of quasi-fiction. Browne's western books — including *Crusoe's Island* (1864) and *Adventures in the Apaché Country* (1869) — were neither exactly factual travel accounts nor romances of adventure, but borrowed elements of both forms in projecting a new version of the literary frontier. The narrator of *Apaché Country*, for example, introduces himself as a modern Don Quixote, passionately interested in "the romance of Spanish history" in North America and eager to retrace the steps of the early conquistadors, that "splendid set of marauders — so fired with chivalry, lust, and fanaticism."[8] Like Charles Stanley and any number of other romantic heroes of western fiction, the narrator's anticipation of adventure and opportunity lures him into *terra incognita*. His expectations are conditioned not by Cooper's Leatherstocking tales, but by even more highly idealized versions of legendary belief: "The very name of 'Arizuma' [Arizona] was fraught with the rarest charms of romance. Here it was that gold and silver existed in virgin masses; here were races of highly-civilized Indians and beautiful women, fair as alabaster, living an Acadian life."[9] Yet the narrator's modern-day quest for El Dorado becomes a lesson in hardship when the Arizona silver lodes turn out to be less lucrative than preliminary reports had indicated. The discouraged silver miner abandons his naive expectations and extends his tour northward through Nevada and northern California, determined, like the narrator of *Yusef*, Browne's 1853 account of travels through the Holy Land, "to disperse the mists of fancy" that surround the popular literary representation of those regions.[10] Thereafter, his narrative blends an impressive interest in detail with occasional flights of undisguised absurdity.

Browne's burlesque travel narratives had appealed to Mark Twain as an effective method for treating western material long before Twain contemplated a western book of his own. As early as

February 1862, he wrote to Jane and Pamela Clemens recommend-
ing Browne's series of essays on the Nevada mining districts, and
he mentioned the series a second time three months later in a letter
written with Orion to the Keokuk *Gate City*.[11] Browne's "A Peep
at Washoe" had appeared a year earlier in *Harper's New Monthly
Magazine*, where readers accustomed to the conventions of western
romance once again encountered an ambitious greenhorn, determined, like his innumerable prototypes, to find fortune and adventure in the Sierran wilderness; and once again the narrator's
adventures take a decidedly unromantic turn in the face of harsh
circumstances. Toward the end of the series, describing conditions
on the route linking Virginia City to California, Browne's disillusioned narrator explains that "the road is five feet deep by one
hundred and thirty miles long, and is composed chiefly of mountains, snow, and mud."[12] Browne's own accompanying illustration
of hazardous winter travel, entitled "Snow Slide,'" appealed to
Twain, who recommended the picture to Pamela and Jane Clemens
in an 1862 letter:

> You want to know something about the route between California
> and Nevada Territory? Suppose you take my word for it, that it is
> exceedingly jolly. Or take, for a winter view, J. Ross Browne's pic-
> ture, in Harper's Monthly, of pack mules tumbling fifteen hundred
> feet down the side of a mountain.[13]

While Twain's recommendation refers specifically to the illustration, his ensuing description of western scenery along the road to
California betrays the marks of literary influence as well. Following Browne's example, Twain deliberately parodies the picturesque
mode of description, reaching for absurdly tall extremes in his
panoramic view of the landscape.

> Why bless you, there's *scenery* on that route. You can stand on some
> of those noble peaks and see Jerusalem and the Holy Land. And
> you can start a boulder, and send it tearing up the earth and crashing
> over trees—down—down—down—to the very devil, Madam. And
> you would probably stand up there and look, and stare and wonder
> at the magnificence spread out before you till you starved to death,
> if let alone. But you should take someone along to keep you moving.

Having composed the Bunker sketch for readers in Keokuk only a week earlier, in late January 1862, Twain was still discovering the descriptive value of tall humor as a method for representing western life, and it seems likely that J. Ross Browne's writings and illustrations played a significant role in that discovery. If there was an important literary influence, however, as several critics have maintained, its effects are noticeable principally in Twain's Washoe writings of the early 1860s.[14] By 1871, as he searched through his file of old letters and *Enterprise* articles for the narrative pattern of his new book, Mark Twain had little to learn about tall humor from Browne or his burlesque precursors. Twain probably scanned the Irishman's Washoe writings for place names and forgotten images of Carson and Virginia City, just as he consulted Albert Richardson's *Beyond the Mississippi* (1867) and other accounts of travel in the West, yet his use of tall humor in *Roughing It* was something new to the burlesque tradition.[15] Whereas literary humorists from John Phoenix to Bret Harte had employed parody and exaggeration for the purpose of debunking romantic conventions, Twain recognized a theme, a potential story, disguised in the very framework of western burlesque. As a literary interpreter of the region, he gave the tall tale a vital role in the story of the frontier by placing the drama of performance and response at the thematic center of a new kind of *Bildungsroman*, one that figures education as a gradual process of unlearning the illusions that inhibit practical vision.

In *The Innocents Abroad*, Twain's narrator had moved freely and unpredictably between quite different narrative poses, adopting an innocent or experienced perspective according to the comic exigencies of the situation. There is still a good deal of unpredictable movement between narrative poses in *Roughing It*, but education replaces travel as the book's primary organizational device, and this change lends thematic coherence to Twain's formerly sporadic use of tall narration. Instead of shifting perpetually between exaggerated states of knowledge and naiveté, the narrator of *Roughing It* describes his gradual disillusionment by adopting the relatively stable perspective of an old-timer. As Henry Nash Smith has explained, the relation between innocence and experience is to some extent fixed by the author's management of the narrative situation:

> When the narrator speaks in the first person, the pronoun "I" links two quite different personae: that of a tenderfoot setting out across the plains, and that of an old-timer, a veteran who has seen the elephant and now looks back at his callow days of inexperience. Both are present in the narrative from the start. The contrast between them, which is an implied judgment on the tenderfoot's innocence and a corresponding claim for the superior maturity and sophistication of the old-timer, is the consequence of precisely that journey which the book will describe.[16]

This acute analysis takes "experience" to be the decisive transforming element in the narrator's education, but Smith overlooks a related component. Twain's tenderfoot earns admission to an exclusive "community of knowers" in the West not only by acquiring experience, but also by mastering a style of narration with which to represent and interpret his experience of the frontier. He must learn to speak and comprehend an idiom that mythologizes and demythologizes the West at the same time, an idiom that relentlessly inflates experience while conveying a latent message to cultural insiders who have "seen the elephant" and who take pleasure in its perpetual readornment.[17] It is here that Twain surpasses Delano and Browne and their burlesque contemporaries, for *Roughing It* demonstrates more than the failure of romantic expectations to conform with the reality of the frontier. Twain treats the disillusionment of the greenhorn not as the climax of his story, but as preparation for a further transformation whereby his narrator acquires a new language, one with its own powers of expression and its own demands for interpretation.

The narrator's initiation to the Far West, and to a form of humor that he finds exceedingly unusual, begins immediately after the overland stage has crossed the Mississippi at St. Joseph. The uneventful trip upriver from St. Louis has already offered the self-assured young traveller an opportunity to display his restrained sense of humor, which he does with a guarded comment about the riverboat pilot's ability to maneuver past snags and sandbars that dot the river: "The captain said she was a 'bully' boat, and all she wanted was more 'shear' and a bigger wheel. I thought she wanted a pair of stilts, but I had the deep sagacity not to say so" (44). The narrator's polite quips, like his white kid gloves and swallow-tail coat, travel only as far as "St. Joe," where the two brothers discover that they must send all their dispensable possessions back to St. Louis before boarding the stage coach bound for Carson City. As the stage pulls away from the states, the narrator receives his first exposure to a different style of humor:

> Almost touching our knees, a perpendicular wall of mail matter rose up to the roof. . . . We had twenty-seven hundred pounds of it aboard, the driver said—"a little for Brigham, and Carson, and 'Frisco, but the heft of it for the Injuns, which is powerful trouble-some 'thout they get plenty of truck to read." (47)

With his impression of the "scholarly Red Man" still intact, the narrator at first finds nothing exceptional in this explanation. When the driver betrays his deadpan delivery with an impressive wink, how-ever, the narrator is forced to reconsider his interpretation:

> But as he just then got up a fearful convulsion of his countenance which was suggestive of a wink being swallowed by an earthquake, we guessed that his remark was intended to be facetious, and to mean that we would unload the most of our mail matter somewhere on the Plains and leave it to the Indians, or whosoever wanted it. (47–48)

The speaker's interpretive difficulty in this passage, of course, is itself exaggerated by the old-timer, whose demythologizing impulse loads every word the tenderfoot can think of to express his naive wonder. Having embarked for the territories armed with an unreli-able Navy revolver and an even more dangerous store of popular myths about the West, the tenderfoot articulates his experience in a language that seems hopelessly inadequate to the task. He speaks not only of scholarly red men, but of "a land of enchantment and . . . mystery," a land that is "dramatically adventurous." In the course of his education, the narrator will learn to reject this sort of inflated language as inauthentic, although his new idiom will rely no less than the old one on hyperbole and exaggeration. He will learn, in other words, to represent the West as "a land of enchant-ment and . . . mystery" by readorning the landscape with a yarn spinner's self-conscious command of fantasy.

The tenderfoot soon forgets his naive disappointment over the loss of the kid gloves he had hoped to wear "at Pawnee receptions in the Rocky Mountains," and just as suddenly he begins to enjoy the stage driver's bizarre sense of humor (45). Although he remains unsure precisely how to interpret the rhetorical intent of the driver's exaggerated tales, the greenhorn finds them increasingly worthy of attention. After camping on the plains a few days out of St. Joseph, he observes that sagebrush "makes a very sociable camp-fire, one around which the most impossible reminiscences sound plausible, instructive, and profoundly entertaining" (55). He remains for the most part a cultural outsider in his new environment, but one with enough insight to remark on the "amazing magnifying properties" of the western atmosphere, which have begun to upset even his own refined sense of proportion (66). Trees that seem to the narrator close at hand are actually miles away, just as stories which begin plausibly enough often end in hilarious improbability.

With such a rudimentary education in the art of tall narrative behind him, the tenderfoot is only marginally equipped to respond to George Bemis's account of his misadventure with a wounded buffalo. Bemis is a "dismally formidable" fellow traveller who packs a "cheerful" Allen revolver in his belt, a weapon so "comprehensive" that, "if she didn't get what she went after, she would fetch something else" (46). When a buffalo-hunting adventure ends in disgrace for Bemis, he becomes sullen for twenty-four hours, after which he offers an irresistible interpretation of what actually occurred "in the dewy freshness" of the previous morning:

> Well, it was not funny. . . . If I had had a horse worth a cent—but no, the minute he saw that buffalo bull wheel on him and give a bellow, he raised straight up in the air and stood on his heels. The saddle began to slip, and I took him round the neck and laid close to him, and began to pray. Then he came down and stood up on the other end for a while, and the bull actually stopped pawing the sand and bellowing to contemplate the inhuman spectacle. Then the bull made a pass at him . . . and then you ought to have seen that spider-legged old skeleton go! (76–77)

When his saddle girth breaks, Bemis is thrown thirty yards off to the left, while his saddle gets a kick that sends it "more than four hundred yards up in the air." Shaken but undaunted, Bemis finds himself "at the foot of the only solitary tree in nine counties adjacent," which he climbs with teeth and nails, all the while "blaspheming my luck in a way that made my breath smell of brim-stone." Perched on a limb forty feet above the ground, he prepares for the worst, cautiously unwinding his lariat from the pommel of his saddle, a move which prompts a seemingly reasonable objection from some member of the audience, possibly the tenderfoot.

> "Your *saddle*? Did you take your saddle up the tree with you?"
> "Take it up the tree with me? Why, how you talk. Of course I didn't. No man could do that. It *fell* in the tree when it came down."
> "Oh — exactly." (78)

The tale approaches its climax when the bull begins gradually to climb the tree, a few inches at a time, gazing hungrily at his adversary, "as if to say, 'You are my meat, friend.'"

> He was within ten feet of me! I took a long breath, — and then said I, "It is now or never." I had the coil of the lariat all ready; I paid it out slowly, till it hung right over his head; all of a sudden I let go of the slack, and the slip-noose fell fairly round his neck! Quicker than lightning I out with the Allen and let him have it in the face. It was an awful roar, and must have scared the bull out of his senses. When the smoke cleared away, there he was, dangling in the air, twenty foot from the ground, and going out of one convulsion and into another faster than you could count! I didn't stop to count, any-how — I shinned down the tree and shot for home. (79)

When his auditors react skeptically, Bemis argues for the legitimacy of the tale by establishing that his account is not necessarily untrue. In response to the narrator's demand for proof, he asks, logically enough: "Proofs! Did I bring back my lariat? . . . Did I bring back my horse? . . . Did you ever see the bull again? . . . Well, then, I never saw anybody as particular as you are about a little thing like that" (79). The tenderfoot is unsure how to react to a narrative that simultaneously impresses him with its ingenuity and offends him with its disingenuousness. His concluding remark expresses considerably more appreciation than he earlier betrayed for the stage driver's humorous convulsion, yet it falls well short of com-plete approval: "I made up my mind that if this man was not a liar he only missed it by the skin of his teeth" (79).

Despite his guarded reaction to the tale, the narrator's attitude toward such wonders of the frontier continues to change, until even he begins to distinguish between his own relatively experienced perspective and that of "the ignorant back home" (84); and, significantly, the distinction rests as much on the narrator's accumulation of experience as on his familiarity with a style of reporting experience to the ignorant. When the party encounters the "first-class curiosity" of alkali water for the first time, as an example, he comments that here is "a thing to be mentioned with éclat in letters" to credulous readers at home in the states (84). With casual rather than bewildered interest, he relates the story of a stage driver on the Southern Overland, "who came near as anything to starving to death in the midst of abundance" because the Apaches "kept him so leaky with holes that he 'couldn't hold his vittles'" (87). The narrator's transformation is uneven and often difficult to measure, for it is never possible to determine with certainty whether his emerging appreciation for tall humor coincides with his experience or issues from the perspective of the old-timer who narrates the tenderfoot's adventures in retrospect. Yet in either event, the narrator experiences a change of perspective as he gradually learns, like a much older Mark Twain, to remember events in vivid detail whether they happened or not.[18] By the time the stage reaches Fort Bridger, the Wyoming outpost named for another famous yarn spinner, the former tenderfoot has acquired considerable skill in the narrative uses of "éclat," so much so that he feels it necessary to reassure his reader: "I am not given to exaggeration, and when I say a thing I mean it" (112).

As the narrator learns to reject his initially naive impressions, aspiring instead to the perspective of a cultural insider, he encounters the unfamiliar values that operate within the community he wishes to join. A rigid social hierarchy exists on the frontier in *Roughing It*, although one that ignores traditional credentials of economic and political distinction. The narrator discovers that two factors alone—the courage to endure life on the frontier with a defiant smile and the ability to narrate the experience with a yarn spinner's straight face—distinguish a citizen of the Far West. And among the characters he encounters during his journey across the plains, no group has "seen the elephant" more times than the perennially talkative stage drivers. With some surprise, the narrator observes that these inveterate yarn spinners are adored by the station keepers and hostlers, who pamper the drivers as if each were "a great and shining dignitary, the world's favorite son, the envy of the people, the observed of the nations" (59). Ignoring formal distinctions of rank, the hostlers treat "the really powerful *conductor* of the coach merely with the best of what was their idea of civility, but the *driver* was the only being they bowed down to and worshipped" (60). In *Life on the Mississippi* (1883), Twain describes the steamboat pilot's seemingly natural authority over *his* official superior, the ship's captain, and again the inversion of rank follows from the pilot's exalted position at the center of a yarn-spinning community. The pilot's specialized knowledge of the river, a knowledge inaccessible to cultural outsiders, and his ability to transform that knowledge into plausible fantasy, make him the "absolute monarch" of the pilot house despite the presence of official superiors.[19]

After the overland journey in *Roughing It*, the former tenderfoot bitterly recalls the humiliation he suffered as a member of the "low and inferior" class of "emigrants," and he regrets the "consumingly ludicrous ignorance" that distinguished him so plainly in the eyes of discerning frontiersmen from "that proudest and blessedest creature that exists on all the earth," the forty-niner (139). As the narrator comes to understand, the old-timer, whether a stage driver, pocket miner, or Mississippi pilot, establishes his nobility by narrating vast experiences in such a way that less knowledgeable listeners find it impossible to distinguish precisely between fact and fiction. The yarn spinner's performance forges a tacit bond among those members of the audience who share a set of experiences and a familiarity with the yarn spinner's genre, and it is within this insular interpretive community that the storyteller enjoys unrivaled authority—the authority, as Twain puts it in *Life on the Mississippi*, of being "always understood."[20] The ultimate cultural insiders of *Roughing It*, of course, are the proud forty-niners, whose memories reach back to the earliest days of the California frontier with a comprehensiveness and a creativity that defy contradiction by those less experienced.

Vestiges of the narrator's old romanticism persist despite his improving insight and an apparent ambition to be revered as an old-timer himself. As the party prepares to cross the alkali desert, for example, the greenhorn fails to contain his excitement, declaring

that "this was fine — novel — romantic — dramatically adventurous — this, indeed, was worth living for, worth travelling for!"
(141). One hour under the wilting sun is enough to convince him
that "the poetry was all in the anticipation — there is none in the
reality." Such lapses in his emerging perspective are infrequent at
this late stage in the journey, however, and in fact the narrator
repeatedly derides his former romantic expectations. In a passage
reminiscent of the attack on fraudulent guidebooks in *The Innocents Abroad*, he blames Cooper and Emerson Bennett for crowd-
ing his naive imagination with false images of the frontier.[21] The
disenchanting reality of living conditions among the Goshoot Indians startles the former "worshipper of the Red Man," who comments that "it was curious to see how quickly the paint and tinsel
fell away from him" (146). The narrator's insight into the fallacy
of his earlier impressions does not, however, complete his transformation. Like Delano's "The Greenhorn" and J. Ross Browne's "A
Peep at Washoe," *Roughing It* describes the displacement of romantic expectations by "one's actual vision"; unlike those others,
however, Mark Twain's book goes on to depict the tall tale's triumph over a potentially wilting and squalid reality. Where the
burlesque tradition culminated with defeated expectations, Twain
proceeds to readorn the landscape according to a new narrative
method, to replace Emerson Bennett's worn-out paint and tinsel
with even louder colors.

By the time the narrator arrives in Carson, he is an accomplished
yarn spinner, still vulnerable to embarrassment at the hands of
legitimate old-timers like "Old Abe Curry," but comfortable with
his emerging position in the frontier community. The earlier contrast of naive and experienced impressions is no longer evident in
his presentation as he slides effortlessly into a new idiom during a
description of Carson and its inhabitants. On his arrival in town,
the narrator meets Mr. Harris, one of Carson's leading citizens,
who begins to introduce himself but then interrupts:

> "I'll have to get you to excuse me a minute; yonder is the witness
> that swore I helped to rob the California coach — a piece of imperti-
> nent intermeddling, sir, for I am not even acquainted with the man."
> Then he rode over and began to rebuke the stranger with a six-
> shooter, and the stranger began to explain with another. When the

> pistols were emptied, the stranger resumed his work . . . and Mr. Harris rode by with a polite nod, homeward bound, with a bullet through one of his lungs, and several in his hips; and from them issued little rivulets of blood that coursed down the horse's sides and made the animal look quite picturesque. I never saw Harris shoot a man after that but it recalled to mind that first day in Carson. (155)

The choice of terms such as "rivulets" and "coursed" implies a subtle parody of the narrator's former style, yet those words perform more than a burlesque function in the tale. The narrator's overland education has supplanted his romantic tendency not with documentary zeal, as was largely the case in J. Ross Browne's travel narratives, but with a yarn spinner's appreciation for extremes, and thus he frequently borrows with ironic intent from precisely the clichéd vocabulary and imagery that once informed his impressions of the West. Experience has inspired a new attitude toward both the old illusions and the reality they claimed to represent, an attitude gleaned from the humorless faces of old-timers in Carson and epitomized in the narrator's own improving deadpan delivery.

The former greenhorn's description of Lake Tahoe's legendary medicinal powers exhibits his increasing command of the yarn spinner's art:

> I know a man who went there [to Tahoe] to die. But he made a failure of it. He was a skeleton when he came, and could barely stand. He had no appetite, and did nothing but read tracts and reflect on the future. Three months later he was sleeping out of doors regularly, eating all he could hold, three times a day, and chasing game over mountains three thousand feet high for recreation. (164)

As the narrator has come to understand, the yarn spinner unites a "community of knowers" by transforming its privations into reasons for laughter and endurance; the artful storyteller acknowledges the fortitude of a community by exaggerating its strengths *and* weaknesses, embellishing real conditions with his extravagant imagery, yet never entirely obscuring the reality of which his tale is an imaginative extension. Twain's narrator objected to nineteenth-century guidebooks in *The Innocents Abroad* because writers such as William C. Prime had willfully distorted "one's actual vision" in their articulation of an image that was "calculated to deceive."[22] Emerson Bennett and other romancers had committed a similar abuse of verisimilitude by asking readers to view the West "through the mellow moonshine of romance" (46). "But," objects the narrator in *The Innocents Abroad*, "if the paint and the ribbons and the flowers be stripped from [the image], a skeleton will be found underneath." In his yarn about Tahoe's irresistible curative powers, Twain quite literally reenacts Prime's guidebook strategy by endowing a skeleton with imaginary vitality, but the tenderfoot's exaggerative language carries a latent affirmation of "one's actual vision." His expansive imagery mythologizes and demythologizes the West at the same time, inflating representations in order to highlight an incongruous contrast with actual conditions.

At least one critic of the book has argued that the narrator's progressive disillusionment fails to instigate a meaningful transformation because "the world of *Roughing It*" lacks "a mature alternative to gullible innocence."[23] In Forrest Robinson's opinion, the moral landscape of the book "grows more confusing and paradoxical as the innocent moves through it."

> His reaction is not to put on knowledge and wisdom. In part, no doubt, this is because there is so little to be found in his environment. In greater part, however, the harsh jokes and brutal revelations which constitute the innocent's education fill him with resentment, deep self-contempt, and render him disillusioned, bitter and cynical.

Whether mature or not by eastern standards, an alternative to gullible innocence does exist in *Roughing It*. The "harsh jokes" that the narrator at first struggles to understand and later learns to perform are not the cause of his bitterness; rather, they demonstrate his capacity to transmute cynicism and disillusionment into humor. The tenderfoot's transformation reaches its conclusion with his ascent to a new status as member of the frontier community, and with his recognition of the part his humor must play in helping to define that community's self-image. Somewhere along the 200-mile road from Carson to Unionville in Humboldt County, he becomes convinced that the very privations that are natural to the frontier can actually contribute, through a yarn spinner's ingenuity, to an appreciation of its glory:

> It was a hard, wearing, toilsome journey, but it had its bright side; for after each day was done and our wolfish hunger appeased with a hot supper of fried bacon, bread, molasses and black coffee, the pipe-smoking, song-singing and yarn-spinning around the evening camp-fire in the still solitudes of the desert was a happy, care-free sort of recreation that seemed the very summit and culmination of earthly luxury. (191)

On his return to Carson, the narrator clearly identifies himself as a cultural insider. No longer confused about the rhetorical intent of the frontier's aggressive brand of humor, he describes Carson's civic contempt for its new territorial attorney, General Buncombe, with the unmistakable authority of an old-timer: "Now the older citizens of a new Territory look down upon the rest of the world with a calm, benevolent compassion, as long as it keeps out of the way — when it gets in the way they snub it" (224). Together with the older citizens, the narrator conspires to snub General Buncombe, an arrogant and unsuspecting Easterner, by exploiting his willingness to believe the worst of his new neighbors. The general is a Washington appointee who considers himself "a lawyer of parts" and who jumps at the opportunity to impress the lawless citizens of the territory by representing Dick Hyde in a real-estate dispute (224). According to Hyde, his ranch was entirely buried when Tom Morgan's property came crashing down the mountainside during a landslide. When Morgan refused to relinquish possession of *his* ranch, despite its new location, Hyde was left with no alternative but to appeal to the learned attorney for assistance. Buncombe finds these circumstances amazing but entirely consistent with his preconceived opinion of territorial idiocy and injustice. He agrees to argue Hyde's case in order to teach the citizens of Carson a lesson about justice.

As Henry Nash Smith has pointed out, the general has as much chance of winning his case as the town-bred dog of Chapter 5 has of overtaking the "deceitful" and "fraudful" coyote, which "glides along and never pants or sweats or ceases to smile."[24] True to his reputation, Buncombe argues his case with relentless zeal, quoting "from everything and everybody" and closing his argument with "a war-whoop for free speech, freedom of the press, free schools, the Glorious Bird of America and the principles of Eternal Justice" (227). Yet despite these exertions, which the crowd finds highly entertaining, ex-governor Roop decides in favor of Morgan on the grounds that "Heaven created the ranches and it is Heaven's prerogative to rearrange them" (228). The decision strikes the general as a colossal affront to reason and justice:

> Buncombe seized his cargo of law-books and plunged out of the court-room frantic with indignation. He pronounced Roop to be a miraculous fool, an inspired idiot. . . . At the end of two months the fact that he had been played upon with a joke had managed to bore itself . . . through the solid adamant of his understanding. (228–29)

To the narrator and his co-conspirators, of course, the general's humiliation reaffirms the cultural sovereignty of the territory. Like the hunting and fishing tales that Nimrod Wildfire performs for Mrs. Wallope in Paulding's *The Lion of the West*, Roop's absurd decree is an expression of defiance, an act of communal self-defense.[25] A tacit bond of sympathy emerges among the members of an elite interpretive community made up of the "older citizens" of the territory, a collectivity that now includes the narrator. His several encounters with solemn practitioners of the yarn spinner's art have taught him at least two things: that experience is paramount on the frontier, and that the imaginative rendering of experience by a skillful storyteller constitutes the frontier community's most effective means of defining itself against "the rest of the world."

Chapter 42 of *Roughing It* opens with a question that would seem to apply equally to the narrator's career and to the course of the narrative itself: "What to do next? It was a momentous question" (265). With the transformation of his tenderfoot essentially complete after only forty-one chapters, Twain's obligation to Elisha Bliss and the American Publishing Company for a 600-page manuscript posed a new problem. The author's solution was to follow his wayward yarn spinner's further transformation into a reporter for the Virginia City *Territorial Enterprise*. The movement to a new perspective, and consequently to a new style of representation, is evident as soon as the narrator exchanges his slouch hat and blue woolen shirt for "a more Christian costume," one befitting his newfound respectability (267). Just as earlier he had been surprised to learn of the exalted stature of stage drivers on the overland route, the reporter now discovers that in Virginia City murderers possess the highest rank of social distinction. He explains that "the reason why there was so much slaughtering done was that in a new mining district the rough element predominates, and a person is not respected until he has 'killed his man'" (306). If one felt squeamish about spilling blood, the second most effective route to social prominence was "to stand behind a bar, wear a cluster-diamond pin, and sell whiskey" (306). Logically enough, the reporter observes that "to be a saloon-keeper and kill a man was to be illustrious" (307).

The narrator's insight into a social order that grants unexpected stature to both stage drivers and homicidal bar keepers links the two parts of *Roughing It*, yet the parallel is especially noteworthy for what it reveals about a shift that has taken place in the narrator's perspective. When he observes that the stage drivers are revered over their official superiors, the conductors, Mark Twain's tenderfoot is engaged in discovering values that conflict with his own, but that attract him powerfully. Conversely, when the *Enterprise* reporter expresses a very similar observation about the importance of bar keepers in Virginia City, he speaks from the perspective of an observer who implicitly rejects the values he describes. The tenderfoot's comment is loaded with anticipation of a life he is about to enter, while the reporter appears to be narrating a past he would like to forget. James M. Cox makes a similar observation about the two parts of the book with his remark that

the past of Mark Twain the reporter is extremely different from the past of Mark Twain the miner—and the difference is not difficult to define. The Mark Twain of volume one moves in a world of anticipation and expectation. The distinguishing feature of that past is that it has a future. But the past of volume two has no future, no real possibility of change, for Mark Twain has moved from the world of memory to the world of record.[26]

Cox's analysis is characteristically suggestive, but it overstates the rupture between *Roughing It*'s two parts, for in his new role as a literate observer Twain's narrator manages some of the book's most humorous episodes. The *Enterprise* reporter's account of his involvement with a fledgling literary journal illustrates the effectiveness of the new pose. Under the editorship of Mr. F., "a felicitous skirmisher with a pen," the Virginia City *Weekly Occidental* undertakes the composition of an original novel, whose chapters are to be prepared separately by members of the staff, including the narrator (325). Chapter 1 belongs to Mrs. F., "an able romanticist of the ineffable school," who introduces the novel's main characters, "a blonde simpleton who talked nothing but pearls and poetry and who was virtuous to the verge of eccentricity," and "a young French Duke of aggravated refinement, in love with the blonde" (326). Subsequent chapters by Mr. F. and Mr. D. introduce a menagerie of typical, if exaggerated, romantic characters, including a "sparkling young lady of high society," a "brilliant young lawyer," "a cloaked and masked melodramatic miscreant," "an Irish coachman with a rich brogue," and

> a Mysterious Rosicrucian who transmuted metals, held consultations with the devil in a cave at dead of night, and cast the horoscope of the several heroes and heroines in such a way as to provide plenty of trouble for their future careers and breed a solemn and awful public interest in the novel. (326)

Franklin R. Rogers speculates that Twain's burlesque thrust in the first three installments may be aimed indirectly at Anthony Trollope, "whose fondness for lawyers is certainly a distinguishing characteristic," and more pointedly at Bulwer-Lytton, whose Rosicrucian had already appeared in popular burlesques by William Thackeray and Bret Harte.[27] Twain's primary targets, of course, were the western serial thrillers that appeared in papers like the *Occidental*, the California *Golden Era*, and other journals that imported Gothic characters and situations into a frontier setting, often without noticing the absurdity of the endeavor. According to one of several conflicting accounts, Virginia City's *Weekly Occidental* did actually begin serializing a novel entitled "The Silver

Fiend, A Tale of Washoe," which survived only three installments and then died a peaceful death, without Mark Twain's help.[28] Other journals, including the *Golden Era*, successfully published numerous serial romances under such intriguing titles as "The Deserted Shaft: A California Romance" and "The Pitt-Smythes, or Life in England, Utah, and California."[29]

It is significant, however, that while the *Weekly Occidental* episode in *Roughing It* is overtly a burlesque of extravagant western romance, it is not the narrator's exaggerative humor that kills the *Occidental* novel. Chapter 4 is entrusted to "a dissolute stranger with a literary turn of mind," whose deadpan earnestness, "pleasing and kindly" manners, and love of whiskey combine to suggest the image of a literate Simon Wheeler or Jim Blaine (326). Like Blaine, whose narrative inspiration comes only when he is "tranquilly, serenely, symmetrically drunk" (344), the stranger does his best writing once alcohol has placed his imagination "in a state of chaos, and that chaos in a condition of extravagant activity" (327). Like Wheeler, whose narrative style is marked by "a vein of impressive earnestness and sincerity," the stranger writes with "singular smoothness, and with a 'dead' earnestness that was funny enough to suffocate a body" (327).[30] The dissolute stranger is a literary yarn spinner of the first order, and his contribution disrupts the novel not simply by denouncing its conventionality, but by pushing an already implausible plot to the brink of absurdity, where romantic excess takes on added dimensions. Setting to work "with all the confidence that whiskey inspires and all the easy complacency it gives to its servants," the stranger proceeds to tie the plot in knots by marrying the coachman to the society young lady "for the sake of the scandal," marrying the duke to the blonde's stepmother "for the sake of the sensation," and then creating a climactic "misunderstanding" between the devil and the Rosicrucian (327). With its "smoke and thunder and smell of brimstone," the stranger's contribution is more worthy of comparison with Bemis's outrageous tale about buffalo hunting on the plains than with Emerson Bennett's *The Trapper's Bride*.

In his delight over the stranger's chapter, the reporter momentarily forgets his professed desire to see the *Occidental* succeed as a literary journal. The other novelists, however, are less attuned to the potential merits of the stranger's style, and they greet his contribution with "a scathing fire of vituperation" (327). In his attempted revision, the stranger reveals only more clearly the unsuitable nature of his narrative method. His tone remains disarmingly sincere, reflecting "that same convincing air of honesty and earnestness that had marked his first work," although the deadpan exterior disguises a tale that is "symmetrically crazy" and "artistically absurd" (328). The revised chapter begins plausibly enough, describing a love affair between the blonde and the lawyer, who are tragically separated during a sailing disaster. The lovers are rescued by different whaling ships, which proceed with the refugees to opposite ends of the globe. Fearing that her true love must be dead, the blonde finally agrees to marry the morally degenerate duke, who is also a refugee aboard her ship. At the precise moment of her resignation, the dashing lawyer lifts his harpoon to strike a whale in the Bering Strait, "five thousand miles away, by the way of the Arctic Ocean, or twenty thousand by the way of the Horn" (330). At this point, the dissolute stranger loses his control over a story that had seemed to be unfolding as a perfectly digestible romance. His old style invades the narrative as soon as the lawyer strikes at the whale, "but not with perfect aim—":

> his foot slipped and he fell into the whale's mouth and went down his throat. He was insensible five days. Then he came to himself and heard voices; daylight was streaming through a hole cut in the whale's roof. He climbed out and astonished the sailors who were hoisting blubber up a ship's side. He recognized the vessel, flew aboard, surprised the wedding party at the altar and exclaimed:
> "Stop the proceedings—I'm here! Come to my arms, my own!" (330–31)

The romance collapses into a tall tale when, under the influence of whiskey, the stranger suddenly introduces a series of absurdities that would dispel even the most indulgent reader's suspension of disbelief. He maintains a deadpan expression to the end, never willing to admit that his tale is anything but gravely serious, and he seems truly disappointed when the other novelists fail to interpret it that way. Like Bemis, he goes so far as to offer "proof" that "the whole thing was within the possibilities," citing Charles Reade's *Love Me Little Love Me Long* and Jonah's story in the Bible as authoritative literary references (331). Yet the irony of this grouping reveals something about the stranger's intention to locate his tale in a rhetorical middle ground by blending plausible with fantastic events.

In terms of the larger structure of *Roughing It*, the narrator's role in the episode is significant. As a fringe member of both the vernacular and literary communities, he is no longer the yarn spinner who trekked between Humboldt and Esmerelda with his pards, nor has he regressed into the perfect greenhorn who boarded the stage at St. Joseph. Rather, the narrator of the *Occidental* episode has become — much like the correspondent of Twain's *Alta* letters from Europe and the Holy Land — a partial spectator, an initiate who chooses rather to observe than to participate in the performances he narrates. As Twain knew from his actual reporting days in Virginia City, the dual perspective of a cultural insider and literate observer simplified the literary presentation of a yarn. His narrator sits conveniently on an interpretive fence: he is literate enough to employ the dissolute stranger's tall tale for burlesque purposes, yet not so literate that he fails, like the *Occidental*'s other novelists, to find the yarn spinner's absurd conclusion thoroughly entertaining. Twain's western *Bildungsroman* has reached a premature and indefinite conclusion by the time the narrator of *Roughing It* learns to blend appreciation with condescension in his journalistic account of the stories he encounters in the West, as in the *Occidental* episode, yet his detachment enables him to achieve some of the book's most effective comedy.

The narrator's dual perspective in the second part of *Roughing It* allowed Twain to fill out his manuscript by drawing his material freely from both vernacular and literate sources, often alternating between the two in order to produce humorous contrasts of the sort he had employed as an *Enterprise* correspondent.[31] That method has inclined most readers to think of the book as a "potpourri" of styles or, as William Dean Howells put it, a "crazy-quilt of homespun fabrics," among which the tall tale participates as just one of many narrative forms, including travelogue, beast fable, character sketch, and historical reporting.[32] In his review of *Roughing It* for the *Atlantic Monthly*, Howells articulated what would become the traditional grab-bag interpretation, commenting that the sheer variety of Twain's narrative devices and perspectives conveys a more accurate impression of life on the frontier than any single genre, like history or romance, could have provided: "A thousand anecdotes, relevant and irrelevant, embroider the work; excursions and digressions of all kinds are the very woof of it, as it were; everything far-fetched or near at hand is interwoven, and yet the complex is a sort of 'harmony of colors' which is not less than triumphant."

Not all readers have resorted to quilt and embroidery metaphors in describing the book. At another critical extreme stands James M. Cox's dramatic remark that "the entire narrative of *Roughing It* is actually the exaggeration, the tall tale of Mark Twain."[33] Tall tales are indeed central to the theme and structure of *Roughing It*, yet neither statement does justice to their role in the narrative. Contrary to the grab-bag interpretation, Twain more or less unified the book's episodic structure by telling the story of his narrator's gradual initiation into a community of cultural insiders. In narrating isolated tales to develop the larger theme of initiation, Twain was departing noticeably from the western burlesque tradition, in which writers like Delano and Browne had employed tall humor primarily as a means of debunking romantic expectations. Cooper receives his comeuppance in *Roughing It*, as he does in virtually every burlesque account of the frontier, but Twain's purpose in stringing together a long series of tall tales is not unlike Cooper's own purpose in the Leatherstocking series: both writers, whether they work within the conventions of western romance or against them, are principally interested in narrating a story about the white man's encounter with the frontier. Twain tells that story by dramatizing his narrator's assimilation of a new style, one that constantly adorns without deceiving, that relentlessly embellishes "one's actual vision" in a communal celebration of hardship and experience.

5

The River as Yarn:
"Old Times on the Mississippi"

Readers of the *Atlantic Monthly* opened the January 1875 issue to meet Roderick Hudson, a promising young sculptor from Northampton, Massachusetts, who decides to embark for Rome on a voyage of artistic liberation. More than thirty years later, Henry James recalled the exhilaration he felt in 1874 and 1875 as a young writer finally ready, like his eponymous hero, to "put quite out to sea" with the serial publication of his first novel:

> I had but hugged the shore on sundry previous small occasions; bumping about, to acquire skill, in the shallow waters and sandy coves of the "short story" and master as yet of no vessel constructed to carry a sail. The subject of "Roderick" figured to me vividly this employment of canvas, and I have not forgotten, even after long years, how the blue southern sea seemed to spread immediately before me and the breath of the spice-islands to be already in the breeze.[1]

Readers who advanced as far as page 69 of the January issue witnessed another auspicious embarkation, but this vessel, unlike James's metaphorical clipper ship, employed no canvas for its locomotion, and its destination was neither Italy nor the exotic South Pacific. With an irony that is all the more pleasing because coincidental, Mark Twain's "cheap, gaudy packet" steamed down the Mississippi from Keokuk, bound for "St. Looey," stirring up life in the slumbering river towns along the way.[2] One thousand miles from the nearest clipper ship in the Atlantic Ocean, 2,000 miles from the port of San Francisco, Mark Twain was in the process of discovering a body of water that would prove as deep and as rich as James's "blue southern sea."

Although Twain had been contemplating a "Mississippi book" since 1866, he committed to the *Atlantic Monthly* project only as a last resort.[3] Having tacked his Sandwich Island notes to the end of *Roughing It* in a frantic effort to satisfy Elisha Bliss, he was entirely out of old newspaper sketches and travel notes, resources that he considered essential to his literary production. In a letter written just after the completion of *Roughing It*, he explained to Livy Clemens that the already long-postponed Mississippi book would have to wait until he could "spend 2 months on the river & take notes, & I bet you I will make a standard work."[4] Still determined that his next book should grow out of carefully recorded observations of travel, Twain wrote to James Redpath that he planned to gather information while spending the fall and winter of 1872 "in England or in Florida or in Cuba."[5] A few months later, he was enjoying an "extravagantly complimentary" welcome in Britain, where plans for a satirical book modeled after *The Innocents Abroad* were rapidly melting in the unexpected warmth of British hospitality.[6] That project was abandoned by late 1872 in favor of a collaboration with Charles Dudley Warner on *The Gilded Age*, a book that includes one of Twain's most memorable characters, Colonel Sellers, but that, in the words of Henry Nash Smith, "did nothing to help Mark Twain find out how to write his own books."[7]

The much celebrated discovery of a promising new subject, one that demanded a different sort of narrative treatment, occurred in the fall of 1874. Howells had been impressed with "A True Story," which he planned to publish in the November issue of the *Atlantic Monthly*, and he contacted Twain in September to ask for a second contribution—"some such story as that colored one for our January number."[8] A second trip to England in 1873 had again yielded no target worthy of extended satire, and Twain felt convinced that the dialect experiment of "A True Story" remained, as he told Howells, "rather out of my line."[9] Frustrated by a lack of workable material, yet apprehensive about the possibility of creating a narrative out of nothing, Twain answered Howells's request on October 24:

My Dear Howells, — I have delayed thus long, hoping I might do something for the January number and Mrs. Clemens has diligently persecuted me day by day with urges to go to work and do that something, but it's no use — I find I can't.[10]

With the pressure for literary production suddenly lifted by this capitulation, Twain almost immediately stumbled across the subject that had seemingly been eluding him. He wrote to Howells only a few hours later:

My Dear Howells, — I take back the remark that I can't write for the Jan. number. For Twichell and I have had a long walk in the woods and I got to telling him about old Mississippi days of steamboating glory and grandeur as I saw them (during 5 years) from the pilot house. He said "What a virgin subject to hurl into a magazine!" I hadn't thought of that before.[11]

The sketches that began arriving on Howells's desk less than a week later, seven in all, bear a distinct formal resemblance to *Roughing It*, although their emphasis suggests a new direction for Mark Twain. Once again the narrator is an old-timer who recalls his initiation into an exclusive interpretive community, and again tall tales play a central role in the educational process. Twain's difficulty in *Roughing It* had been to balance the anecdotal quality of his material against the developmental theme, ideally sustaining a digressive, exaggerative style of humor and thematic coherence at the same time. In "Old Times on the Mississippi," he finessed that difficulty by subordinating the tall tale's anecdotal content to the interpretive play that surrounds the performance of a yarn. In other words, he removed the uneasy balance between anecdote and rhetorical drama, between episode and theme, by focusing on the tall-tale situation, often dramatizing a yarn-spinning confrontation while neglecting the content of the yarn itself. The shift in emphasis enabled Twain to examine more thoroughly than before the privileged interpretive status of the tall tale's "community of knowers" and to begin articulating an epistemological ideal based on the collusive activity of this privileged community. Perhaps most important, the shift in emphasis enabled Twain to give his disruptive humor a thematic coherence that had been lacking in each of his extended travelogues.

The narrator of *Roughing It* begins to identify himself as an old-timer somewhere along the road to Humboldt, where he finally arrives at the "very summit and culmination of earthly luxury" during a series of yarn-spinning performances beside the evening campfire.[12] In "Old Times," such interpretive privilege is inextricably related to professional knowledge, so that the tenderfoot's figurative "summit" reappears in the imposing image of the pilot house. Echoing the narrator of *Roughing It*, Twain's cub pilot boards a "big New Orleans boat" and exclaims: "When I stood in her pilot-house I was so far above the water that I seemed perched on a mountain" (45). To enter the pilot house, the metaphorical "summit" or mountaintop of interpretive privilege, one first must learn the river, and then must learn to talk about the river, for there exists more than a figurative parallel between the cub's formal instruction as a pilot and his informal introduction to the art of yarn spinning. In fact, among themselves the pilots speak a private language, one that the narrator later identifies with the river itself, "a dead language to the uneducated passenger" but a living idiom to those experienced enough to comprehend its tacit or concealed significance. It is the language of the river and of the tall tale, an idiom that implies more than it states and that depends heavily on the interpretive activity of cultural insiders for its effective operation. The cub goes on to draw an explicit connection between a certain method of storytelling and the profession of river running when he explains that the more luxurious boats are always full of unemployed pilots, who enjoy free room and board while purportedly studying conditions on the Mississippi. This elite company convenes every day in the pilot house, "a sumptuous glass temple," with "leather cushions and a back to the high bench where visiting pilots sit, to spin yarns and 'look at the river'" (220). The pilots themselves seem aware that the exclusivity of their profession depends as much on a certain narrative and interpretive dexterity as on the art of piloting a steamboat, for, as the cub remarks, "all pilots are tireless talkers, and as they talk only about the river they are always understood" (221).

During the course of his gradual initiation into the pilot-house community, the cub encounters more than a few "tireless talkers," yet the reader hears very little of their talk, for Twain is more interested in dramatizing a series of interpretive confrontations than in narrating isolated yarn-spinning performances. Before the narrator has even contracted to learn the river, for example, he receives indirect exposure to the elite society of the pilot house by attaching himself to the night watchman, a river man of the lowest rank, who has plenty of time to talk and who possesses a seductively convincing style. Significantly, the cub relates the watchman's tale indirectly to the reader, first preparing an elaborate context and then summarily touching on the substance of the story. Twain actually omits the yarn spinner's climax, preferring throughout to describe his narrator's reaction to the performance rather than present the "text" of the story itself.

> I drank in his words hungrily, and with a faith that might have moved mountains if it had been applied judiciously. . . . As he mellowed into his plaintive history his tears dripped upon the lantern in his lap, and I cried, too, from sympathy. He said he was the son of an English nobleman — either an earl or an alderman, he could not remember which, but believed he was both. . . . [A]nd from that point my watchman threw off all trammels of date and locality and branched out into a narrative that bristled all along with incredible adventures; a narrative that was so reeking with bloodshed and so crammed with hair-breadth escapes and the most engaging and unconscious personal villainies, that I sat speechless, enjoying, shuddering, wondering, worshiping. (73)

John C. Gerber has pointed out that Twain deliberately exaggerated the narrator's youth and inexperience, putting his age at about sixteen when in fact Sam Clemens was already a well-travelled twenty-one-year-old man in 1857, the year he asked Horace Bixby to teach him the river.[13] In extending the cub's naiveté, Twain was of course preparing a context for his humor, establishing a dramatic relationship between the forces of innocence and experience. He had done something quite similar in *The Innocents Abroad* and *Roughing It*, articulating audience response as a way of embedding his humorous material within a larger story of confrontation and discovery. Yet here context, the drama of performance and response, receives more attention than the humorous material it serves to embed. Because the cub's narration focuses on gesture and reaction, the anecdotal interest of the watchman's bristling adventures never engages the reader. The yarn-spinning episode serves mainly to expose the protagonist's character and to foreshadow his struggle for acceptance into a community that defines itself through adherence to conventions of narrative performance and interpretation. In effect, Twain gives the tall tale's rhetorical drama a thematic relevance that eclipses the potential anecdotal interest of the watchman's yarn.

To enter the pilot house is to become a master of interpretation in more than one sense, for the same characters who exchange yarns in the ship's "sumptuous glass temple" daily confront the river's interpretive challenge as well. In fact, the watchman's false yet convincing sentimentality anticipates the hazardous romantic appeal of the river, and the cub's credulous reception of the yarn with "a faith that might have moved mountains" parallels his subsequent, and frequent, misreading of the river's language. The cub's education in river running thus entails a series of interpretive challenges that follow the pattern of a tall-tale encounter, except that here it is the river that wears a yarn spinner's deadpan expression. Anecdotal interest necessarily yields to rhetorical drama as the Mississippi itself provides the "text" over which rival interpreters encounter one another, as when Bixby instructs the cub in "water-reading." Bixby asks:

> Do you see that long slanting line on the face of the water? Now that's a reef. Moreover, it's a bluff reef. There's a solid sand bar under it that is nearly as straight up and down as the side of a house. There's plenty of water close up to it, but mighty little on top of it. If you were to hit it you would knock the boat's brains out. (286)

Under the pilot's direction, the cub steers over a low place in the reef where the ship finds barely enough water to crawl through. On the following afternoon, Bixby leaves his pupil alone in the pilot house, promising to return before the cub enters an unfamiliar stretch of river. When the pilot fails to appear, the cub is content to steam "vaingloriously" along, "getting prouder and prouder," until another long slanting line stretches its "deadly length" across the face of the river.

My head was gone in a moment; I did not know which end I stood on; I gasped and could not get my breath; I spun the wheel down with such rapidity that it wove itself together like a spider's web; the boat answered and turned square away from the reef, but the reef followed her! I fled, and still it followed — still it kept right across my bows! I never looked to see where I was going, I only fled. The awful crash was imminent — why didn't that villain come! If I committed the crime of ringing a bell, I might get thrown overboard. But better that than kill the boat. So in blind desperation I started such a rattling "shivaree" down below as never had astounded an engineer in the world before. (287)

Bixby, who has been hiding behind a chimney, calmly enters the pilot house to prevent serious damage, for in an effort to miss the bluff reef the cub has sent the ship careening directly for shore. After inquiring sarcastically about the cub's reason for attempting an unscheduled landing, Bixby asks:

"Why, what could you want over here in the bend, then? Did you ever hear of a boat following a bend up-stream at this stage of the river?"

"No, sir, — and I wasn't trying to follow it. I was getting away from a bluff reef."

"No, it wasn't a bluff reef; there isn't one within three miles of where you were."

"But I saw it. It was as bluff as that one yonder."

"Just about. Run over it." (288)

Just as the narrator's exaggerated confidence earlier ran aground against the appearance of mortal danger, so does his exaggerated terror become ridiculous when the ship slides over the alleged reef "like oil." Bixby explains:

"Now don't you see the difference? It wasn't anything but a wind reef. The wind does that."

"So I see. But it is exactly like a bluff reef. How am I ever going to tell them apart?"

"I can't tell you. It is an instinct. By and by you will just naturally *know* one from the other, but you will never be able to explain why or how you know them apart." (288)

Reality continually retreats beneath a series of veils as the cub learns that dangers lurking beneath the apparently tranquil water may themselves be illusory. Knowledge of the river, including the ability to distinguish between fact and fantasy, belongs finally and exclusively to a community of old-timers—pilots who have dedicated their lives to the mastery of an interpretive art—because experience alone teaches one the subtleties inherent to "the language of this water" (288). It is a language, as Bixby admits, that never makes meaning present—a language that invites privileged interpreters to reconstruct an implied significance, but that never entirely relinquishes its deadpan expression. To the eyes of a greenhorn or romantic traveller, the river puts on a "faint" and "simple" expression that only conceals the "grimmest and most dead-earnest of reading-matter" (288). Bixby performs the role of a tight-lipped cultural insider and passive accomplice as the cub buys into the river's illusions with too much or too little confidence, but even Bixby cannot articulate the knowledge that eludes his cub. When the narrator's mistaken interpretation identifies him as a greenhorn, members of the pilot-house community have reason to enjoy a self-congratulatory laugh at his expense, for the cub's response at once confirms their mastery of the river and their command of an idiom that celebrates experience by mocking expectation.

It is important to note that although the bluff-reef episode includes no unit of narrative that could be compared with George Bemis's buffalo tale, the situation in which Bixby and the cub encounter each other bears all the elements of a dramatized tall-tale performance. The invitation for credulous misjudgment, the exploitation of a willing and naive listener for the entertainment of an elite group, the demand for an interpretive choice based on incomplete knowledge, and the contest of wits in which experience outweighs all other virtues—these are the unmistakable hallmarks of a tall-tale performance. The only thing missing is the tale itself, which has been abstractly embodied in the unpredictable, inscrutable, and deceptive river. This movement from anecdote to interpretive drama, a movement that preserves the tall tale as only a trace, was already in progress when Twain inserted "the boys" into the revised version of his *Alta* correspondence as a way of knitting the episodic humor of the letters into a more coherent story of travel in *The Innocents Abroad*. In "Old Times" the balance has clearly shifted from an anecdotal to a primarily thematic and situational use of tall narrative. Twain's humor continues to operate between the poles of innocence and experience, but as he focuses more on the yarn-spinning situation than on the yarn itself, those terms begin to assume imaginative shape beyond the range of travel-book literature.

In concentrating his attention on the drama of performance and response, Twain sacrificed some of the frantic energy that had earned him a reputation as the Wild Humorist of the Pacific Slope, but the shift also enabled him to extend his characterization of humorous types. He knew from experience that he could present the comedy of defeated expectations with impressive results by describing his narrator's momentary encounters with unnamed Parisian barbers and anonymous western stage drivers. In *The Innocents Abroad* and *Roughing It*, the journey itself knitted such minor figures together without the need for extended characterization. Because it dispenses with the journey as a structuring device, "Old Times on the Mississippi" required a more elaborate experiment in characterization, with the result that an enduring fictional relationship between Bixby and his naive pupil focuses the humor and organizes the action of the *Atlantic Monthly* sketches. In the two perspectives that collide throughout the story, Mark Twain successfully revives and sustains the old antagonism between Mr. Brown and his romantic friend, Mr. Twain, but the two parts of the comic juxtaposition no longer serve primarily as means to a humorous end.[14] Whereas the Twain–Brown character axis of the Sandwich Islands letters existed for the sake of the contrast it brought into focus, Bixby and his cub are more like individuals who encounter each other in a series of mutually revealing interpretive contests.

As in the bluff-reef episode, the river itself usually brings the book's central personalities into conflict and thus presents occasions for extended characterization. When the wounds incurred on the imaginary bluff reef have healed, for example, the cub returns to his apprenticeship with all his naive overconfidence restored. Bixby retires from the pilot house as the boat enters "the plainest and simplest crossing in the whole river," and his rejuvenated pupil happily takes the wheel, "brimful of self-conceit and carrying [his] nose as high as a giraffe's" (573). The cub's confidence in his ability to navigate the "bottomless crossing" begins to waver, however, when a small audience gathers outside the pilot house. Its members exchange guarded looks and nervous whispers.

> Presently the captain stepped out on the hurricane deck; next the chief mate appeared; then a clerk. Every moment or two a straggler was added to my audience; and before I got out to the head of the island I had fifteen or twenty people assembled down there under my nose. I began to wonder what the trouble was. As I started across, the captain glanced aloft at me and said, with a sham uneasiness in his voice, —
> "Where is Mr. Bixby?" (574)

The narrator refers to "my audience," implying that he is in control of the performance, yet Bixby is the silent orchestrator of this farce, and he once again casts his unwitting cub in the role of naive victim. The captain and mate join in the conspiracy by reporting imaginary perils to both starboard and port, and "then came the leadsman's sepulchral cry: 'D-e-e-p four!'" Next, a series of false soundings threatens to dismantle the cub's reason entirely:

> "Quarter twain! Quarter twain! *Mark* twain!"
> I was helpless. I did not know what in the world to do. I was quaking from head to foot, and I could have hung my hat on my eyes, they stuck out so far.
> "Quarter *less* twain! Nine and a *half*!"
> We were drawing nine! My hands were in a nervous flutter. I could not ring a bell intelligibly with them. I flew to the speaking tube and shouted to the engineer, —
> "Oh, Ben, if you love me, *back* her! Quick, Ben! Oh, back the immortal soul of her!"
> I heard the door close gently. I looked around, and there stood Mr. Bixby, smiling a bland, sweet smile. Then the audience on the hurricane deck sent up a thundergust of humiliating laughter. I saw it all, now, and I felt meaner than the meanest man in human history. (574)

If there is a tall tale lodged somewhere in this encounter between innocent expectations and private knowledge, that tale is the river itself, for the shifting channels and hidden shoals of the Mississippi mount the interpretive challenge over which Bixby and his cub confront each other. Literally speaking, there is no yarn present in the episode, yet the characters, including an audience filled with cultural insiders, participate as players in a tall-tale performance in which the river serves as an ostensible "text." Inside knowledge amounts to nothing less than the vast experience necessary to distinguish a bluff reef from a wind reef, or a bottomless crossing from shoal water. The narrator's failure to distinguish correctly, of course, contributes to his gradual disillusionment and brings him one step closer to the pilot house. When the excitement has settled, Bixby makes the educational purpose of the episode explicit by warning the cub never again to allow anyone "to shake your confidence" in knowledge that is grounded in experience (574).

The failure of dreams to conform to reality, according to James M. Cox, is the "substance of Mark Twain's humor," and one might add that it is also the substance of Bixby's advice to the cub.[15] As Bixby admits during the bluff-reef episode, not even an experienced pilot can articulate the distinction between appearance and reality; yet inhabitants of the pilot house must possess an intuitive sense of where that distinction lies, and they must be able to "talk about the river" in such a way that the thin line separating expectation from experience is never obvious, but always implicit and accessible to the well informed. Learning to read the river thus means learning to react appropriately in a tall-tale situation and to speak in such a way that one is "always understood" by privileged interpreters in one's audience.

Twain recognized the power of an interpretive disposition that seems to escape the inevitable mediation of language—the power, that is, of being "always understood." In a late work, "Refuge of the Derelicts," one of his most venerable seamen, Admiral Stormfield, reprimands a young poet by exclaiming: "Hang it, what you understand a person to say hasn't got anything to do with what the person says, don't you know that?"[16] This playful skepticism about the possibility of meaningful communication becomes progressively darker through the course of Twain's career, yet in 1875 he still felt that the yarn spinner engages in a privileged form of discourse, a discourse that is "always understood" by those listeners who are culturally attuned enough to bridge the gaps and indeterminacies that fracture the yarn spinner's performance. As Twain moved reluctantly from travelogue in the direction of imaginative fiction, the status of this privileged community and its claim to an inarticulate knowledge became more important to him than the tall tale itself, and that is why "Old Times on the Mississippi" contains many more interpretive confrontations than actual yarns. The storyteller's performance had become, and would remain in his later fiction, less a digressive and isolated event than a means of developing the author's enduring interest in the role of interpretation as a social activity with the power to affirm a community and its values.

6

The Contest for
Narrative Authority in
The Adventures of Tom Sawyer

During the winter and early spring of 1875, as Twain worked to produce regular serial installments for "Old Times on the Mississippi," a 400-page fragment of what would become his first novel lay incomplete on his writing desk. The manuscript had bogged down some time during the preceding year, when its author experienced a shortage of what he called his "stock of materials." Twain later explained his belief that "when the tank runs dry you've only to leave it alone and it will fill up again in time, while you are asleep—also while you are at work at other things and are quite unaware that this unconscious and profitable celebration is going on."[1] An unconscious celebration apparently was in progress while Twain composed "Old Times," for he needed only two months to complete the unfinished manuscript when he returned to it in May 1875. On July 5, he wrote to Howells that he had "finished the story . . . about 900 of MS, and maybe 1000 when I've finished 'working out' the vague places."[2]

Although Twain relished the image of an imaginative "tank" that only time could refill, in fact his decision to pigeonhole *The Adventures of Tom Sawyer* (1876) repeatedly during its composition owed as much to generic confusion as to a shortage of material or inspiration. Even during the productive spring of 1875, as he rapidly brought the manuscript to a conclusion, he remained unsure about exactly what sort of book he was writing, a parody of romantic expectations in the manner of "Old Times" and *Roughing It*, or a boyhood romance containing elements of parody.[3] When he sent a completed draft to Howells in July 1875, he seemed convinced that the book was a satire rather than a romance, for he declared emphatically that "it is *not* a boy's book, at all. It will only be read by adults. It is only written for adults."[4] Two sentences from his friend, however, were enough to effect a complete reversal of opinion. Howells considered the book an outstanding romance of boyhood adventure, and he advised Twain to temper the satirical tone in order to attract an adolescent rather than an exclusively adult audience: "I think you should treat it explicitly *as* a boy's story. Grown-ups will enjoy it just as much if you do; and if you should put it forth as a study of boy character from the grown-up point of view, you'd give the wrong key to it."[5]

Despite Howells's suggestions for revision, or perhaps in part because of them, Twain's indecision on the question of an audience is audible throughout the finished manuscript. Like the novel's author, the narrator of *Tom Sawyer* appears suspended between two attitudes toward his material—one detached and ironic, the other engaged and romantic—and he remains peculiarly uncommitted to either. He is reluctant to invite suspension of disbelief from his readers, yet he remains attuned to what Twain much later in his career described as "the exigencies of romantic literature."[6] Those exigencies called for a dose of heightened pathos in the aftermath of Injun Joe's death by starvation, which the narrator presents straightforwardly in language that seems ripe for a deflating rejoinder:

> The poor unfortunate had starved to death. In one place near at hand, a stalagmite had been slowly growing up from the ground for ages, builded by the water-drip from a stalactite overhead. The captive had broken off the stalagmite . . . to catch the precious drop that fell once in every three minutes with the dreary regularity of a clock-tick. . . . That drop was falling when the pyramids were new; when Troy fell; when the foundations of Rome were laid. . . . It is falling now; it will still be falling when all things shall have sunk down the afternoon of history, and the twilight of tradition, and been swallowed up in the thick night of oblivion. . . . [T]o this day the tourist stares longest at the pathetic stone and that slow dropping water when he comes to see the wonders of McDougal's cave.[7]

This is the sort of associationist hyperbole that Twain had employed frequently for comic effect as a travelling correspondent, but here there is no Mr. Blucher or Mr. Brown present to interrupt the exaggerated eulogy with a horse-sense comment. The romancer's attempt at pathos is apparently sincere, and his overstated images of antiquity betray no hint of irony. Nevertheless, Twain cannot quite resist the temptation to poke fun at his own inflated rhetoric as he moves from Injun Joe's eulogy into an angry satire of precisely the same brand of tear-soaked sentimentalism that the narrator has just finished expressing. Having established Joe's demise within a historical context that reaches from ancient Egypt to the present, the narrator turns to the subject of a petition for Joe's pardon, and his extraordinary sympathy turns suddenly into parody:

> The petition had been largely signed; many tearful and eloquent meetings had been held, and a committee of sappy women been appointed to go into deep mourning and wail around the governor and implore him to be a merciful ass and trample his duty underfoot. Injun Joe was believed to have killed five citizens of the village, but what of that? If he had been Satan himself there would have been plenty of weaklings ready to scribble their names to a pardon-petition and drip a tear on it from their permanently impaired and leaky water-works. (240–41)

After twenty years of exploiting credulity in fools, Twain found it difficult in *Tom Sawyer* to sustain a romantic attitude without occasional lapses, and critics have traditionally focused on this apparent confusion of the narrator's attitude as the novel's principal shortcoming. Bernard DeVoto's important introduction to his 1939 edition persuasively identified the generic vacillation beyond boyhood romance and adult parody as the book's "gravest limitation," although similar opinions had been appearing in reviews of the novel since its publication in 1876.[8] Forrest G. Robinson is the most recent critic to approach *Tom Sawyer* in terms of what he deems its author's "bad faith" in the project of romance. Commenting on the "leaky water-works" passage, he writes that

> Mark Twain's ironic indignation is more the product of his own self-indulgence than of superior self-knowledge or integrity. . . .

[A]s narrator of the tale Mark Twain has demonstrated a more urgent itch for melodrama than the one he condemns in the crowd. Perhaps it began to dawn on him that his scorn, if fully unleashed, would inevitably find its way back to its source. If we grant him the intimation that the angry exposure of others threatened to reveal the same fault in himself, we can begin to make sense of his hasty retreat to higher ground. For then Mark Twain's apparent return to superior detachment from village hypocrisy appears in its true colors as an uneasy truce with his own bad faith.[9]

While Robinson's verdict on the novel is harsher than most, it departs only in intensity from the traditional assumption that Twain was either unconscious of his narrator's conflicting attitudes or simply unable to control them. Yet these two narrative faces — one expressing romantic indulgence and the other commonsense parody — had been providing the raw material for Mark Twain's comedy since the 1850s, and it seems unlikely that in writing *Tom Sawyer* the veteran humorist suddenly forgot how to manipulate his favorite comic poses. In fact, a large part of the novel's charm and complexity lies precisely in its author's ability to juxtapose the attitude of the romancer against that of the straight-faced yarn spinner in a subtle competition for narrative authority. That competition is reflected in the narrator's tendency to undercut his own inflated sentimentalism, although an even fiercer contest of attitudes occurs between the narrator and the novel's other principal spokesman, Tom Sawyer. In his role as an amateur storyteller and showman, Tom indirectly deflates the narrator's purple prose with a subtler brand of the same poison that Mr. Brown employed with his verbal jibes at the romantic "Mr. Twain" in the author's Sandwich Island letters. It is certain, as Robinson and others have objected, that Tom's knack for undermining the narrator's style effectively prevents Twain from arriving at the kind of consistency of perspective that might constitute "good faith," yet it is this lack of symmetry that generates much of the novel's humor and complexity.[10]

Because the narrator frequently sneers at the excessive sentimentalism of his characters — often immediately after having indulged in a soppy reverie of his own — his attitude toward the story remains difficult to pin down. One constant feature of his performance, however, is the perfect omniscience with which he observes the life of St. Petersburg. His descriptions appear to be drawn from a great distance, and the terrific scope of his perspective is constantly reflected in diction that smacks of the picturesque and association- ist mode Twain had parodied effectively in *The Innocents Abroad* and elsewhere. In the narrator's vision, for example, Jackson's Is- land becomes a self-contained fictional world whose remoteness from the limiting conditions of reality suggests a parallel with Cooper's Lake Otsego and other classic settings of American ro- mance:

> It was the cool gray dawn, and there was a delicious sense of repose and peace in the deep pervading calm and silence of the woods. Not a leaf stirred; not a sound protruded upon great Nature's meditation. Beaded dewdrops stood upon the leaves and grasses. A white layer of ashes covered the fire, and a thin blue breath of smoke rose straight into the air. (106)

Twain's already wide reputation as a humorist in 1876 rested largely on his ability to construct such picturesque scenes by imper- sonating a naively romantic perspective. The punchline usually ar- rived with a sudden interruption or revision by some more experi- enced character, an old timer whose understated realism chastens the deluded romantic and explodes the illusion. But the corrective explosion that might alter the narrator's image of Jackson's Island never occurs in *Tom Sawyer*. There is significantly no interruption when the narrator indulges in the sort of scene painting that Twain knew so effectively how to ridicule. Instead, the novel's official narrator invites his reader to enter an imaginary world by conform- ing to its laws, ignoring for the time being, as A. C. Bradley puts it, "the beliefs, aims, and particular conditions which belong to you in the other world of reality."[11]

Within the self-contained fictional world created by the narrator, however, there exist other voices, one of which constantly chal- lenges the narrator's creative endeavor by describing the same scenes and adventures according to very different narrative princi- ples. The reader learns in Chapter 1—where Tom returns from a day of hookey "in time to tell his adventures to Jim"—that Tom Sawyer's love of play is inseparably linked to his gift for narration (3). He and Joe Harper obtain "glittering notoriety" in St. Petersburg, for example, not by performing feats of heroism on Jackson's Island, but by narrating exaggerated heroics to the credulous folks at home: "They began to tell their adventures to hungry listeners — but they only began; it was not a thing likely to have an end, with imaginations like theirs to furnish material" (138). Tom's hungry listeners are the citizens of St. Petersburg, and their eagerness to suspend disbelief encourages Tom to stretch the facts every time he describes his escapades. Hence while the reader experiences the adventure in McDougal's cave as an adolescent love story, reported from the narrator's omniscient perspective, the novel's fictional audience receives a very different version of the same events, one for which perfect suspension of disbelief is a dangerous enterprise: "Tom lay upon a sofa with an eager auditory about him and told the history of the wonderful adventure, putting in many striking additions to adorn it withal" (234). Even among friends, Tom cannot resist embellishing the facts. After his midnight visit to town from the hideout on Jackson's Island, Tom "recounted (and adorned) his adventures" for his comrades, Huck and Joe (118). Virtually every adventure in the novel receives such double treatment, being first presented as romance by the narrator to the reader, and second narrated as an oral tale by Tom, with "striking additions to adorn it withal," to a living audience.

Tom's propensity for storytelling is really the narrative extension of what James M. Cox has called his "commitment to play," and Tom's games, like his stories, embellish and transform the narrator's world.[12] Thus the woods surrounding St. Petersburg alternately become Sherwood Forest or the Spanish Main according to Tom's, not the narrator's, intentions, and although those imaginary settings are borrowed from literary romance, under Tom's creative authority they never masquerade as anything but play. Whereas the narrator depends on the illusion generated by his fictional setting, Tom's imaginary landscapes invite suspension of disbelief only from his naive victims, whose mistaken credulity ironically mirrors the reader's own imaginative investment in the project of romance. Tom's pirate and Indian games are romances tinged with enough consciousness of their own fictionality that the boys can shift instantaneously from one game to another when boredom threatens to destroy the fun (127). When members of the gang shout elaborate nautical orders at one another in order to enhance the sense that their raft is actually an oceangoing pirate vessel, the narrator comments that "it was no doubt understood that these orders were given only for 'style,' and were not intended to mean anything in particular" (101).[13]

Similarly, Tom's embellished retelling of events in the novel is a form of game playing, and his stories, like his games, are a conscious transformation of the narrator's romance rather than a rival romance. In effect, Tom's stories are tall tales that he performs within the narrator's fictional context, not for the reader's entertainment exactly, but for the benefit of *his* audience, the population of St. Petersburg. And although a portion of that audience consists of wide-eyed "innocents" whose fate is to be "slaughtered" by Tom's fabrications, most of its members recognize his role as a yarn spinner and expect him to perform it well (15). Aunt Polly, for example, frequently plays the victim, admitting at one point that "old fools is the biggest fools," yet even in that capacity she is an enthusiastic participant in the interpretive game that surrounds each of Tom's narrative performances (2). She expects him to embellish the truth and does her best to "trap him into damaging revealments" whenever she can (3). When Tom passes up the opportunity to gild the facts, as in his first encounter with the schoolmaster, St. Petersburg is confused and disappointed (53).

Tom Sawyer's peculiar brand of creativity provided Twain with a tentative solution to a problem he had been writing about without attempting to solve for many years. His extensive training in burlesque during the 1850s and 1860s taught him the useful lesson that romance and the tall tale are irreconcilable forms, better suited for humorous contrast than for compromise. The two genres presuppose in their respective audiences such entirely different attitudes toward the enterprise of storytelling that combinations of tall tale and romance, like the ill-fated *Occidental* novel in Chapter 51 of *Roughing It*, are bound to create confusion, and Twain was an expert at exploiting the humor of such confusion without risking it himself.[14] He loved to celebrate the moment of ultimate disillusionment, the moment when the tenderfoot or cub enters a new phase of life and a new interpretive community by dispensing with false romantic expectations. Yet here the challenge was to gratify the "exigencies of romantic literature" while subverting them at the same time. Following Howells's advice, Twain intended to engage his readers imaginatively with a story of boyhood adventure, yet he sought to do so without concealing his relentless parodic impulse, an impulse toward the disillusioned laughter of the pilot house in "Old Times on the Mississippi."

As the novel's premier yarn spinner, Tom Sawyer thus assumes the role previously reserved for figures such as Horace Bixby and Simon Wheeler, Twain's old-timers, storytellers capable of affirming a "community of knowers" by playing tacitly to its inside knowledge of experience during a tall-tale encounter. Juxtaposing Tom's creative project against the narrator's romantic performance, Twain initiates a renegotiation of the narrator's claims to authority—a renegotiation, moreover, in which the reader plays a vital role.[15] In effect, romance and the tall tale perform an impromptu dance together in a novel that cannot decide whether to invite or exploit suspension of disbelief.

Twain's indecision about the nature of his own performance undeniably produces moments of confusion within the text, but he manages in general to juxtapose the novel's competing voices by establishing two separate audiences, which approach the story with very different expectations, so that the interpretive efforts of one group reflect ironically on those of the other. Thus although the narrator seems perfectly reasonable in soliciting his reader's confidence in a romantic picture of the river—that "vast vague sweep of the star-gemmed water" (102), which in daylight becomes "the shallow limpid water of the white sand-bar" (107)—Tom is simultaneously engaged in "slaughtering" those members of *his* audience, the citizens of St. Petersburg, who buy into his tales with the reader's degree of romantic indulgence. The demands made on the two audiences—the narrator's readers and Tom's listeners—are completely different, so that interpretive success in one case amounts to failure in the other, and vice versa. In essence, Tom and the narrator are one more formulation of the Mr. Brown–Mr. Twain character axis with the crucial difference that here the two antagonists never confront each other directly.[16] The old battle between the yarn spinner and the romantic, between Wheeler and his pedantic listener, between Bixby and the cub, here emerges indirectly as a contest for narrative authority between two figures with highly dissimilar approaches to storytelling. Unlike Mr. Brown's rude critique of his companion's inflated rhetoric, Tom's creative adorn-ments offer a subtle yet persistent challenge to the romancer's narrative project, for even the most romantically inclined reader is aware that Tom mercilessly exploits precisely the kind of voluntary credulity that the narrator expects from *his* audience.

This is not to suggest that readers are victimized for their willingness to experience the novel on the narrator's terms, as a romance. On the contrary, it is the subtlety with which the text sustains the conflict of styles and interpretive assumptions that signals an important departure for Mark Twain as a writer. The narrator of *Tom Sawyer* of course solicits the reader's suspension of disbelief, but Tom's counterperformance effectively dislocates the narrator's creative project by enacting an alternative model of performance and response, implicitly warning against an interpretive strategy that mimics the credulity of his victims. Thus the effect of Tom's exaggerated retelling of the narrator's story is to make the novel less a romantic tale than what might be called a conditional romance, for through Tom the novel relentlessly parodies its own demands for imaginative investment from the reader.[17] Unlike the *Occidental* episode in *Roughing It*, where the tall tale's deflating wit utterly confounds the authors of a popular romance, here Tom's habit of elaborate storytelling provides an ironic counterbalance to the narrator's performance without explicitly discrediting or burlesquing that performance. The tall tale, as Tom Sawyer's natural idiom, becomes a means of engaging the debate over narrative authority in a novel that manages to be a romantic adventure without committing itself to the assumptions endorsed by its romantically inclined narrator.

While Tom never explicitly critiques the narrator's performance, his "spectacles" repeatedly serve to expose the sham quality of the narrator's brand of inflated rhetoric.[18] For example, he frequently subverts the performances of rival speakers whose eloquence or affected passion commands the respect, but not the interest, of the St. Petersburg audience. Mr. Walters, the Sunday-school superintendent, is only the first of several pious and upright orators in the novel to adopt an artificially elevated style for official occasions: "Mr. Walters was very earnest of mein, and very sincere and honest of heart; and he held sacred things and places in such reverence, and so separated them from worldly matters, that unconsciously to himself his Sunday-school voice had acquired a peculiar intonation which was wholly absent on week-days" (32). Mr. Walters's style of Sunday dress, like the "peculiar intonation" of his speech, "unconsciously" confuses reverence with affectation: "[H]is boot toes were turned sharply up, in the fashion of the day, like sleigh-runners—an effect patiently and laboriously produced by the young men by sitting with their toes pressed against a wall for hours together" (32).

When Tom trades his fish hooks for Sunday-school tickets, he is of course expressing a similar concern about style and "effects," for it is "the glory and éclat" associated with earning a Bible, rather than the Bible itself, that he covets (31). Unlike Mr. Walters, however, Tom deludes neither himself nor his audience with false pretenses toward humility, and when he takes center stage to receive his prize, he is entirely conscious of the sensation he hopes to produce. Judge Thatcher's insistence that Tom name Christ's first two disciples places the hero in a difficult predicament, but it also gives him the opportunity to disrupt Mr. Walters's laboriously choreographed performance with a climax that is more appropriate to Tom's spontaneous and self-conscious style. If he answers correctly or names the wrong two apostles, Tom will have contributed to the superintendent's sham spectacle by further falsifying the game without exposing its hypocrisy. When he finally shouts "DAVID AND GOLIAH!" to the expectant audience, however, he reveals that not only his own performance but the entire event is inspired by vanity and sustained through careful affectation. Just as Tom frequently challenges the narrator's authority by retelling the story of his adventures according to a yarn spinner's rather a romancer's method, here he steals the stage from Walters by pushing an unacknowledged fiction to the limit of absurdity. Tom's pride and naughtiness are finally no different from Walters's artificial piety except in that, like a yarn spinner, Tom plays to an inside audience, one that tastes before it swallows, and he therefore makes no effort to conceal the nature of his performance from those who can appreciate it.

The narrator draws "the curtain of charity over the rest of the scene" before it becomes clear how Tom's audience will react to his absurd rejoinder, but in general St. Petersburg is relieved and appreciative when he interrupts the course of conventional oratory (36). Judith Fetterley has called Tom a "sanctioned rebel," noting that the community actually demands his irreverence "because it provides excitement and release, and because the ultimate assimilation of the rebellion constitutes a powerful affirmation of their values."[19] St. Petersburg is indeed a captive audience for the novel's official windbags, and although its citizens sneer at behavior not sanctioned by officialdom's platitudes, they are starved for diversion and regard Tom, without admitting it, as their deliverer. At the church service that follows Sunday school, Tom's boredom extends to the entire St. Petersburg audience, and his antidote to ennui simultaneously cripples the sermon and inspires a communal spirit of laughter among the congregation. The narrator pays special attention to the minister's "peculiar style" of oratory, which, like Mr. Walters's "Sunday-school voice," exhibits its own studied affectation:

> His voice began on a medium key and climbed steadily up till it reached a certain point, where it bore with strong emphasis upon the topmost word and then plunged down as if from a spring-board. . . . The minister gave out his text and droned along so monotonously through an argument that was so prosy that many a head by and by began to nod—and yet it was an argument that dealt in limitless fire and brimstone and thinned the predestined elect down to a company so small as to be hardly worth saving. (39–40)

When Tom releases his pinchbug and disrupts Mr. Sprague's sermon, he creates a spectacle that draws the sleepy and fragmented audience together into a true congregation. The victim in this episode is neither religion nor piety nor even Sprague himself, but an unnatural style of speaking that has earned the minister a great reputation while adding nothing to the spiritual life of the community. The minister's ornate and seemingly passionate style, like Mr. Walters's "peculiar intonation," is part of a grand cultural delusion against which, according to Satan in "The Chronicle of Young Satan," the human race possesses "unquestionably one really effective weapon—laughter."[20] Tom's counterperformance, like his retelling of the narrator's story, undermines Sprague's affected fire and brimstone by unleashing an "unholy mirth" of which Satan himself would have approved (43).

In his address at the funeral service for Tom, Huck, and Joe, the minister relies more on sentimental than apocalyptic hyperbole, and this time his presentation more successfully exploits the congregation's hunger for sensationalism. The eulogy is loaded down with fictions that the audience willingly accepts because they enhance the entertainment value of the performance. The episode functions almost like a commentary on the reader's own interpretive endeavor, for what is at stake is the validity of suspension of disbelief as a response to narrative invention.

> As the service proceeded, the clergyman drew such pictures of the graces, the winning ways and the rare promise of the lost lads, that every soul there, thinking he recognized these pictures, felt a pang in remembering that he had persistently blinded himself to them, always before, and had as persistently seen only faults and flaws in the poor boys. . . . The congregation became more and more moved, as the pathetic tale went on, till at last the whole company broke down and joined the weeping mourners in a chorus of anguished sobs, the preacher himself giving way to his feelings, and crying in the pulpit. (131)

The image of Sprague crying over his extravagantly "pathetic tale" suggests a curious parallel with the narrator's own highly sentimental, and seemingly nonironic, eulogy for Injun Joe toward the end of the novel. Both eulogies invite heavy doses of emotional investment in an exaggerated representation, and both end with the image of a community apparently united in anguish (tourists, in the later passage, who stare teary eyed at Joe's "pathetic stone"; "weeping mourners" in the earlier passage). Yet although the narrator's creative authority seems to insulate his performance and to guarantee his hyperbole, Sprague's inflated rhetoric explodes as soon as a rival performer arrives on the scene. The minister fails to realize until too late that his "pathetic tale" is predicated on even larger fiction, one that invites suspension of disbelief only in order to mock those credulous enough to offer it. Despite the persuasiveness of Sprague's embellished "pictures," Tom again steals center stage — and again in the manner of a yarn spinner — by exposing the congregation's exaggerated sentimentality for what it really is. As the boys make their triumphant entrance into the church, the "'sold' congregation" unites in appreciation of the joke, admitting that "they would almost be willing to be made ridiculous again to hear Old Hundred sung like that once more" (131–32). Of course,

Tom's performance at the funeral does not involve an actual tall
tale (only later does he embellish the story of his adventures on
the island), yet he successfully orchestrates a tall-tale situation by
playing on the credulous expectations of his audience. Two kinds
of fiction come directly into conflict — the minister's (and, by association, the narrator's) sentimental hyperbole on the one hand, and
Tom's pretended death on the other — and the game triumphs by
exposing the sham.

Tom's most successful subversion of the novel's several official
rhetorics occurs at the "Examination Evening" ceremony, where
the village schoolchildren are enlisted to entertain their parents and
friends with literary and oratorical performances. Tom has been
selected to deliver "the unquenchable, indestructible 'Give me liberty or give me death' speech," and he approaches the stage full
of his usual vanity and confidence (155). But Tom's rhetoric of
adornment and exaggeration, the rhetoric of the tall tale, is useless
on this stage, and he is seized with a fit of anxiety that leaves him
uncharacteristically speechless. Members of the audience offer a
"weak attempt at applause" but quickly forget their disappointment
when the next several orators deliver a series of "declamatory
gems" (156). The evening's star performers are the young ladies
who read from "original 'compositions'" on such subjects as "Memories of Other Days," "Religion in History," and "Dream Land,"
always applying an appropriately "laboured attention to 'expression' and 'punctuation.'" The narrator comments that

> a prevalent feature in these compositions was a nursed and petted
> melancholy; another was a wasteful and opulent gush of "fine lan-
> guage;" another was a tendency to lug in by the ears particularly
> prized words and phrases until they were worn entirely out; and a
> peculiarity that conspicuously marked and marred them was the
> inveterate and intolerable sermon that wagged its crippled tail at the
> end of each and every one of them. (156)

The narrator's opinion of "the glaring insincerity of these ser-
mons" is explicit enough, although it is difficult finally to see in
what way his own "fine language," which he never hesitates to
invoke, differs from that of the young ladies. Indeed, his eulogy
for Injun Joe — "Did this drop fall patiently during five thousand

years to be ready for this flitting human insect's need?" — might easily bear one of the saccharine titles he satirizes earlier (240). Despite his condescension toward the fluffy poetics of the "Examination Evening," the narrator is responsible for having transformed the Mississippi River into "the vast vague sweep of the star-gemmed water," and Tom's miserable failure to imitate passion during his recital therefore signals an important difference between his own and the narrator's creative abilities and intentions. The narrator practices a different art from that of his hero, and the contrast between their two approaches to language and narrative emerges in large part through the narrator's frequent, although apparently inadvertent, commentary on his own style.

Having suffered humiliation on what might be called the narrator's stage of conventional literary performance, Tom fares more gallantly in his own element. The boys stage a performance of their own when they contrive to remove the teacher's wig and expose his gilded pate to the delighted audience (160). Just as in an earlier scene Tom's mischief "crippled" Mr. Sprague's fire-and-brimstone sermon, he and his friends successfully deflate the evening's "fine language" through an act of interruption and exposure, the two principal gestures that define Tom's relation to the rest of St. Petersburg. The prank functions like a tall tale in its insistence that illusions, both linguistic and cosmetic, are to be laughed at rather than soberly revered as substitutes for truth; and, as in church, laughter proves more effective than either the teacher's or the narrator's loftiest eloquence at uniting the community behind a common sentiment. The yarn spinner — unlike the romancer, the pedant, the Sunday-school superintendent, or the minister — invites suspension of disbelief only from his naive victims, and his triumph occurs through a humorous affirmation of reality that takes place, to the delight of all St. Petersburg, upon the teacher's embarrassed face and across his blazing skull.

Tom's performance resembles the teacher's own ostentatious display in that it is motivated by vanity, but the two performers differ significantly in their choice of tactics. Forrest Robinson has suggested that "St. Petersburg society is a complex fabric of lies," in which "Tom is exceptional only in the sheer quantity of his showing off."[21] Indeed, Tom encounters formidable competition in his bid to remain the town's center of attraction, not least from Aunt

Polly, who reveals on page 1 that Tom's obsession with "effects" may have a genetic explanation: "The old lady pulled her spectacles down and looked over them . . . they were her state pair, the pride of her heart, and were built for 'style,' not service" (1). As Robinson suggests, the rest of adult St. Petersburg seems equally driven by a desire to occupy the spotlight. Judge Thatcher's presence at the Sunday-school presentation inspires such excitement that the preening becomes virtually epidemic:

> Mr. Walters fell to "showing off," with all sorts of official bustlings and activities. . . . The librarian "showed off" — running hither and thither with his arms full of books. . . . The young lady teachers "showed off" — bending sweetly over pupils that were lately being boxed. . . . The young gentlemen teachers "showed off" with small scoldings. . . . The little girls "showed off" in various ways, and the little boys "showed off" with such diligence that the air was thick with paper wads and the murmur of scufflings. And above it all the great man sat and beamed a majestic judicial smile . . . for he was "showing off" too. (33–34)

Despite such stiff competition, Tom consistently distinguishes himself as the town's leading attention getter, *not* because he shows off more but because he shows off differently than the rest of St. Petersburg. Tom has a yarn spinner's gift of self-consciousness, and when he creates an "effect," he does so without losing sight of the reality from which his performance departs.[22] Unlike Mr. Walters, who mistakes his Sabbath-day affectations for sincere piety, Tom refuses to be sold by his own or his society's fictions. Aboard the raft with Huck and Joe Harper, he knows that his piratical orders are "not intended to mean anything in particular" (101). Similarly, his public "spectacles" are staged to produce a sensation, but they invariably do so by exposing rather than perpetuating the town's pet hypocrisies. As Fetterley suggests, Tom's frequent adornment of the truth, his "rebellion" from the behavior sanctioned by society's platitudes, finally constitutes "a powerful affirmation" of the community's underlying commitment to unpretentious common sense.[23] St. Petersburg rallies around Tom not because he is a more persistent or effective master of affectation than either Walters or Sprague, but because he is a gamesman and yarn spinner who is capable of entertaining the community with a self-conscious fiction, a fiction that celebrates rather than obscures experience through a process of narrative embellishment.

The unstable discrepancy between Tom's self-conscious style of performance and the narrator's brand of literary romance undoubtedly complicates the reader's interpretive task, yet this discrepancy may also be read as a measure of Twain's increasing dexterity as a writer. There persists throughout the novel a "tension," to use Wolfgang Iser's term, between the role the narrator asks us to play and the role we naturally wish to adopt as culturally attuned members of Tom's, as opposed to the narrator's, audience.[24] As so many critics have noticed, this tension becomes a source of confusion in the novel, yet by placing different interpretive demands on Tom's listeners and the narrator's readers, Twain manages to coordinate an ingenious compromise between the literary romance and the tall tale. In effect, he indulges in the narration of a romantic story that begs for the reader's unqualified suspension of disbelief while at the same time mocking his narrator's request. The novel is a romance with an escape hatch, an engaging story of courtship and adventure whose yarn-spinning hero continually laughs at the very interpretive conventions its narrator appears to take for granted.

Twain remained susceptible throughout his career to what Henry Nash Smith called "infection from 'wildcat literature,'" although he found it difficult to commit himself entirely to a form of storytelling that makes facile demands on the reader's confidence.[25] What he primarily rejected, as his essays on Cooper's literary offenses much later made clear, was not romantic fiction itself, but the excesses of certain romancers, those like Emerson Bennett — a favorite target — who regarded the reader's suspension of disbelief as an automatic response, something owed the storyteller rather than something earned. In *The Adventures of Tom Sawyer*, the tall tale provided Twain with a counterfiction that operates as a corrective to romantic indulgence without entirely invalidating the project of romantic narration itself. James M. Cox has called Tom Sawyer's character "an index to Mark Twain's inability to 'believe' in conventional fiction," and indeed one of the hero's primary tasks in the novel is to subvert the sham language and behavior that both he and Twain associate with insipid romantic indulgence.[26] The yarn-spinning hero's explicit targets are easily identified and defeated, although his most formidable challenge comes indirectly from the narrator himself. Tom's subversive tactics — his knack for timely interruption and ability to adorn the narrator's story according to his own creative impulse — allowed Twain to question the method of his novel as he wrote it, to laugh with Tom at a form of interpretive indulgence in the very act of indulging himself.

7

The Disembodied Yarn Spinner and the Reader of *Huckleberry Finn*

Toward the end of "Old Times on the Mississippi," Mark Twain explains that the river pilot of the 1840s and 1850s was to be envied because, unlike even a king, "his movements were entirely free."[1] The river pilot before the war was "an absolute monarch," the one man on earth who answered to no higher authority, who was "absolute in sober truth and not by a fiction of words" (91). Twain drives his point home by noting the inevitable contingency of alternative forms of authority:

> Kings are but hampered servants of parliament and people; parliaments sit in chains forged by their constituency; the editor of a newspaper cannot be independent, but must work with one hand tied behind him by party and patrons . . . no clergyman is a free man and may speak the whole truth . . . writers of all kinds are manacled servants of the public. . . . In truth, every man and woman and child has a master, and worries and frets in servitude; but, in the day I write of, the Mississippi pilot had *none*. (90)

To enjoy absolute authority, the author implies, is to live outside the jurisdiction not only of rival authority but of the restraining voice of a socially conditioned conscience as well. The Mississippi pilot, much like the narrator of Twain's bizarre fantasy "The Facts Concerning the Recent Carnival of Crime in Connecticut," attains his sovereignty by circumventing conscience, by subduing all challenges to his authority, including those that come from within.

There is no question that the romantic image of a solitary river pilot, unfettered by convention and responsible to no one, weighed heavily on Mark Twain's imagination, and it is tempting to read virtually everything he wrote as a sort of fantasy of evasion and liberation, albeit in many cases an aborted fantasy. Indeed, the monarchs of the river anticipate the satanic figures of Twain's late career in that they appear to stand above the distinctly human conflict between natural autonomy and social conditioning, between instinct and training, or — as Twain put it describing Huck's dilemma — between a sound heart and a deformed conscience. Huckleberry Finn himself might be pictured as a promising candidate for the piloting profession, a potential cub who has not yet found, and perhaps never will, a Mr. Bixby to lead him into the pilot house and out of contingency. Instead, Huck learns the river together with Jim, whose desire to "own himself" constitutes an economic variant of their mutual quest for perfect autonomy. As they maneuver their raft over bluff reefs and through dangerous stretches of river, the two fugitives seem at least as determined as the cub pilot of "Old Times" to attain a version of the "boundless authority" that makes actual pilots "the only unfettered and entirely independent human beings that [live] in the earth" (90).

Although the picture of the solitary monarch in "Old Times" helps to make sense of the imaginative impulse that carries Huck and Jim downriver — presumably the same impulse that tempts Huck to light out for the territory once the first quest has ended in an ambiguous liberation for Jim — that romantic picture reveals only one important quality of the pilot house. After describing the river monarch as a nearly divine individual who seems to epitomize the robust spirit of self-reliance, the narrator of "Old Times" goes on in the very next chapter to tell a quite different story about the failure of individual pilots to challenge the authority of their own fledgling union. Full of their characteristic professional arrogance, the best and most respected pilots on the river initially scorn the formation of a "Pilots' Benevolent Association," just as they denounce all other attempts to trespass on their authority. But the association manipulates the marketplace so effectively that even the most stubborn and independent pilots are finally compelled to relinquish their autonomy and to forfeit large sums of capital as well. It turns out that there is a power before which even the solitary monarch must kneel, and that power is the piloting community, the impious congregation that gathers each day in the "sumptuous glass temple" of a "big New Orleans boat" to "spin yarns and 'look at the river'" (45). This concession to a higher authority does not really diminish the stature of the Mississippi pilot, for he remains an iconic figure in the larger culture, and the narrator of "Old Times"—himself a former river man—actually celebrates the association's triumph as a solidification, rather than a compromise, of power. Acting as a union, the pilots are able to command higher prices for their services, and the association's rigid exclusivity serves to institutionalize their monopoly on authority. The unconditional autonomy once wielded by individual despots is not diminished but transformed into an equally unconditional corporate power as the pilots collaborate in establishing "perhaps the compactest, the completest, and the strongest commercial organization ever formed among men" (96).

Twain's curious juxtaposition of individual and corporate power in "Old Times on the Mississippi" suggests that the pilot house of his imagination was not the solitary throne critics have often taken it to be. Autonomy of the sort that Twain associated with his years on the river, and of the sort that Huck and Jim pursue, has an essential communal dimension, for the power that belongs uniquely to pilots in "Old Times" is really the same as that wielded by the older citizens of Virginia City: the power of being "always understood" in an interpretive transaction that privileges certain individuals over others. More than a throne or pedestal, the pilot house is a forum for tireless talkers and a proving ground for potential members of the yarn spinner's "community of knowers." Although he is often described as a prototypal "American Adam," Huck Finn runs from "lonesomeness" and cruelty in search of just such a community. He never expresses an Adamic desire to become "an individual standing alone," as R. W. B. Lewis puts it, "self-reliant and self-propelling, ready to confront whatever [awaits] him with the aid of his own inherent and unique resources."[2] Rather, Huck is after the sort of autonomy that comes with interpretive competence, the sort of power enjoyed by a cultural insider. In effect, his journey down the Mississippi is less an evasion of authority than a

quest for the authority of membership in an interpretive community—the authority that comes with a seat in the pilot house
beside men such as Sam Clemens, Bill Bowen, and Horace Bixby:
monarchs, to be sure, but "tireless talkers," "deliciously easygoing," full of "irreverent independence," and always ready with a
story (93).

The pilot house possessed special symbolic value for Mark
Twain, but the peculiar intimacy shared by its inhabitants surfaces
wherever the tireless talkers of his fiction convene to spin yarns.
Far from the "sumptuous glass temple" of a big New Orleans boat,
out on the not so sumptuous road to Humboldt, the narrator of
Roughing It and his companions reproduce a version of the pilot
house by transforming their toil into celebratory narratives that
only a fellow sufferer can fully appreciate. Ballou, Oliphant, Cla-
gett, and the narrator at first constitute an unlikely wilderness
team—"a blacksmith sixty years of age, two young lawyers, and
myself"—but harsh conditions along the 200-mile journey encourage the travellers to forge a small and resilient community, a community bound by its shared experience of hardship and affirmed
through its ability to transform such experience into interpretive
play.[3] Twain wrote in glowing terms of his own experience as a
cultural insider during the three months he spent in Jim Gillis's log
cabin in Jackass Gulch, "that serene and reposeful and dreamy and
delicious sylvan paradise."

> Every now and then Jim would have an inspiration, and he would
> stand up before the great log fire, with his back to it and his hands
> crossed behind him, and deliver himself of an elaborate impromptu
> lie—a fairy tale, an extravagant romance—with Dick Stoker as the
> hero of it as a general thing. . . . Dick Stoker, grey-headed and
> good-natured, would sit smoking his pipe and listen with a gentle
> serenity to these monstrous fabrications and never utter a protest.[4]

Regardless of whether the physical surroundings were splendid
or squalid, the performance of an impromptu yarn before a group
of cultural insiders stood as a paradigmatic social event in Mark
Twain's imagination. The implicit understanding between a teller
and his audience, epitomized in the relationship between Gillis's
grave expression and Dick Stoker's "gentle serenity," appealed to

Twain as a special instance of communication — a form of understanding made perfect because it remains inarticulate. Language, Twain believed, except the language of dreams, is never transparent, yet the yarn spinner's veiled intentions become very nearly so for a particular segment of his audience. Like the pilots in "Old Times," Gillis is "always understood" because his "monstrous fabrications" invite tacit interpretive collaboration from certain qualified members of his audience, like Dick Stoker, whose serene attention implies a thorough understanding of the game Gillis is playing. Late in his career, Twain reserved the power to escape linguistic contingency only for his transcendent characters, figures such as Satan and No. 44, who effortlessly achieve a pilot's perfect understanding by speaking in a language of essences rather than of mere representations. During most of his career, however, the yarn spinner is the figure who, for Twain, wields the power to generate and sustain a community through his use of language — a community, moreover, that mirrors the Pilots' Benevolent Association in being among "the compactest, the completest, and the strongest" ever formed by men.[5]

In the summer of 1876, Mark Twain decided to send Huckleberry Finn and a fugitive slave down the Mississippi River in search of such a community. Huck and Jim themselves forge what Lionel Trilling has called "a primitive community," a "community of saints," but, as Trilling's wording implies, their relationship is more a fragile obstruction to impinging social realities than a viable and sustaining refuge.[6] Laughter of the sort enjoyed in the security of the pilot house and around the evening campfire is noticeably lacking in Huck and Jim's most intimate moments:

> We catched fish, and talked, and we took a swim now and then to keep off sleepiness. It was kind of solemn, drifting down the big still river, laying on our backs looking up at the stars, and we didn't ever feel like talking loud, and it warn't often that we laughed, only a little kind of a low chuckle.[7]

The laughter of the pilot house embodied for Twain the affirmation of a yarn-spinning community that celebrates its exclusivity by exploiting the credulous expectations of outsiders. Although he frequently played the victim himself, Twain's writing had always celebrated the defeat of credulity as a communal triumph, often a triumph that helps prepare the chastened victim, like the cub of "Old Times" or the tenderfoot of *Roughing It*, for eventual assimilation into the group. Yet the refuge that the pilot house and the campfire consistently offer to Twain's early vernacular heroes eludes Huck and Jim, whose flight from persecution becomes a hopeless search for precisely the combination of corporate and individual power that the author's pilots, stage drivers, and forty-niners enjoy as members of an insular yarn-spinning community. The two outcasts repeatedly display narrative resourcefulness of the sort that qualifies those early figures for admission to a cultural inner circle, yet Huck and Jim remain eager candidates for inclusion within a folk community that is no longer viable in the world of *Huckleberry Finn*. There is laughter associated with the novel, but it occurs outside Huck's Mississippi Valley, in the imaginative space where the reader and implied author collaborate over interpretive possibilities suggested by Huck's performance. A new pilot house, generated in response to Huck's narration but ironically closed to Huck himself, emerges from this collaborative arrangement between the reader and implied author, who participate together as the novel's only cultural insiders, privileged in their response to a tall-tale performance in which the deadpan narrator is his own first victim.[8]

To understand how Twain transfers the pilot-house ideal of tacit interpretive collaboration from the text of his early writings to the reading situation of *Huckleberry Finn*, it is helpful to recall his early style as a platform entertainer and the literary persona that evolved out of his lecturing career. According to contemporary reviews and evidence contained in newspaper transcripts of his speeches, Mark Twain on stage was the consummate yarn spinner that he described in "How to Tell a Story." In that essay he maintained that "the humorous story," as conceived and performed only in America, "is told gravely; the teller does his best to conceal the fact that he even dimly suspects that there is anything funny about it."[9] Writing to James Redpath, Twain explained that his lecture technique relied for its humorous effect "chiefly on a simulated unconsciousness and intense absurdity," stylistic features that combined to produce a peculiarly understated humor, filled with placid expressions of "ludicrous exaggeration."[10] After attending a perfor-

mance of the Sandwich Islands lecture in 1866, Noah Brooks remarked that Twain's listeners were riveted and amazed by "his
slow, deliberate drawl, the anxious and perturbed expression of
his visage, the apparently painful effort with which he framed his
sentences, and above all, the surprise that spread over his face
when the audience roared with delight."[11] Contemporary reviewers
commonly noted that Twain never smiled or laughed during a performance, and one writer in Chicago claimed that the more the
audience laughed, "the more he looked as if about to cry, . . . as
solemn as an undertaker screwing down a coffin lid."[12]

The lecturing technique that Noah Brooks and others found so
completely original of course owed a great deal to Artemus Ward,
whose deadpan absurdities Twain had witnessed and appreciated in
Virginia City.[13] Even more importantly, though, Twain's platform
technique was a direct and uncomplicated extension of the yarn-
spinning style he had known since childhood. The persona he invented for the stage was that of a tall-tale teller who speaks gravely
but knows better. His drawling speech and affected seriousness
served as an invitation to excessively naive listeners — if any such
listeners could really have existed — to adopt a correspondingly
grave interpretation of his words, while the yarn spinner shared a
tacit joke with those members of the audience who saw through
the deadpan and appreciated its crafted absurdity. Twain was apparently worried that the yarn-spinning technique would misfire in a
lyceum setting because he could not be sure that his audience would
know how to perform its part correctly.[14] To guard against a too
literal interpretation of his deadpan presentation, he actually
prepped friends in the crowd before his first lecture in San Francisco, providing cues that would ensure him of at least a small
community of insiders whose laughter he hoped might infect the
rest of the audience, even if at first people did not know what they
were laughing about. He never resorted to the cues, either because
the San Francisco crowd already understood this kind of humor,
or because his deadpan expression was transparent enough to suit
the occasion. For whichever reason, the persona succeeded impres-
sively by holding in suspension two apparently conflicting attitudes
toward Twain's subject matter: outwardly the speaker projected
the "anxious," "perturbed," "solemn," and "grave" demeanor of an
undertaker, while inwardly a very different personality betrayed a

keen sense of the "intense absurdity" permeating the narration, seemingly despite the undertaker's demeanor.

The literary persona who calls himself "Mark Twain" is a less consistent, but very similar character. As John C. Gerber has demonstrated, the works narrated by "Mark Twain" reveal a wide variety of narrative points of view — Gerber describes seven separate "comic poses" that employ the pseudonym — each of which corresponds roughly to the persona Twain had already developed for the stage.[15] Whether he pretended to superiority (as what Gerber calls "the Gentleman," "the Moralist," "the Sentimentalist," "the Instructor") or to inferiority (as "the Sufferer," "the Simpleton," "the Tenderfoot"), Twain was essentially employing a deadpan expression that allowed him to exercise his stage technique in writing. All these characters share an utter insensitivity to humor, a grave seriousness that suggests the presence of a comic alter ego somewhere behind the mask. In each of his different poses, the literary persona — like his platform counterpart — combines outward solemnity with an implicit sense of humor, so that one never pities a character like the Sufferer of "Journalism in Tennessee," essentially because the personality of the tall humorist is implicit in everything the Sufferer says and does. Much like the undertaker of Twain's stage performances, the unfortunate journalist who calls himself "Mark Twain" wears a straight face that conceals, without quite obscuring, the part of his character that laughs inaudibly with the reader at the Sufferer's exaggerated misfortune.

As Huck points out on the first page of his narrative, *Huckleberry Finn* is not another deadpan performance by "Mr. Mark Twain" (1), but an autobiographical account by a semiliterate boy who, had he known what trouble it would be to write a book, "wouldn't a tackled it" in the first place (362). Critics have made much of the transfer of narrative responsibility, with its liberating implications for Twain's style and imagination, but what actually occurs is less a revolutionary discovery in perspective than a subtle division of the formerly unified stage and literary persona. The "Mark Twain" who so impressed Noah Brooks and others operated by sustaining apparently contradictory attitudes within a single character, producing a sort of condensed version of the old Twain-Brown confrontation.[16] That binary persona breaks down in *Huckleberry Finn* when the deadpan attitude ceases to function as a mere pose for the implied humorist and instead comes to life as something dynamic, creative, and independent. Huck combines the dubious attributes of the Simpleton, the Tenderfoot, and the Sufferer, and his grave seriousness makes him appear "innocently unaware" of the humor and hypocrisy his tale expresses. Like Mark Twain on stage, he is "anxious and perturbed"; he sometimes frames his sentences with a "painful effort"; he finds little to laugh at and much to worry about; in short, Huck's narration places a straight face over the occasionally comic, more often cruelly absurd, world of Mark Twain's Mississippi Valley. But the twin characteristics of the yarn-spinning persona, the grim demeanor and the smile it conceals, no longer belong to the same character. Huck, as the novel's grave expression, is a rhetorical posture made real. He does not qualify exactly as a yarn spinner himself, because he enjoys no access to the perspective of the implied humorist and because his solemn performance is never posed.[17] He is a disembodied yarn spinner, the deadpan attitude come to life as part of a yarn-spinning strategy, often comically mistaken in his literal judgments and his grave outlook, but genuinely rather than affectedly ignorant of his mistakes.[18]

Because Huck, unlike the deadpan poses of Twain's other writings, remains entirely cut off from the perspective of the implied humorist, Mark Twain as an authorial commentator remains equally cut off from Huck's narrative consciousness. Gerber notes that Twain's best writing occurred when the pose placed limitations on the humorist—that is, when the demands of characterization forced Twain "to make his satire implicit" and to "avoid authorial underlining."[19] On stage and in the writings narrated by versions of the stage persona, Twain's satire tended to be heavy-handed, if not explicit, for the humorist was never very far behind the solemn mask through which he spoke. With Huck in the role of deadpan narrator, however, satire and humorous commentary are forced farther beneath the surface. Huck articulates absurdities solemnly, in a manner befitting Simon Wheeler or Jim Baker of *A Tramp Abroad*, but Huck's seriousness operates comically only for the reader and his interpretive cohort, the implied humorist, whose powerful sense of irony places constant pressure on the reader's interpretive endeavor without penetrating or undermining the hero's conscious narration.[20] As a result—and as Huck comments on the raft — laughter remains curiously outside the text, much as the humor of a tall tale emerges more from what cultural insiders are able to infer about the yarn spinner's performance than from the "text" of his performance itself.

This is another way of making a point that critics have insisted on for many years: the point that *Huckleberry Finn* is really two stories — one narrated by Huck, the other reconstructed by readers — and that the distance between these two stories is the source of Twain's power as an ironist and a humorist. Commenting on the novel's use of dramatic irony, Wayne Booth observes that Huck's explicit narration encourages the reader to collaborate with the implied author in producing a parallel, unwritten text:

> Huck's version of his motives and feelings differs considerably from the one we reconstruct; the story Mark Twain tells us is consequently quite different from the story that Huck thinks he is telling, and of course the distance between the two is in itself our most interesting (and amusing) information about the events and about Huck's own character.[21]

James M. Cox makes essentially the same point when he explains that Huck's vernacular narration carries with it "implied norms," which act as "means of control within the reader's mind."[22] These norms, according to Cox, "exist outside the novel," where they function as implicit conventions, intended to guide the reader's reconstruction of Huck's narrative. For both Cox and Forrest Robinson, such collusive activity amounts to a conspiracy designed to avoid difficult moral issues, an attempt by Twain and his reader to congratulate each other for endorsing moral platitudes. Yet there is something powerfully affirmative, for Twain at any rate, in the joint fictive project through which an implied author, performing much like a yarn spinner, invites tacit interpretive cooperation from his reader. That collusive project may indeed foster the repression that Robinson and Cox find so sinister, but it does so in order to revive a version of the yarn-spinning "community of knowers," a community that repeatedly fails to materialize for Huck within the novel, but that still holds some of its former authority for Mark Twain. The gap that Booth identifies between two stories, one narrated gravely by Huck and the other reconstructed implicitly by Mark Twain and the reader, generates humor in the same way that a tall tale entertains cultural insiders in the speaker's audience; but in generating humor according to the pattern of a tall tale, the novel anticipates the ultimate frustration of Huck's own desire for inclusion within the elite interpretive circle that his performance helps to define. Twain backs away from this realization at the end of the novel, but as long as Huck actualizes the outlook of the deadpan expression, as long as his grave demeanor remains more than a transparent pose, Huck's fate as a permanent cultural outsider is tragically secure.

Huck's rhetorical predicament is reflected throughout the novel at the thematic level, where the pilot-house ideal of tacit communication repeatedly fails to offer the refuge that he and Jim seek. By the time the novel was completed in 1883, the notion of communal affirmation in "the brotherhood of man"—a favorite phrase in the late writings—had become dangerously problematic for Twain. He found it increasingly difficult to imagine a medium through which human beings might establish meaningful bonds of communication, bonds of the sort that earlier transported the tenderfoot of *Roughing It* to "the very summit and culmination of earthly luxury." Whereas the yarn spinner's artful dissimulation had once suggested the possibility of a transparent language, the possibility of being "always understood," after *Huckleberry Finn* Twain began to conceive of transparency as a quality belonging exclusively to meta-languages, dream dialects that embody rather than represent meaning.

Nevertheless, a trace of the pilot house survives in *Huckleberry Finn*, not just in the reading situation but in the novel itself. Twain's brooding on human nature and the limitations inherent to language had not hardened into acute skepticism when he composed the 1876 chapters of the novel, and it is in this section, roughly Chapters 1 through 17, that the oral community of his earlier books clings to a tenuous existence. That existence was made even more tenuous by the author's decision to accommodate his new publisher, Charles Webster, by excising the episode that has come to be known as the "Raftsmen's Chapter" in order to shorten the manuscript. Following Bernard DeVoto's initiative in 1942, and supplementing DeVoto's aesthetic decision with evidence of Twain's probable intentions, the editors of the Mark Twain

Project have restored the Raftsmen's Chapter to its original position as Chapter 16 of their definitive edition of the novel—a decision that deserves mention because, without the episode, the object of Huck's quest never comes fully into view.[23] The events of that episode, especially when examined in direct contrast with Huck's subsequent experiences in Bricksville, effectively illustrate the purpose of his journey and foreshadow its inevitable frustration at the end of the novel.

As with virtually every episode in the book, Huck's casual observations about the setting in Chapter 16 carry almost mystical significance and exert a powerful influence over the mood and action of the scene. The raftsmen's "monstrous long" craft acquires a ceremonial air as it glides slowly into view, drifting past the encamped runaways, "as long going by as a procession" (106). After shoving off at night behind the awesome raft, Huck mentions that a ceiling of clouds obscures the moon and stars, while the heavy timber on the river's banks blocks off any light from shore, causing this stretch of the river to appear hermetically isolated. Unlike the terrifying fog of the previous chapter, here the image of darkness and isolation describes a natural refuge that temporarily encloses the two rafts within a single frame: "We went drifting down into a big bend, and the night clouded up and got hot. The river was very wide, and was walled with solid timber on both sides; you couldn't see a break in it hardly ever, or a light" (106).

Huck swims to the great raft to listen for information about Cairo, the key to Jim's freedom, yet as he waits in the shadows he witnesses a scene that has important consequences for his own quest as well. Crouching in the shadows at the edge of the raft, he observes a version of the "pipe-smoking, song-singing, and yarn-spinning" scene that took place around the evening campfire on the road to Humboldt; yet unlike the tenderfoot of *Roughing It*, Huck watches from a significant distance as the raftsmen engage in a series of ritual performances that both frighten the stowaway and attract him powerfully. With his own raft drifting inexorably south rather than westward toward the frontier, Huck passively witnesses but never quite reaches the tenderfoot's summit:

There was thirteen men there—they was the watch on deck of course. And a mighty rough-looking lot, too. They had a jug, and

tin cups, and they kept the jug moving. One man was singing—
roaring, you might say; and it wasn't a nice song—for a parlor
anyway. He roared through his nose, and strung out the last word
of every line very long. When he was done they all fetched a kind of
Injun war-whoop, and then another was sung. (107)

The drinking and singing aboard the raft soon lead to a comic
showdown between a pair of cowardly ring-tailed roarers, "the
Child of Calamity" and the "copper-bellied corpse-maker," whose
extended battle of words and abbreviated battle of fists in turn
yield to more singing and, finally, to a series of storytelling performances. Huck remains hidden in the shadows as the raftsmen exchange yarns about the river:

> The man they called Ed said the muddy Mississippi water was whole-
> somer to drink than the clear water of the Ohio; he said if you let a
> pint of this yaller Mississippi water settle, you would have about a
> half to three quarters of an inch of mud at the bottom, according to
> the stage of the river, and then it warn't no better than Ohio water—
> what you wanted to do was to keep it stirred up—and when the
> river was low, keep mud on hand to put in and thicken the water up
> the way it ought to be. (112)

The Child of Calamity endorses Ed's opinion by offering an even
more surprising illustration:

> [H]e said there was nutritiousness in the mud, and a man that drunk
> Mississippi water could grow corn in his stomach if he wanted to.
> He says:
>   "You look at the graveyards; that tells the tale. Trees won't grow
> worth shucks in a Cincinnati graveyard, but in a Sent Louis grave-
> yard they grow upwards of eight hundred foot high. It's all on
> account of the water the people drunk before they laid up. A Cincin-
> nati corpse don't richen a soil any." (112–13)

As he listens intently to the raftsmen's tales, Huck crouches at
the remote fringes of a yarn-spinning community, much as the
frame narrators of old southwestern humor eavesdropped on vernacular performances in order to present their tall humor indirectly, in an authentic-sounding idiom.[24] But the narrative frame in

Huckleberry Finn functions less as a traditional insulating device for the narrator than as an obstacle to Huck's participation in an ironically remote version of the pilot-house ideal. Critics have often emphasized Huck's determination to occupy the margins of "sivilization," his urge to stand alone like a Mississippi pilot, the absolute and unfettered monarch of his own fate. Yet from the very beginning of the novel, Huck makes explicit his desire to perform the role of a cultural insider rather than that of a loner: he is "most ready to cry" when Tom threatens to exclude him from the gang in Chapter 2 (10); his chronic attacks of "lonesomeness" frequently leave him "down-hearted" and wishing for company (4); he often invents stories in which he portrays himself as a member of a close-knit family;[25] and he constantly laments his isolation by projecting his sadness onto nature. After the raftsmen discover him hiding among their provisions, Huck proves himself a worthy candidate for inclusion within the community of cultural insiders by nimbly distorting the truth with a yarn spinner's finesse: challenged to explain his presence on the raft or face harsh punishment for spying, he answers with precisely the right degree of absurdity by impersonating the deceased Charles William Allbright in a comic performance that instantly diffuses a potentially dangerous situation and converts the wrath of his audience into roaring laughter.

Yet despite his dexterity as a humorist and his desire to belong to such a community, Huck is denied membership in the raftsmen's interpretive circle. As they laughingly propose to divide Ed's fantastic tale about Charles William Allbright into equal parts, each man agreeing to "swaller a thirteenth of the yarn," Huck remains a conspicuous fourteenth member of the audience (120). Crouching at the edge of the narrative frame, he witnesses the raftsmen's intimacy without entering into the community defined through their yarn-spinning performances. Throughout the rest of the novel, Huck never comes closer to a meaningful initiation than in this early episode, where his experience with the raftsmen ironically dashes both his own and Jim's chances for a successful flight. Once Cairo is past and the timber along the banks begins to break up, revealing the lights of sordid towns along the shore, Huck and Jim can only prolong the inevitable disappointment of their quest for parallel forms of freedom.

As the two runaways approach Bricksville in Chapter 21 of the novel—with their new passengers, the king and duke, aboard the raft—Huck's description of the setting presents a stark contrast with the hermetic stretch of river that seemed to caption and insulate the events of Chapter 16. Unlike the raftsmen's mighty craft, which floats ceremonially along in harmony with the river's current, Bricksville looms precariously over the Mississippi's edge, subject to the devastating effects of the river's perpetual rising and falling:

> On the river front some of the houses was sticking out over the bank, and they was bowed and bent, and about ready to tumble in. The people had moved out of them. The bank was caved away under one corner of some others, and that corner was hanging over. People lived in them yet, but it was dangersome, because sometimes a strip of land as wide as a house caves in at a time. Sometimes a belt of land a quarter of a mile deep will start in and cave along and cave along till it all caves into the river in one summer. Such a town as that has to be always moving back, and back, and back, because the river's always gnawing at it. (183)

Like the town itself, Bricksville's residents and visitors from the country offer a striking contrast with the community that exists aboard the great raft. At first, the town's popular diversions appear identical to those of Chapter 16, for Huck observes that "there was considerable whiskey drinking going on, and I seen three fights" (183). Yet violence in Bricksville fails as a precondition for harmony. The bruises suffered by the corpse-maker and the Child of Calamity are, in George Monteiro's words, "a small price to pay for the sake of peace and the establishment of order"; in Bricksville, however, and in the gloomy towns all along the shore, violence is destructive of social order.[26] The people prefer actual suffering to the spectacle of confrontation, and, unlike the raftsmen, they require a victim for their entertainment.

When Boggs arrives in town "for his little old monthly drunk," Huck witnesses an explicit parallel to the confrontation of long-winded braggarts in Chapter 16, although a breakdown of communication between the participants in Bricksville's version of the same game determines a very different outcome. Boggs is a loud-mouthed coward in the ring-tailed roarer tradition, and his colorful threats, uttered from horseback as he tears through town, make him a worthy adversary for either of Chapter 16's aggressive boat-men: "Cler the track, thar. I'm on the war-path, and the price uv coffins is a gwyne to raise. . . . Meat first, and spoon vittles to top off on. . . . Whar'd you come f'm, boy? You prepared to die?" (184). The loafers who line Bricksville's main street are amused at Boggs's regular sprees, and they recognize him as "the best-naturedest old fool in Arkansaw—never hurt nobody, drunk nor sober" (184). They tolerate the fifty-year-old, red-faced drunk, be-cause they are "grateful for the noise" he brings monthly to a town that is otherwise deadly silent, yet no member of this audience is willing to participate in Boggs's verbal game by actively responding with a counterboast. Instead, they deride his performance with jeers: "Everybody yelled at him, and laughed at him, and sassed him" (184). Unlike the wild soliloquies of the Raftsmen's Chapter, Boggs's ritual boasting does nothing to affirm "the establishment of order" in Bricksville. Rather than inspiring active and imagina-tive engagement, his hysterics only provide a passive diversion from the community's daily routine.

The murder of Boggs is a crisis in the oral community, a com-plete breakdown of the unspoken, reciprocal agreement that in Twain's writing always characterizes the relationship between a yarn spinner and cultural insiders in his audience. The "gentle se-renity" of Dick Stoker's face as he listened to Jim Gillis's outra-geous impromptu lies, in which Stoker customarily played the lead-ing role, epitomized that reciprocal agreement for Mark Twain, who observed their relationship with fascination at Angel's Camp in 1865 and never forgot its curious strength. The same intimacy emerges in the holy places of his early fiction: in the pilot house, on Lake Tahoe, beside the evening campfire, and wherever yarns, boasts, and exaggerated threats are exchanged among insiders. The potentially binding force of this collusive humor misfires in Bricks-ville, where "gentle serenity" is replaced by derisive mockery in the expressive faces that line the town's main street. Colonel Sherburn, Boggs's chosen antagonist, refuses to participate in this corrupt-ed version of the raftsmen's game, not because he misinterprets Boggs's comic threats or misreads the old man's essential good nature; rather, as Sherburn himself puts it, "I'm tired of this" (184). The colonel's cold-blooded intolerance emerges out of his insight into a degenerate relationship between the folk performer and his audience, a relationship characterized by derision and cruelty, with no affirmative significance for the community as a whole.

A new alignment between the entertainer and the entertained, already foreshadowed in the town's jeers, emerges clearly in the frantic rush to catch a glimpse of the dying man through the drugstore window. Anxious spectators, apparently pleased that this month's spree has culminated with an added diversion, compete not with the performer in a verbal contest but with one another for the best view of the performer's dying body:

> I rushed and got a good place at the window, where I was close to him, and could see in. . . . Pretty soon the whole town was there, squirming and scrouging and pushing and shoving to get at the window and have a look, but people that had the places wouldn't give them up, and folks behind them was saying all the time, "Say, now, you've looked enough, you fellows; 'taint right and 'taint fair, for you to stay thar all the time, and never give nobody a chance; other folks has got their rights as well as you." (187)

Earlier, as Huck crouched alone at the edge of the raftsmen's craft, he was an outsider watching an insular community in action. In Bricksville, the entire community stands with Huck at the extreme periphery of a literal frame, where they observe with apparent pleasure the suffering of a lone entertainer. The insular community has dissolved because the tall talker's audience, instead of thirteen hungry raftsmen ready to swallow a yarn, now consists entirely of cultural outsiders, including Huck. Sherburn's cold-blooded intolerance only formalizes a divorce that has already taken place between the vernacular entertainer and his listeners, for Boggs's performance long ago degenerated into nothing more than a tiresome sideshow, attended for only passive diversion. Not coincidentally, Huck and the rest of Bricksville move directly from one attraction to the next, abandoning the murder scene in favor of an actual circus, where the townspeople again observe ritualized cruelty from a safe and passive distance.

When an anonymous witness to Boggs's murder suggests that Colonel Sherburn ought to be hanged, it becomes plain what happens to such an audience when it begins to feel the strength of its numbers. With no binding knowledge or shared experience to define its limits, no generally accepted mode of expression to affirm its values, Bricksville's "community" quickly degenerates into a lynch mob. Huck describes the swelling current of violence as it moves like a wave, purposefully but uncontrollably, through the street:

> [E]verything had to clear the way or get run over and tromped to mush, and it was awful to see. Children was heeling it ahead of the mob, screaming and trying to get out of the way; and every window along the road was full of heads. . . . They swarmed up in front of Sherburn's palings as thick as they could jam together, and you couldn't hear yourself think for the noise. . . . Some sung out, "Tear down the fence! tear down the fence!" Then there was a racket of ripping and tearing and smashing, and down she goes, and the front wall of the crowd begins to roll in like a wave. (189)

Walter Blair has convincingly demonstrated that Twain's reading on the French Revolution contributed to his image of the wantonly destructive mob, yet Colonel Sherburn's confrontation with the citizens of Bricksville remains a decidedly local event.[27] Neither the rights of a privileged class nor the demands of a hungry populace are at stake; rather, the conflict in Sherburn's yard pits the colonel's hardened will against the once powerful and affirmative collective will of the community in a test of strength. Unlike General Buncombe of *Roughing It*, who faces similar if less violent communal opposition from the citizens of Virginia City, Sherburn effortlessly disperses the mob and effectively announces the demise of the folk community as a force that might institute and sustain its own social order. In one of very few instances in the novel, Huck's voice wears thin, and Mark Twain becomes plainly audible as Sherburn vanquishes the crowd with his biting sarcasm: "The idea of *you* lynching anybody! It's amusing. The idea of you thinking you had pluck enough to lynch a *man*! Because you're brave enough to tar and feather poor friendless cast-out women that come along here, did that make you think you had grit enough to lay your hands on a man?"

Colonel Sherburn's philippic on the capacity of the willful individual to defy the community signals a new balance of power in the novel, one that bears heavily on the outcome of Huck's journey, for events in Bricksville anticipate the violent breakup of folk communities all along the river. Huck never finds or creates an effective analogue for Mark Twain's pilot house, yet Twain invites the reader of *Huckleberry Finn* to participate in an abstract version of the yarn-spinning community of his earlier books. Regardless of the level of sympathy one extends to Huck, his performance induces readers to engage in a collaborative effort with the novel's implied author, for Huck's naive narration requires extensive reconstruction by a perspective that is detached from the biases of antebellum Mississippi Valley culture. The reader, in effect, goes behind Huck's back to conspire with Mark Twain over the significance of Huck's performance, much as cultural insiders tacitly consult the figure behind the deadpan mask in formulating their response to a tall tale.[28] Huck never enjoys the intimacy that such tacit collaboration entails, yet Twain resurrects his old dream of a transparent language and an ideal oral community by making Huck's performance a pretense for the reader's assimilation into a new interpretive community, a new pilot house, constituted — like the old one — by silent collusion among interpretive cohorts.[29] When readers interpret Huck's avowed willingness to go to hell for saving Jim as evidence of the narrator's virtue, to take the most obvious example of dramatic irony in the novel, they join Mark Twain in reformulating the expressed meaning of Huck's narration in a way that none of the characters, least of all the deadpan narrator, is capable of doing. By reading through the deadpan expression, as Huck himself cannot, the reader ironically enjoys an opportunity to become like a member of the raftsmen's nighttime watch — that is, to participate in the event of narrative performance by tacitly filling in gaps and indeterminacies that separate the words of the deadpan from the perspective of the humorist.[30] In responding like true cultural insiders to one another's yarns, the raftsmen actually offer a program for experiencing the novel on its own terms, not because *Huckleberry Finn* is a collection of tall tales about the Mississippi River, but because it is a novel that employs dramatic irony as a way of engaging its reader's interpretive participation according to the pattern of tall-tale performance and response.

Some of the novel's most aggressive critics maintain that the reader's assumption of such a privileged interpretive perspective recapitulates a pattern of evasion worked out in the novel, whereby an ailing society ritually denies its gravest problems. Indeed, it may be inevitable that at some level of social consciousness the peculiarly American penchant for yarn spinning belies a cultural tendency to participate in what Forrest Robinson calls "the dynamics of bad faith." What Robinson perhaps overlooks in his effort to uncover symptoms of evasion in the novel, however, is that the reader's complicitous role in *Huckleberry Finn* recapitulates another dynamic structure as well, the structure of tall-tale performance and response, in which interpretive collaboration among cultural insiders has the power to produce meaningful communal affirmation. By the time he finished the novel in 1883, Twain no longer entirely believed in the power of the oral community to redeem the "sivilized" individual, and this loss of confidence helps to explain why Huck's journey fails to produce a socially construed version of *Roughing It*'s "summit and culmination of earthly luxury." The yarn spinner's performance still embodied for Twain the possibility of a transparent medium of communication, and thus the possibility of a viable oral community, but the ideal had become increasingly problematic and abstract.[31] Indeed, while Huck's narrative performance invites the reader to enter a privileged interpretive community, Huck himself becomes a victim of Twain's growing despair over the possibility that such a community could exist among self-interested mortals. It is this tension between the ideal of unmediated communication—the dream of being "always understood"—and the novel's seeming disavowal of the ideal that troubles many of *Huckleberry Finn*'s critics and that helps to explain the novel's endless power to engage its readers, a tension between the dynamics of the tall tale and the dynamics of bad faith.

Conclusion

The Eclipse of Humor

"His Exaggeration-mill A-working":
A Connecticut Yankee in King Arthur's Court

After *Adventures of Huckleberry Finn*, the tall tale survives as an echo in Mark Twain's writing, a strategy for communal affirmation that never quite succeeds. That echo is heard throughout *A Connecticut Yankee* (1889), although the movement from Huck's relatively consistent deadpan narration to the more overtly satirical tone of the later novel carried Twain even farther from the spirit of the yarn spinner's art. In fact, as he first envisioned his tale of a nineteenth-century time traveller in Arthur's England, Twain intended his hero to win power and wealth by exercising narrative as well as technical ingenuity. Outlining the projected story for an audience on Governors Island in 1886, he explained that the Yankee, then called Robert Smith, was to have ignored the king's invitation to rescue sixty captive princesses from a local ogre, opting instead to "tell a majestic lie about" it, "like the rest of the knights."[1] Much like the revered Mississippi pilots of "Old Times on the Mississippi," Arthur's knights gather regularly to tell "lies of the stateliest pattern," and they remain "reading and willing to listen to anybody else's lie."[2] Clarence also proves himself a capable dissimulator by spinning a yarn that members of the court eagerly "seize" and "swallow" (46), and even the Demoiselle Alisande la Carteloise impresses Hank with a narrative style that is distinctly reminiscent of that of Jim Blaine in *Roughing It*. Her "horizonless transcontinental sentences" (127), much like Blaine's drunken non sequiturs, produce incessant narratives that "generally began with-

161

out a preface, and finished without a result" (212). As Hank aptly exclaims, "there never was such a country for wandering liars" (88).

Such casual traces of the yarn spinner's technique surface everywhere in the novel, yet Twain initially intended to do more than embed echoes of the tall tale throughout the text of *A Connecticut Yankee*. By February or March 1886, when he suspended composition on the novel for nearly a year and a half, he had completed three chapters and the introductory "Word of Explanation," and the evidence contained in this portion of the completed text suggests that Hank Morgan's narrative performance was to have been modeled after Huck's deadpan autobiography.[3] Both characters are vernacular storytellers who narrate their adventures in a matter-of-fact style that inadvertently deflates romantic social customs of the land through which they travel.[4] Like Huck, the Yankee initially performs the role of a deadpan social commentator whose observations betray a limited range of ironic understanding. Judith Fetterley concurs that Twain originally conceived of Hank Morgan as "a successor to Huck Finn, a character who would adopt the latter's role of traveling through a corrupt world and exposing its corruption."[5] This process of exposure was to have been, as in *Huckleberry Finn*, largely incidental to the hero's conscious narrative intentions, for as Twain told his illustrator, Dan Beard, he originally considered the Yankee "a perfect ignoramus," a figure whose narrow angle of vision makes him capable of suggesting a contrast that he fails to appreciate entirely himself.[6] In the novel's prospectus, which Twain either wrote or edited some time in 1889, the author continued to describe his vernacular hero as a deadpan performer created in Huck's image, perhaps shorn of Huck's natural compassion and simplicity, but still innocently unaware of the indignation conveyed by his performance: "Without knowing it the Yankee is constantly answering modern English criticism of America, and pointing out the weakness and injustice of government by a privileged class."[7]

Despite this explanation of the novel's deadpan strategy for producing dramatic irony, anyone who has read through Chapter 8 of *A Connecticut Yankee* recognizes that Hank Morgan possesses more satirical understanding than his author originally intended to give him. Already in Chapter 4, which Twain wrote when he returned to the manuscript during the summer of 1887, the Yankee contradicts the image of an ignoramus who answers modern England "without knowing it." Hank's perspective had apparently broadened considerably during the year and a half he spent pigeonholed in Twain's writing desk, for in the opening pages of the 1887 portion of the novel he reveals an impressive literary background — he has read *Tom Jones*, *Roderick Random*, "and other books of that kind," including the novels by Sir Walter Scott — and he is perfectly capable of connecting his observations about sixth-century England with a critique of modern British laws and manners (32). In Chapter 4, he maintains on the basis of his reading of English literature that although the Arthurians habitually employ language that "would have made a Commanche blush," it is furthermore true that "the highest and first ladies and gentlemen in England had remained little or no cleaner in their talk, and in the morals and conduct which such talk implies, clear up to a hundred years ago; in fact clear into our own nineteenth century" (32).

By Chapter 8, the inconsistency in Hank's deadpan expression has produced a noticeable shift in Twain's narrative strategy. As he solidifies his political power and begins to contemplate reforms, Hank for the first time displays his capacity for direct invective against British institutions: "Why, dear me, *any* kind of royalty, howsoever modified, any kind of aristocracy, howsoever pruned, is rightly an insult" (64). Hank continues to employ the language of an ignoramus, capable at times of thinly masking the implied author's satirical intentions, but his own growing indignation oversteps the conceptual limitations inherent to an effective deadpan presentation. Henry Nash Smith explains that the author has "tried not merely to transform the vernacular value system into a political ideology, but to make it the conceptual framework for a novel embodying his philosophy of history and using this philosophy to interpret nineteenth-century civilization."[8] Finally, according to Smith, "the comic fable proved too fragile to sustain the burden of thought and emotion Mark Twain imposed on it."

There is little point in beating Hank Morgan over the head, as so many critics have done, because he fails to reproduce Huck's deadpan performance, yet Mark Twain was more effective as a literary yarn spinner than as a literary satirist, and a brief comparison of parallel passages from the two novels will help to illustrate this evaluative claim. When Huck observes the king and duke preying on the confidence of innocent mourners in the Wilks episode, he comments in a memorable passage that "it was enough to make a body ashamed of the human race."[9] Huck's explicit meaning, his disapproval of the king's performance, is plain enough, yet the reader is left to decide whether the shame does not belong equally to members of the king's indulgent audience who, like their counterparts in Bricksville, so eagerly swallow his story in order to gratify their desire for sensational diversion. Here and throughout the novel, Huck's narration suggests ironic possibilities that he simply overlooks himself, so that the deadpan narrator becomes the unwitting spokesman for a vision that contains far more indignation than he is capable of expressing directly.

Toward the beginning of his adventures in Camelot, Hank expresses an identical attitude toward the human race, although the effect of his performance is very different:

> It is enough to make a body ashamed of his race to think of the sort of froth that has always occupied its thrones without shadow of right or reason, and the seventh-rate people that have always figured as its aristocracies—a company of monarchs and nobles who, as a rule, would have achieved only poverty and obscurity if left like their betters to their own exertions. (64)

The silent interpretive partnership that was necessary to reconstruct ironic possibilities emerging from Huck's avowal of shame never develops in response to the Yankee's speech. His "trite but passionate invective," as Henry Nash Smith puts it, precludes the reader's interpretive collusion by suggesting that Hank already knows exactly where to direct his rage.[10] Moreover, whereas the power of Huck's indignation is augmented by the fact that he remains unconscious of its full scope, Hank's rage seems almost too loud. The distance between the implied humorist and his vernacular spokesman has disappeared, and thus Hank cannot generate the same broad ironic effect that Huck achieves with his deadpan presentation. As the direct spokesman for Mark Twain's indignation, Hank must shout loud and long to convey an emotion that Huck captures in a single breath.

Speaking before an audience at Yale University in June 1888, as *A Connecticut Yankee* awaited its final phase of composition,

Twain explained that the moral responsibility of the American humorist consisted in "the deriding of shams, the exposure of pretentious falsities," and "the laughing of stupid superstitions out of existence"—all of which contributed to make the humorist "the natural enemy of royalties, nobilities, privileges, and all kindred swindles, and the natural friend of human rights and human liberties."[11] His notes for the novel, written at about the same time, include high praise for the distinctively irreverent American press, suggesting that whenever straight-shooting newspapers "laugh one good king to death, they laugh a thousand cruel and infamous shams and superstitions into the grave," for "irreverence is the champion of liberty and its only sure defense."[12] Mark Twain's irreverence was running high in 1888, so high in fact that the character he created to vent his growing indignation became a virtual spokesman for the pen warmed up in hell instead of a novelistic device capable of converting that indignation into humor. Earlier in his career, the tall tale had supplied the basic recipe for such a conversion; as he speculated on the American humorist's iconoclastic calling in 1888, however, Twain found the yarn spinner's art increasingly irrelevant to his purposes as a writer. He had begun to locate his humor in a bolder form of irreverence, one that makes no pretense at being "innocently unaware" of its subversive project.

Reading and Complicity in
The Tragedy of Pudd'nhead Wilson

Twain returned to "the matter of Hannibal" in *Pudd'nhead Wilson*, and in a sense he returned to the tall tale as well, although the form no longer implied the affirmation of an ideal interpretive community. It is well known that the novel grew from a comic seed planted in 1869, when Twain composed an extravagant sketch entitled "Personal Habits of the Siamese Twins."[13] In that tale, a freakish congenital ligature forces two radically opposed personalities, Chang and Eng, to endure each other's company through an endless series of annoyances. Chang, a teetotaling member of the Good Templars, becomes "drunk as a lord" when his profligate brother swills hot whiskey, until "it was not possible to tell which was the drunkest" (211). Twain delights in extending the situation comedy to absurd limits, explaining that the brothers fought on opposite sides during the Civil War and eventually took each other prisoner at Seven Oaks, "though a general army court had to be assembled to determine which one was properly the captor, and which the captive" (209). According to the logic of the tale's humor, individual volition and responsibility become hopelessly problematic when two wills operate within a single body, or when identity is understood as a complex of forces rather than as a unified structure. With a yarn spinner's knack for understated absurdity, the narrator casually explains that despite their radical differences, the twins are a model of perfect companionship and "even occupied the same house, as a general thing" (209).

In 1891, the Siamese twins Giovanni and Giacomo Tocci toured America, and Twain could not resist the opportunity to tap public excitement over the "youthful Italian 'freak' — or 'freaks' — " by recasting the twenty-year-old jokes of his early tale in an updated mold.[14] He replaced the names Eng and Chang with the Italianate Angelo and Luigi Cappello and substituted for the original ligature an anatomically accurate description of the Tocci twins: a creature, or creatures, "consisting of two heads and four arms joined to a single body and a single pair of legs" (119). With these modifications in place, he contemplated a timely and "extravagantly fantastic little story" that was to have enacted a contrast of political affiliations, religious beliefs, smoking and drinking habits, and the like precisely in the manner of the 1869 yarn (119). This "little story" eventually became the massive Morgan Manuscript, an early version of *Pudd'nhead Wilson* that includes the dizzying coincidence of three major plots: a tall yarn about Siamese twins from Italy, the Cappello brothers; a fingerprinting detective story featuring the eccentric country lawyer Pudd'nhead Wilson; and a changeling–miscegenation plot instigated by the slave Roxana. When his publisher, James Hall, insisted that the manuscript would profit from a major revision, Twain performed the celebrated "literary Caesarean" that produced the final version of the novel by separating the Siamese twins, thus removing the substance of the yarn that had suggested the novel in the first place (119).

For all its graphic appeal, the image of a literary caesarean is not entirely accurate to describe the operation that Twain performed on the Morgan Manuscript in the early summer of 1893. In fact, the final revision amounted less to a sanitary operation than to a messy subversion of the original tall tale and of the identity riddle that the Cappello twins were intended to embody. Many passages that Twain originally composed to exploit the comic situation of the tale retain an implicit sense of the Siamese-twin identity problem, even though the twins no longer inhabit a single body in *Pudd'nhead Wilson*.[15] In the manuscript, for example, when Luigi is asked to explain his motivation for acting heroically during an attack on Angelo's life, he reiterates the argument that fuels the situation comedy of the tale: "suppose I hadn't saved Angelo's life, what would have become of mine? If I had let the man kill Angelo, how many hours would I have survived? I saved my own life, you see."[16] In *Pudd'nhead Wilson*, Twain severs the twins but leaves them in such close proximity that Luigi's original point about their melded identities remains implicit in the passage: "suppose I hadn't saved Angelo's life, what would have become of mine? If I had let the man kill him, wouldn't he have killed me, too? I saved my own life, you see" (52). The physical manifestation of two personalities contained within a single body has disappeared, but the logic of the farce remains as a shadowy reminder that identity in the novel is never reducible to simple and distinct components.

Virtually all of Twain's revisions during this last phase of work on the novel were directed toward rooting out the original tall tale, although in many instances the altered passages — like the one above — retain a latent or implicit sense of the identity problem that generated the comedy of the tale. In the manuscript, for example, Pudd'nhead's straight-faced joke about killing half a dog is only one of several statements explicitly intended to underscore his sympathy for the Siamese twins and to foreshadow his unique grasp of identity problems raised by their fluid, undifferentiated condition. In the revised version, where that condition no longer pertains, Pudd'nhead's joke is curiously irrelevant to the plot except as a bizarre signal that the logic of the tale survives despite the absence of the farcical twins themselves. Their Siamese condition has been edited out of the novel, but the substance of Wilson's aphoristic insight — the notion of complex interdependence — retains a latent suggestiveness that operates throughout the novel like a covert secret, shared by Wilson, the narrator, and the novel's reader.

This privileged circle develops very early in the novel, also in part as a result of revisions made in the early summer of 1893. One of the simplest yet most revealing changes of that late stage in the novel's composition involved Twain's decision to alter the title of his preface. Some time after he elected to sever the Siamese twins, the author performed a seemingly unrelated operation on his preface by replacing the original "Note Concerning the Legal Points" with "A Whisper to the Reader." He made only minor stylistic alterations within the text of the original "Note," yet the choice of a new title is interesting because it suggests that Twain was aware that his revised plan for the novel had occasioned a new rhetorical situation. The "Whisper" immediately alerts readers to their role in a private communicative relationship with "Mark Twain," the jackleg author of the preface who employs specious legal jargon in his attempt to claim an ancient lineage of "Cerretani senators and other grandees" (2). When the English edition of *Pudd'nhead Wilson* appeared in 1894, a reviewer for the *Athenaeum* praised the novel for "the really excellent picture of Roxana," but went on to note that "the humor of the preface might very well be spared; it is in bad taste."[17] Leaving the question of taste aside, Twain's prefatory note to *Pudd'nhead Wilson* cannot well be "spared," for it serves an important rhetorical purpose by helping to shape the reader's attitude toward the novel's jackleg author. The discreetly whispered exaggerations of the revised preface establish an interpretive partnership that will eventually exclude the humorless citizens of Dawson's Landing, whose "vision" — as the narrator later explains — "was not focused for [irony]" (25).

One character, however, earns admission to the novel's interpretive inner circle: David Wilson enters Dawson's Landing with "a covert twinkle of a pleasant sort" in his "intelligent blue eye," and — much like the narrator — he immediately whispers to the reader by confounding his fictional auditors with a polished deadpan delivery (5). Speaking with the earnest expression of "one who is thinking aloud," Wilson utters the apparently absurd remark that confirms his standing as both a cultural outsider in Dawson's Landing and a cultural insider in the novel's rhetorical drama. The reader, who receives privileged information about Wilson's character, perceives the "covert twinkle" in his eye and thus easily construes his statement about the dog as a veiled assertion of the interdependence of parts in a living organism.[18] The ironic stranger's immediate audience, on the other hand, searches his face with curiosity, "with anxiety even," but finds "no light there, no expression they could read," and Wilson consequently receives the unofficial title of Pudd'nhead by unanimous decision of his victims in the comic exchange (5). Only the reader and narrator recognize his unflattering sobriquet as what it really is: a perfectly appropriate name for the deadpan expression that disguises, to Wilson's apparent satisfaction, the covert light in his eye.[19]

Wilson plays the role of an ironist in the Morgan Manuscript as well, but there his irony only articulates the point that the twins, themselves a physical manifestation of complex identity, make over and over: the point that reductive answers to questions about identity are doomed to misfire with humorous consequences. Even such simple-minded characters as Betsy Hale and Aunt Patsy enjoy enough insight into the condition of the Siamese pair to side with Pudd'nhead in the comic debate over Luigi's responsibility for the assault (151–53). In the published version of the novel, the principle of interdependence no longer asserts itself explicitly through the twins, and — as the community's response to Wilson's "fatal remark" demonstrates — no one in Dawson's Landing shares Pudd'nhead's covert insight into the complex nature of identity. The same fictions of law and custom that were openly ridiculed in the situation comedy of the Morgan Manuscript's tall tale go unchallenged in the novel, except by Wilson, for the twins no longer present a physical parable to contradict legal provisions that arbitrarily fracture identity and concretize the naming process. Instead of a mere articulation of the story's comic situation, Wilson's position on questions of identity thus becomes the substance of a private understanding he shares with the reader and narrator. In rooting out the farce, Twain in effect establishes rhetorical boundaries that exclude the citizens of Dawson's Landing from the novel's interpretive inner circle, where insight into human interdependence — the humorous concept at the heart of the deleted tall tale — is shared tacitly among those participants in the story's narrative performance whose vision *is* "focused for irony."

Although Twain presents Wilson as a character who comprehends irony, Pudd'nhead never becomes a transcendent figure, and the reader's interpretive partnership with him carries no exemption, for either Wilson or the reader, from the novel's relentless ironies.

In fact, the compelling image of David Wilson as the straight-faced author of an ironic calendar threatens to draw the reader into complicity with the novel's arch legislators as soon as Wilson lowers his deadpan mask during the novel's climax. His defense of the mistakenly accused twins in the final courtroom scene initially suggests a direct parallel with his ironic performance in the novel's opening episode, for his advocacy of the twins challenges the prosecution's effort to pin a false label on an innocent victim. But Wilson's argument against reductive naming actually culminates in another, equally insidious, attribution of simple identity. For the first time since his misappropriation of the "pudd'nhead" label in Chapter 1, Wilson lowers his deadpan mask, finally contradicting the town's mistaken verdict on him, when he successfully uncovers the fiction of identity that Roxy authored when she reversed the babies in their cribs; and in challenging this arbitrary attribution of identity, he inadvertently buys into a larger fiction of law and custom by conferring legitimacy on precisely those reductive legal discriminations that inspired Roxy's action in the first place. At one time content to play the part of an ironic victim, Pudd'nhead relinquishes his disguise when he brilliantly restores the "true" Tom Driscoll to his rightful title. Yet at the same instant, Wilson reveals himself as what he has been all along, an expert lawyer and perpetrator of the sham by which Dawson's Landing confers identity on its citizens.

As Pudd'nhead triumphantly renounces his twenty-year-old label in the final recognition scene, his formerly veiled irony becomes a veiled complicity that threatens to implicate the reader as well. This important player in the interpretive drama has been conditioned by the novel's rhetorical structure to perform the role of Wilson's interpretive cohort and fellow ironist, a role that encourages the reader to endorse Wilson's challenge of the legal establishment, and through which the reader shares Wilson's apparent detachment. Yet as Twain is perfectly aware, the reader who applauds Pudd'nhead's discovery of the changeling plot becomes like one of the simple-minded jurors at the impromptu trial in Chapter 1, eager to confer identity on the culprit under the auspices of a legal system that pursues a comically rigid approach to questions about human nature and volition. In the excitement that Pudd'nhead quite consciously orchestrates in the courtroom with his pauses and carefully timed revelations, the reader forgets to ask whether it was the human three-fifths or the canine two-fifths of the accused that should be held responsible for the murder of Judge Driscoll. This was precisely the question that the Siamese-twin yarn raised over and over in order to demonstrate the ridiculous simplicity of such legal distinctions, yet Twain invites his reader, along with the citizens of Dawson's Landing, to overlook the trace of the tall tale in the novel's climactic revelation scene. Contrary to the impression created by the author's "Whisper to the Reader," an impression of mutual and privileged objectivity, the language of jurisprudence with which the first families of Dawson's Landing maintain their hold on power finally entangles the reader in a web of ironies that offers no perfectly guiltless point of reference.

Many readers are understandably uncomfortable with such a predicament, as Mark Twain hoped they would be, and it is for this reason that so much critical energy has been expended in attempts to explain where and why the author became "confused" about the moral implications of his story. Some of the novel's most astute critics operate on the assumption that Twain intended to provide his reader with an objective and consistent point of view, and that ill-conceived plot developments and imperfect revisions thwarted this intention, producing instead a tangled monstrosity. George Toles, for example, writes that *Pudd'nhead Wilson* "is a novel which would like to lead the reader out of itself (out of its myriad confusions and unresolved conflicts) into a secure framework of shared knowledge and belief, but it is finally unable to do this."[20] Lee Clark Mitchell takes a similar approach to the novel's contradictions, arguing that "Twain was unable to fulfill his initial intentions" because his satire of racial assumptions became confused with an incompatible point about social training.[21] Frustrated by the novel's inability to "lead the reader out of itself," Twain's critics customarily either blaze their own trails toward a secure and detached objectivity or concur with Toles that "the form of closure Twain adopted could not resolve the many 'voices' that are intermittently heard in *Pudd'nhead Wilson* into one, unified voice."[22]

The incessant discussion of "flaws" in the novel, together with attempts to place the reader of *Pudd'nhead Wilson* in a more tenable interpretive position by correcting those flaws, bears out Walker Gibson's impressive insight into the nature of critical judgment. Gibson argued that the book we reject as "bad" is often one "in whose mock reader we discover a person we refuse to become,

a mask we refuse to put on, a role we will not play."[23] The role
Mark Twain asks his reader to play in *Pudd'nhead Wilson* is one
with serious difficulties, not because Twain failed to produce closure, but because that role entails complicity with the novel's reductive argument. The reader who assumes ironic distance from the
novel's antebellum setting inevitably becomes an unwitting victim,
a credulous stranger who accepts the narrator's confidential "whisper" for all it seems to imply. Only toward the end of the novel
does the reader's illusory detachment collapse in a revelation that
ironically betrays the shadowy presence of the original tall tale
and the comic idea that made it work. The reader's inadvertent
complicity with the court, as it reassigns identities according to
fictions no less arbitrary than the one it condemns, confirms the
notion that Twain began to explore when the original Siamese
twins, Chang and Eng, were accused and then acquitted of a series
of minor crimes: the notion that guilt, like identity itself, is somehow always shared among separate parts of the complex social or
biological organism. As the reader cheers Pudd'nhead's progress
toward a conviction in the final trial scene, it becomes painfully
apparent that no objective point of analysis exists — or ever has
existed — from which the reader can ironically denigrate the humorless citizens of Dawson's Landing, for the reader's own interpretive
activity has become entangled with the town's insidious process of
naming.

Evan Carton, one critic who accepts the tainted role Twain offers his reader rather than attempting to rewrite it, explains that
the novel's "ultimate mimetic feat" lies in "the consubstantiality of
its characters with its author and readers."[24] All participate in a
drama that echoes the rhetorical pattern of a tall-tale performance,
a drama in which the reader draws the unlucky part of the naive
victim. Carton describes the drama succinctly:

> Twain's novel implicates us in its community of disingenuousness
> and guilt and, by so doing, facilitates our realization of that commu-
> nity (ourselves) and its possible redemption through us. We and
> Twain, in the end, are neither wholly masters nor wholly slaves;
> rather, I think, the novel would have us take on a more difficult
> mediatory position — the assumption of responsibility — as it has
> done by providing a medium in which responsibility may be recog-
> nized and shared.

The "community of knowers" that possessed such cultural authority in Twain's early writings is now, in Carton's words, a "community of disingenuousness and guilt," and its redemption has become
a seriously problematic affair. Traces of the tall tale continue to
circulate throughout the author's late work, but the yarn spinner's
art no longer provides the "medium in which responsibility may be
recognized and shared" as a bond of sympathy among interpretive
collaborators. Collective guilt has replaced the yarn spinner's inside
perspective as the cultural glue that might unite a modified version
of Twain's old yarn-spinning community—what he now calls, with
bitter irony, "the brotherhood of man."

Wish Fulfillment and the Uses of Transcendence
in Mark Twain's Late Writings

With its endlessly implicating ironies, *Pudd'nhead Wilson* gestures
toward the notion that, as Twain later put it in his autobiography,
to speak one's "whole frank mind" is "a thing which is wholly
impossible to a human being."[25] Language, ironically the primary
instrument of both social training and self-expression, preempts all
efforts to transcend the provincial morality of Dawson's Landing,
for the town's leading citizens, together with Wilson and the reader, remain locked into a vocabulary that contains the permanent
inscription of traditional injustices. The yarn spinners of Twain's
early career, by contrast, escape what James Cox has called *Pudd'n-
head Wilson*'s "total irony" by practicing a self-conscious art of
dissimulation, turning the inevitable duplicity of language toward
their own rhetorical ends rather than pretending, like Wilson, to
have overcome it.[26] The stage drivers and forty-niners of *Roughing
It* enjoy an exalted cultural status because they manage precisely what Twain later felt it was "wholly impossible" for a human being to do. In defiance of linguistic horizons that block transparent expression in articulate discourse, a "community of knowers"
emerges in the silent space of agreement, at the metaphorical "summit and culmination of earthly luxury," where privileged interpreters join the yarn-spinning performer in collusive laughter.

This is a model of transcendence that begins to break down in
Huck Finn's Mississippi Valley, where potential interpretive com-

munities repeatedly fail to materialize in response to narrative performance. After Huck, the yarn spinners of Twain's fiction never
regain the interpretive privilege they enjoyed as elite residents of
the pilot house, where men such as Horace Bixby were sure of
being "always understood" by their colleagues. Such transparency
becomes increasingly rare in Twain's writing after 1885, for what
had been the yarn spinner's redemptive power of narrative performance belongs in the late work exclusively to supernatural figures,
mysterious strangers who alone stand above complicity in social
fictions. It is as though the transcendent hero who dominates the
major creative efforts of Twain's last fifteen years enabled the
author to repossess, as a kind of wish fulfillment, the ideal of a
guiltless interpretive perspective. *Pudd'nhead Wilson* dramatized
Twain's belief that to live within a culture's verbal horizons is to
abet, even in silence, that culture's crimes against humanity, for
the users of a language inscribed with traditional prejudices, including users privileged with a keen sense of irony, can never entirely escape implication. To repossess the pilot house, therefore,
Twain had to look beyond culture, beyond man, to a figure who
stands outside any conceivable verbal horizon. Not coincidentally,
the mysterious strangers of the late fiction invariably possess linguistic powers that defy human comprehension (No. 44 seasons his
discourse with "strange words and phrases, picked up in a thousand
worlds"), for the late hero, like the yarn spinners of the early writings, must grasp and control every articulate and inarticulate nu-
ance of language.[27]

Vernacular storytellers continue to perform yarns in the late
works, but their power to affirm a human community through
self-conscious dissimulation has been absorbed and transformed
by the transcendent figure. Twain draws a coy parallel between
priestcraft and the yarn spinner's craft in "No. 44, The Mysterious
Stranger," for example, implying through August Feldner's naive
narration that faith in the Church's miracles amounts to excessive
credulity in the presence of a skillful storyteller. Much like a tall
tale, Father Peter's story about the "miracle of Turin" employs
graphic details and a curious logic in order to make events of the
most "unusual nature" seem entirely plausible.[28] Similarly, Edmund
Aubrey entertains his fictional listeners in *Personal Recollections
of Joan of Arc* (1896) with such wildly exaggerated tales of blood-

shed and heroism that they mockingly rename him "the Paladin" because of "all the armies he was always going to eat up some day."[29] Aubrey's outrageous threats and stories echo the language of Twain's raftsmen in *Huckleberry Finn*, but the Paladin plays an essentially cameo role in *Joan of Arc*, and his narrative performances, like Father Peter's miracles, are thoroughly insignificant as agents of social transformation in the novel. Aubrey's colorful idiom enlivens the story of Joan's life, but his language is contained by that of the genteel narrator, the Sieur Louis de Conte, who describes the storyteller's performances for the reader. James Cox explains that Aubrey, acting as the novel's perfunctory yarn spinner, provides

> an earthy touch to the reverent narrative, thereby brightening up with a kind of comic relief the pathetic history of the martyred maiden. But [his] presence in the narrative confirms rather than threatens the essential gentility of the Sieur's reverent pose, giving his unctuous tale at best a proper whimsicality—something in the manner of a minister's anecdote to salt the sermon.[30]

Significantly, it is not the tall-talking Paladin who enjoys a privileged interpretive position in the novel, but the mystical and clairvoyant heroine herself, Twain's first authentic mysterious stranger and transcendent redeemer of man. Yet there is really no hope of redemption for the damned human race in *Joan of Arc*. With his decision to locate what was formerly the yarn spinner's interpretive privilege outside human discourse entirely, in a region where social training and the "Moral Sense" are powerless to distort understanding, Twain made no effort to resolve the unstable ironies of *Pudd'nhead Wilson*. Rather, he gratified a consuming wish by identifying himself with a perspective that transcends that novel's irony, a perspective that laments man's depraved condition without enduring it. The Conte's closing remarks clearly suggest that what interests Twain most about Joan is her ability to escape Pudd'nhead's inevitable complicity—her ability, in effect, to release Twain's imagination from the entangled ironies of his earlier novel:

> I have finished my story of Joan of Arc, that wonderful child, that sublime personality, that spirit which in one regard has no peer

and will have none—this: its purity from all alloy of self-seeking, self-interest, personal ambition. In it no trace of these motives can be found, search as you may, and this cannot be said of any other person whose name appears in profane history.[31]

The cultural insiders of Twain's late fiction are indeed no longer the profane pilots and stage drivers of his early career, but rather gods, angels, and saints, characters who enjoy enough detachment from human affairs to laugh with perfect disinterest at the perpetually tenderfooted human race. Lacking such detachment, Twain's human characters possess what Satan calls "a bastard perception of humor," for laughter has become the province of an otherworldly elite.[32] In a fantastic sketch entitled "Sold to Satan," this group includes individuals who in life shared a devastating insight into the degraded human condition—Voltaire, Goethe, Homer, Socrates, Confucius—and who now convene in hell, like the pilots of "Old Times on the Mississippi," to laugh at the world and at man's dull vision. In "The Chronicle of Young Satan," Satan wonders whether mankind will someday redeem itself by learning to laugh with these transcendent old-timers, and his answer, an expression of Mark Twain's despair, leaves little reason for hope: "Will a day come when the race will detect the funniness of these juvenalities and laugh at them?—and, by laughing at them, destroy them? . . . No, you lack the sense and courage."[33]

Through the figure of the mysterious stranger, Twain was able to repossess the interpretive detachment that made his laughter possible, the detachment he had enjoyed earlier in his career as the implied humorist behind the deadpan mask of Mark Twain. But the same power of disengagement that generates a new "community of knowers" in the later writings also signals the end of Mark Twain's creative engagement with the tall tale as a form of storytelling. The elite group that convenes in the late fiction to laugh at man's imperfection looks like another yarn-spinning community; but membership in this interpretive elite belongs exclusively to figures like Satan and Howard Stephenson of "The Man That Corrupted Hadleyburg," characters who explicitly do *not* participate in the human rhetorical drama whose disturbing ironies pervade the worlds of *Huckleberry Finn* and *Pudd'nhead Wilson*. The tall tale's characteristic relationship of privileged to underprivileged interpretive stances persists in many of the late stories, but that opposition no longer serves to enact a dramatic encounter between a performer and his audience. Instead of challenging his credulous listeners to an interpretive confrontation, the Satan figure laughs at his audience from a metaphysically secure distance, insisting on an inflexible distinction, as Cox puts it, "between the audience who is judged and the narrator who exposes."[34] With that distinction in force, satire displaces the tall tale, and anger displaces pleasure as the impulse behind Mark Twain's humor.

NOTES

Introduction

1. Benjamin Franklin, *Benjamin Franklin's Letters to the Press*, ed. Verner W. Crane (Chapel Hill: U of North Carolina P, 1950) 262–64.

2. For a good introduction to the satirists of the Revolutionary period, see Lewis P. Simpson, "The Satiric Mode: The Early National Wits," *The Comic Imagination in American Literature*, ed. Louis D. Rubin, Jr. (New Brunswick: Rutgers UP, 1973) 49–62.

3. The collected writings of Lowell's most popular crackerbarrel philosopher, Hosea Biglow, first appeared in 1848 as *The Biglow Papers*. Locke's *The Nasby Papers* appeared in 1864.

4. Lewis Leary, "Benjamin Franklin," *The Comic Imagination in American Literature*, ed. Louis D. Rubin, Jr. (New Brunswick: Rutgers UP, 1973) 47.

5. Franklin, *Franklin's Letters to the Press* 30–32.

6. Franklin, *Franklin's Letters to the Press* 32–35.

7. Nils E. Enkvist, *Caricatures of Americans on the English Stage Prior to 1870* (Port Washington, N.Y.: Kennikat P, 1951) 27–46.

8. The note on armaments appeared in the *Public Advertiser* of May 14, 1765, four days before the same paper reported on Spain's purchase of 25,000 Canadian ax-heads.

9. George Santayana, "The Genteel Tradition in American Philosophy," *Santayana on America*, ed. Richard C. Lyon (New York: Harcourt, Brace & World, 1968) 46–49.

10. Walter Benn Michaels, "The Interpreter's Self: Peirce on the Cartesian 'Subject,'" *Georgia Review* 31 (Summer 1977): 385.

11. Charles S. Peirce, *The Essential Writings*, ed. Edward C. Moore (New York: Harper & Row, 1972). See especially the essays "Questions Concerning Certain Faculties Claimed for Man," 66–84, and "Some Consequences of Four Incapacities," 85–118.

12. Peirce, *Essential Writings* 115–18.

13. Josiah Royce, *The Problem of Christianity* (1913; rpt., Chicago: U of Chicago P, 1968) 57–98.

14. Royce, *Problem of Christianity* 315–17.

15. James Hall, *Letters from the West* (1828; rpt., Gainesville, Fla.: Scholars' Facsimiles, 1967) 349.

16. Stanley Fish, "Interpreting the *Variorum*," *Critical Inquiry* 2 (Spring 1976): 465–85; Jonathan Culler, *Structuralist Poetics: Structuralism, Linguistics, and the Study of Literature* (Ithaca: Cornell UP, 1975); David Bleich, *Subjective Criticism* (Baltimore: Johns Hopkins UP, 1978); Peter Rabinowitz, *Before Reading: Narrative Conventions and the Politics of Interpretation* (Ithaca: Cornell UP, 1987).

17. Quoted in Louis J. Budd, *Our Mark Twain: The Making of His Public Personality* (Philadelphia: U of Pennsylvania P, 1983) 158.

18. Samuel L. Clemens, "To Orion and Mary E. Clemens," 19 October 1865, *Mark Twain's Letters, Volume 1: 1853–1866*, ed. Edgar Marquess Branch, Michael B. Frank, and Kenneth M. Sanderson (Berkeley: U of California P, 1988) 322–24.

19. Franklin Meine, ed. and introduction, *Tall Tales of the Southwest* (New York: Knopf, 1930) xv.

20. Bernard DeVoto, *Mark Twain's America* (Boston: Houghton Mifflin, 1932) 176.

21. Bernard DeVoto, *Mark Twain at Work* (Boston: Houghton Mifflin, 1942) 3.

22. Alan Gribben, *Mark Twain's Library: A Reconstruction*, 2 vols. (Boston: Hall, 1980). See also Louise Schleiner, "Romance Motifs in Three Novels of Mark Twain," *Comparative Literature Studies* 13 (December 1976): 330–47.

23. Evan Carton, "*Pudd'nhead Wilson* and the Fiction of Law and Custom," *American Realism: New Essays*, ed. Eric J. Sundquist (Baltimore: Johns Hopkins UP, 1982) 93.

24. DeVoto, *Mark Twain's America* 176.

Chapter 1

1. Isaac Weld, *Travels Through the States of North America, During the Years 1795, 1796, 1797* (London, 1800) 143–44.

2. Quoted in Walter Blair and Hamlin Hill, *America's Humor* (New York: Oxford UP, 1978) 7.

3. H. W., "Slick, Downing, Crockett, Etc.," *London and Westminster Review* December 1838: 136–45; rpt. in *Critical Essays on American Humor*, ed. W. B. Clark and W. C. Turner (Boston: Hall, 1984) 21–22.

4. Mody C. Boatright, *Folk Laughter on the American Frontier* (New York: Macmillan, 1949) 87–88.

5. H. W., "Slick, Downing, Crockett, Etc." 21.

6. H. W., "Slick, Downing, Crockett, Etc." 20.

7. Alexis de Tocqueville, *Democracy in America*, ed. J. P. Mayer, trans. George Lawrence (1835; rpt., New York: Anchor, 1969) 488.

8. Louis D. Rubin, Jr., "The Great American Joke," *The Comic Imagination in American Literature*, ed. Louis D. Rubin, Jr. (New Brunswick: Rutgers UP, 1973) 12. William Hazlitt advanced a similar explanation for what he perceived to be tendencies toward sensationalism and exaggeration in American literature. Whereas England possessed "an old and solid ground in previous manners and opinion for imagination to rest upon," according to Hazlitt, the American literary imagination enjoyed no such foundation on which to build, and it therefore had to be "excited by overstraining." American literature and humor thus understandably tended to be overdrawn and unnatural (Hazlitt, *Edinburgh Review* 50 [October 1829]: 126–27). See also David S. Reynolds, *Beneath the American Renaissance: The Subversive Imagination in the Age of Emerson and Melville* (Cambridge: Harvard UP, 1989) 191.

9. Rubin, "Great American Joke" 15.

10. Carolyn S. Brown, *The Tall Tale in American Folklore and Literature* (Knoxville: U of Tennessee P, 1987) 11.

11. Ernest W. Baughman, *Type and Motif-Index of the Folktales of England and North America*, Indiana Folklore Series, no. 20 (Bloomington: Indiana UP, 1966) xvii.

12. Brown, *Tall Tale in American Folklore and Literature* 12.

13. Although the tall tale was indeed a "national" form of humorous storytelling in the sense that it belonged to no single region, the form was not favored by all Americans. Most tales were told by men to all-male or predominantly male audiences, and this is generally true also of written tall humor. With the exception of such characters as Sally Fink and Sally Ann Thunder Ann Whirlwind Crockett, who are in every way equal to their tall-talking male counterparts, women rarely play important roles in tall stories. Even more significantly, very few women have written tall tales, and only occasionally does a woman appear in the role of native yarn spinner. Carolyn S. Brown's research uncovered one female storyteller who was named "Champion Liar of Nebraska" in 1925, although interestingly the woman presented her tall stories as having been told to her by a male relative. Two recent studies of women's humor offer compelling explanations for the virtually exclusive maleness of so much nineteenth-century American humor: Nancy A. Walker, *A Very Serious Thing: Women's Humor and American Culture* (Minneapolis: U of Minnesota P, 1988); and Nancy Walker and Zita Dresner, eds., *Redressing the Balance: American Women's Literary Humor from Colonial Times to the Present* (Jackson: UP of Mississippi, 1988). These critics acknowledge that tall

humor has always appealed more to American men than women, and that
fact is reflected throughout the literary development of the form. An
interesting study of this phenomenon is Kay Lorraine Cothran, "Women's
Tall Tales: A Problem in the Social Structure of Fantasy," *St. Andrews
Review* 87 (1974): 340–56. For specific examples of women in tall tales,
see Norris W. Yates, *William T. Porter and "The Spirit of the Times"*
(Baton Rouge: Louisiana State UP, 1957) 127–36; and Boatright, *Folk
Laughter on the American Frontier* 34–46.

14. *The Spirit of the Times, A Chronicle of the Turf, Field Sports,
Literature and the Stage* 18 (1848): 439.

15. H. P. Grice, "Logic and Conversation," *Syntax and Semantics*, ed.
Peter Cole and Jerry L. Morgan (New York: Academic P, 1975) 41–58;
David R. Sewell discusses Grice's principle in a related context in *Mark
Twain's Languages: Discourse, Dialogue, and Linguistic Variety* (Berke-
ley: U of California P, 1987) 131.

16. Brown, *Tall Tale in American Folklore and Literature* 33.

17. Wayne C. Booth, *A Rhetoric of Irony* (Chicago: U of Chicago P,
1974) 100.

18. Quoted in Walter Blair, *Native American Humor, 1800–1900* (New
York: American Book, 1937) 285.

19. Wolfgang Iser, *The Act of Reading: A Theory of Aesthetic Response* (Baltimore: Johns Hopkins UP, 1978) 108.

20. Walter J. Slatoff, *With Respect to Readers: Dimensions of Literary
Response* (Ithaca: Cornell UP, 1970) 30.

21. Walter J. Ong, "The Writer's Audience Is Always a Fiction," *PMLA*
90 (1975): 11.

22. Ong, "Writer's Audience Is Always a Fiction" 11–12.

23. Samuel L. Clemens, *The Autobiography of Mark Twain*, ed.
Charles Neider (New York: Harper & Row, 1959) 197.

24. Stanley Fish, "Literature in the Reader, Affective Stylistics," *New
Literary History* 2 (Autumn 1970): 123.

25. Reynolds, *Beneath the American Renaissance* 202.

26. Tocqueville, *Democracy in America* 474.

27. Fish discusses the notion of "meaning as event" in "Literature in the
Reader" 123.

28. Walter Blair, "Mark Twain's Other Masterpiece: 'Jim Baker's Blue-
Jay Yarn,'" *Studies in American Humor* 1 (1975): 135.

29. Quoted in Constance Rourke, *American Humor* (New York: Harcourt, Brace, 1931) 34.

30. Samuel Peters, *The Works of Samuel Peters of Hebron, Connecticut*, ed. K. W. Cameron (Hartford: Transcendental Books, 1972) 43.

31. Peters, *Works of Samuel Peters* 39.

32. Thomas D. Clark, *The Rampaging Frontier* (Bloomington: Indiana UP, 1939) 209. Contemporary reactions to Peters's book are discussed in K. W. Cameron's preface to Peters, *Works of Samuel Peters* 4.

33. James Hammond Trumbull, *The True Blue-Laws of Connecticut and New Haven and the False Blue-Laws Invented by the Rev. Samuel Peters* (Hartford, 1876).

34. Samuel Peters, *General History of Connecticut*, ed. Samuel Jarvis McCormick (New York: Appleton, 1877).

35. E. D. Hirsch, Jr., *Validity in Interpretation* (New Haven: Yale UP, 1967) 55.

36. Quoted in Curtis D. MacDougall, *Hoaxes* (New York: Dover, 1940) 229.

37. Poe's comments on Locke appear in his *Essays and Reviews*, ed. G. R. Thompson (New York: Library of America, 1984) 1221; Reynolds discusses the relationship between the two writers in *Beneath the American Renaissance* 241–42.

38. Bernard DeVoto, *Mark Twain's America* (Boston: Houghton Mifflin, 1932) 243.

39. Yates, *William T. Porter and "The Spirit of the Times"* 150.

40. James E. Caron, "Mark Twain and the Tall Tale Imagination in America," diss., U of Oregon, 1983, 83.

41. Henry James, *The American* (1877; Boston: Houghton Mifflin, 1962) 100.

42. James M. Cox, *Mark Twain: The Fate of Humor* (Princeton: Princeton UP, 1966) 12.

43. Harold H. Kolb, Jr., personal interview, 20 April 1986.

44. Frederick Marrayat, *Second Series of a Diary in America with Remarks on Its Institutions* (Philadelphia, 1840); Frances Trollope, *Domestic Manners of the Americans* (London, 1832).

45. Estwick Evans, *Pedestrian Tour, 1818* (Cleveland, 1904) 284.

46. Timothy Flint, *Recollections of the Last Ten Years* (1826; rpt., Carbondale: Southern Illinois UP, 1968) 28.

47. T. D. Bonner, ed., *The Life and Times of James T. Beckworth* (New York: Harper, 1858); Christian Schultz, *Travels on an Inland Voyage* (New York, 1810).

48. James Hall, *Letters from the West* (1828; rpt., Gainesville, Fla.: Scholars' Facsimiles, 1967) 359.

49. James Kirke Paulding, *Letters from the South*, 2 vols. (New York, 1817) 2:10–11.

50. James Kirke Paulding, *The Lion of the West*, ed. J. N. Tidwell (1831; Stanford: Stanford UP, 1954) 14–15. The play was revised by John Augustus Stone before it was first performed as *The Lion of the West* for

a New York audience in 1831. An English adaptation by William Bayle Bernard opened in London in 1833 under the title *The Kentuckian, or A Trip to New York*, and it is this third version of the original Paulding play that survives today (Nelson F. Adkins, "James K. Paulding's *Lion of the West*," *American Literature* 3 [November 1931]: 249).

51. Paulding, *Lion of the West* 62.

52. William T. Porter, ed. and introduction, *The Big Bear of Arkansas, and Other Tales* (Philadelphia: Carey, Hart, 1845) vii.

53. Porter, *Big Bear of Arkansas* vii–viii.

54. Porter, *Big Bear of Arkansas* vii.

55. Blair, *Native American Humor* 91.

56. Yates, *William T. Porter and "The Spirit of the Times"* 155.

57. Kenneth S. Lynn has thoroughly explored the politics of the tall tale's literary assimilation in *Mark Twain and Southwest Humor* (Boston: Little, Brown, 1959).

58. "A Trip to Possum Walk," *Spirit* 18 (1848): 241–42.

59. Esperance, "Chills and Fever," *Spirit* 22 (1852): 529.

60. Peter Zigzag, "A True Story," *Spirit* 19 (1849): 484.

61. Paulding, *Lion of the West* 62.

62. Other California tales in a similar style include "A Valentine," *Spirit* 19 (1849): 13; and "A Profitable Poultry Yard," *Spirit* 19 (1849): 570.

63. Pascal Covici, *Mark Twain's Humor: The Image of a World* (Dallas: Southern Methodist UP, 1962) 7–8.

64. Covici, *Mark Twain's Humor* 9.

65. George W. Kendall, "Bill Dean, The Last Texan Ranger," *Spirit* 16 (1846): 229.

66. Henry James, "The Novels of George Eliot," *Atlantic Monthly* October 1866: 485.

67. William P. Hawes, "A Bear Story," *Sporting Scenes and Sundry Sketches*, 2 vols., ed. H. W. Herbert (New York: Gould, Banks, 1842); rpt. in *A Quarter Race in Kentucky*, ed. W. T. Porter (Philadelphia: Carey & Hart, 1846) 188–96.

68. Samuel L. Clemens, *Mark Twain's Letters*, 2 vols., ed. Albert Bigelow Paine (New York: Harper, 1917) 2:504.

Chapter 2

1. "A Tough Story," *Journal* (Hannibal, Mo.), 10 December 1847, quoted in Edgar Marquess Branch, *The Literary Apprenticeship of Mark Twain* (Urbana: U of Illinois P, 1950) 5.

2. "A Tough Yarn," *Western Union* (Hannibal, Mo.), 7 August 1851, quoted in Branch, *Literary Apprenticeship of Mark Twain* 6.

3. Walter Blair, "Mark Twain's Other Masterpiece: 'Jim Baker's Blue-Jay Yarn,'" *Studies in American Humor* 1 (1975): 135.

4. Samuel L. Clemens, "How to Tell a Story," *Selected Shorter Writings of Mark Twain*, ed. Walter Blair (Boston: Houghton Mifflin, 1962) 239–40.

5. David E. Sloane distinguishes between the literary comedians and the comic tradition of the Old Southwest, noting that the former exhibited "a thoroughly different and substantially more humane spirit" (1). His distinction is valid and useful, yet in terms of the gradual emergence of techniques for literary yarn spinning, the two traditions can be thought of as separate stages in a single development (Sloane, *Mark Twain as a Literary Comedian* [Baton Rouge: Louisiana State UP, 1979]).

6. The importance of Clemens's stage technique in this process of literary discovery should not be overlooked, yet a thorough consideration of his parallel career on the lecture platform falls outside the scope of the present study. Mark Twain's flexibility as a literary persona capable of playing any number of roles certainly derived in part from Clemens's experience as a platform entertainer. His professional lecturing career did not begin until October 1866, yet by then he was well versed in various techniques of oral presentation, and many of those techniques had already begun to inform his experiments in writing. In *The Authentic Mark Twain: A Literary Biography of Samuel L. Clemens* (Philadelphia: U of Pennsylvania P, 1984), Everett Emerson maintains that Sam Clemens delivered his first successful comic performance at a printer's banquet in January 1856, and it seems likely that subsequent modifications to the stage persona paralleled his development of an effective literary persona. Artemus Ward, whom Twain met in Virginia City in December 1863, was undoubtedly the predominant influence in this area, for it was Ward who first demonstrated to the young reporter the impressive power of deadpan narration as a means of comic presentation. Later in life, Twain criticized Ward's lack of spontaneity on stage, but he never ceased to admire the humorist's ability to drop a studied remark "apparently without knowing it, as if [he] were thinking aloud." Twain sought to cultivate Ward's "simulated unconsciousness" in his own stage performances, and although the literary Mark Twain more often plays the victim than the yarn spinner, his heroes often possess Ward's gift for deadpan narration. For more on the relation of Twain's platform career to his writing, see Fred W. Lorch, *The Trouble Begins at Eight: Mark Twain's Lecture Tours* (Ames: Iowa State UP, 1966); Samuel L. Clemens, *Mark Twain Speaking*, ed. Paul Fatout (Iowa City: U of Iowa P, 1976); John A. Barsness, "Platform Manner in the Novel: A View from the Pit," *Midcontinent American Studies Journal* 10 (Fall 1969): 49–59; and Sloane, *Mark Twain as a Literary Comedian*.

7. Quoted in Blair, "Mark Twain's Other Masterpiece" 142.

8. Reprinted in Minnie M. Brashear, *Mark Twain: Son of Missouri* (Chapel Hill: U of North Carolina P, 1934) 167–68.

9. Describing the method of his "magical realism," for example, Gabriel García Márquez explains that "if you say that there are elephants flying in the sky, people are not going to believe you. But if you say that there are four hundred and twenty-five elephants in the sky, people will probably believe you." In place of the yarn spinner's deadpan expression, García Márquez describes the writer's "brick face" (George Plimpton, ed., *Writers at Work*, 6th ser. [New York: Penguin, 1984]).

10. Samuel Johnson, *Lives of the Poets* (London, 1779–81); rpt. in John Donne, *John Donne's Poetry*, ed. A. L. Clements (New York: Norton, 1966) 107–8.

11. Richard A. Dwyer and Richard E. Lingenfelter, *Lying on the Eastern Slope: James Townsend's Comic Journalism on the Mining Frontier* (Miami: UP of Florida, 1984) 42.

12. Samuel L. Clemens, *The Adventures of Thomas Jefferson Snodgrass*, ed. Charles Honce (Chicago: Pascal Covici, 1928) 23–24.

13. Samuel L. Clemens, *Adventures of Huckleberry Finn*, ed. Walter Blair and Victor Fischer (1885; Berkeley: U of California P, 1985) 130.

14. Branch, *Literary Apprenticeship of Mark Twain* 41.

15. Clemens, *Adventures of Thomas Jefferson Snodgrass* 6.

16. Samuel L. Clemens, *Life on the Mississippi* (1883; New York: Heritage, 1944) 290.

17. Isaiah Sellers, "Steamboat and River Intelligence," *True Delta* (New Orleans), 7 May 1859, quoted in Samuel L. Clemens, *The Works of Mark Twain: Early Tales and Sketches*, 2 vols., ed. E. M. Branch and R. T. Hirst (Berkeley: U of California P, 1979) 1:128.

18. Clemens, "River Intelligence," *Early Tales* 1:131–33.

19. Clemens, *Life on the Mississippi* 291.

20. Clemens, "The Burial of Sir Abner Gilstrap, Editor of the Bloomington *Republican*," *Early Tales* 1:106.

21. Mikhail Bakhtin, *The Dialogic Imagination: Four Essays*, ed. Michael Holquist, trans. Caryl Emerson and Michael Holquist (Austin: U of Texas P, 1981) 76.

22. George Feinstein explores the effect of this kind of storytelling on Twain's approach to narrative in general in "Mark Twain's Idea of Story Structure," *American Literature* 18 (1946): 161.

23. Samuel L. Clemens, *Mark Twain in Eruption*, ed. Bernard DeVoto (New York: Harper, 1922) 359; Twain praised this style of narration on several occasions, some of which are listed in Blair, "Mark Twain's Other Masterpiece" 146.

24. Samuel L. Clemens, Notebook 14 (1879), Mark Twain Papers, Ban-

croft Library, University of California, Berkeley; quoted in Blair, "Mark Twain's Other Masterpiece" 137.

25. Both letters are reprinted in Samuel L. Clemens, *Mark Twain's Letters, Volume 1: 1853–1866*, ed. Edgar Marquess Branch, Michael B. Frank, and Kenneth M. Sanderson (Berkeley: U of California P, 1988) 132, 136. Franklin R. Rogers discusses Clemens's revisions in the introduction to *The Pattern for Mark Twain's "Roughing It"* (Berkeley: U of California P, 1961).

26. Rogers, *Pattern for Mark Twain's "Roughing It"* 12.

27. Blair, "Mark Twain's Other Masterpiece" 142.

28. A version of the same episode appears in Chapter 64 of *Roughing It*, ed. Paul Baender and Franklin R. Rogers (1872; Berkeley: U of California P, 1972), where a horse named Oahu demonstrates some of Bunker's traits of personality.

29. Clemens, *Mark Twain's Letters, 1853–1866* 147.

30. Mark Twain employed this brand of incongruity in some of his most memorable yarns, including the Tom Quartz tale in the second part of *Roughing It* and Jim Baker's yarn about the blue jays in *A Tramp Abroad*.

31. Clemens, "How to Tell a Story," 241.

32. Rogers, *Pattern for Mark Twain's "Roughing It"* 13.

33. Quoted in Albert Bigelow Paine, *Mark Twain: A Biography*, 4 vols. (New York: Harper, 1912) 4:203.

34. Clemens, *Roughing It* 269–70.

35. Clemens, *Roughing It* 268.

36. Clemens, *Roughing It* 268.

37. Clemens, "Petrified Man," *Early Tales* 1:155; Clemens, "A Bloody Massacre near Carson," *Early Tales* 1:320.

38 Clemens, "Over the Mountains," *Early Tales* 1:293–95.

39. Samuel L. Clemens, *Mark Twain's Letters*, 2 vols., ed. Albert Bigelow Paine (New York: Harper, 1917) 1:401.

40. Walter Blair and Hamlin Hill, *America's Humor* (New York: Oxford UP, 1978) 345.

41. Sydney J. Krause, "The Art and Satire of Twain's 'Jumping Frog' Story," *American Quarterly* 16 (Winter 1964): 562–76.

42. Quoted in T. Edgar Pemberton, *The Life of Bret Harte* (New York: Dodd, Mead, 1903) 74.

43. Clemens, "The Only Reliable Account of the Celebrated Jumping Frog of Calaveras County," *Early Tales* 2:273.

44. Clemens, "Angel's Camp Constable," *Early Tales* 2:279.

45. Clemens, "Jim Smiley and His Jumping Frog," *Early Tales* 2:282.

46. Joseph Hopkins Twichell, "Mark Twain," *Harper's New Monthly Magazine* 92 (May 1896): 818.

47. Bernard DeVoto, *Mark Twain's America* (Boston: Little, Brown, 1932) 251.

48. Emerson, *Authentic Mark Twain* 20.

49. George Santayana, "The Genteel Tradition in American Philosophy," *Santayana in America*, ed. Richard C. Lyon (New York: Harcourt, Brace & World, 1968) 46–47.

Chapter 3

1. Royall Tyler, *The Yankey in London* (New York: Isaac Riley, 1809) 103–4.

2. James Kirke Paulding, *The Bucktails; or Americans in England* (1813; Philadelphia, 1847), quoted in Perley Isaac Reed, "The Realistic Presentation of American Characters in Native American Plays Prior to Eighteen Seventy," *Ohio State University Bulletin* 22 (May 1918): 89.

3. Thomas Chandler Haliburton, *The Sam Slick Anthology*, ed. Walter S. Avis (Toronto: Clarke, Irwin, 1969) 156.

4. Haliburton, *Sam Slick Anthology* 163.

5. Haliburton, *Sam Slick Anthology* 79.

6. James Kirke Paulding, *John Bull in America; or the New Munchausen* (New York: Wiley, 1825) viii.

7. Paulding, *John Bull in America* 6–7.

8. In commenting only on the effectiveness of Paulding's yarn as a parody of British expectations, I do not mean to appear insensitive to its brutal characterization of the "black servant." That such a story could have been considered entertaining and, even to an extent, "plausible" is enough to rule out its humorous effect for most readers today.

9. Henry Nash Smith discusses the origins of an "associationist" tradition of American travel literature in *Mark Twain: The Development of a Writer* (Cambridge: Harvard UP, 1962) 26. Associationist theory, he explains, held that "a writer could endow a landscape with aesthetic value by evoking images of past events connected with it in his mind."

10. J. Ross Browne, *Yusef; or, The Journey of the Frangi: A Crusade in the East* (New York: Harper, 1853) iv.

11. Samuel Fiske, *Mr. Dunn Brown's Experiences in Foreign Parts* (Boston: Jewett, 1857) 87.

12. Fiske, *Mr. Dunn Brown's Experiences* iv.

13. Samuel L. Clemens, *The Innocents Abroad, or the New Pilgrims Progress* (1868; New York: Signet, 1966) 15. Subsequent page references to this edition appear in the text.

14. Albert Bigelow Paine, *Mark Twain: A Biography*, 4 vols. (New York: Harper, 1912) 1:383.

15. Twain wrote a total of fifty-eight letters concerning his voyage: fifty for the *Alta*, one for the Naples *Observer* (later reprinted in the *Alta*), one for the New York *Herald*, and six for the New York *Tribune*. All of them are reprinted in Daniel Morley McKeithan, ed., *Traveling with the Innocents Abroad: Mark Twain's Original Reports from Europe and the Holy Land* (Norman: U of Oklahoma P, 1958).

16. McKeithan, *Traveling with the Innocents Abroad* 54–55.

17. McKeithan, *Traveling with the Innocents Abroad* 97.

18. J. W. DeForest had employed this device in *Oriental Acquaintance, Or Letters from Syria* (New York, 1856), where he asked: "How can a man think about Joshua or the valley of Jehoshaphat, when fifty indefatigable little bores are sharply reminding him of the actual and suffering present" (65–66).

19. Bruce Michaelson, "Mark Twain the Tourist: The Form of *The Innocents Abroad*," *American Literature* 49 (1977): 395. Franklin Walker discusses J. Ross Browne's decision not to revise his travel correspondence for book publication in *Irreverent Pilgrims: Melville, Browne, and Mark Twain in the Holy Land* (Seattle: U of Washington P, 1974) 82–83.

20. Michaelson, "Mark Twain the Tourist" 395.

21. McKeithan, *Traveling with the Innocents Abroad* 25–26.

22. Samuel L. Clemens, *Mark Twain's Letters, Volume 2: 1867–1868*, ed. Harriet Elinor Smith and Richard Bucci (Berkeley: U of California P, 1990) 119.

23. McKeithan, *Traveling with the Innocents Abroad* 209.

24. McKeithan, *Traveling with the Innocents Abroad* 55–56.

25. McKeithan, *Traveling with the Innocents Abroad* 44.

26. McKeithan, *Traveling with the Innocents Abroad* 44–45.

27. Leon T. Dickinson, "Mark Twain's Revisions in Writing *The Innocents Abroad*," *American Literature* 19 (May 1947): 155.

28. Samuel L. Clemens, "How to Tell a Story," *Selected Shorter Writings of Mark Twain*, ed. Walter Blair (Boston: Houghton Mifflin, 1962) 239.

29. James M. Cox, *Mark Twain: The Fate of Humor* (Princeton: Princeton UP, 1966) 41.

30. Forrest G. Robinson, "Patterns of Consciousness in *The Innocents Abroad*," *American Literature* 58 (March 1986): 54.

31. Robert Regan, "The Reprobate Elect in *The Innocents Abroad*," *American Literature* (May 1982): 241–42.

32. Henry Nash Smith and William M. Gibson, eds., *Mark Twain–Howells Letters: The Correspondence of Samuel L. Clemens and William D. Howells, 1872–1910*, 2 vols. (Cambridge: Harvard UP, 1960) 1:256.

33. For a thorough discussion of Twain's use of humorous counterpoint in *The Innocents Abroad* and later works, see Franklin R. Rogers, *Mark*

Twain's Burlesque Patterns: As Seen in the Novels and Narratives, 1855–1885 (Dallas: Southern Methodist UP, 1960) 26–94.

34. Rogers discusses Twain's effort to dramatize the confrontation between pilgrims and sinners in *Mark Twain's Burlesque Patterns* 55.

35. Cox, *Mark Twain* 47.

36. Robinson, "Patterns of Consciousness in *The Innocents Abroad*" 61, 51.

Chapter 4

1. Emerson Bennett, *The Trapper's Bride; or, Spirit of Adventure* (Cincinnati: Straton and Barnard, 1848) 9.

2. See, for example, Sam Clemens, "To Jane L. Clemens," 20 March 1862, *Mark Twain's Letters, Volume 1: 1853–1866*, ed. Edgar Marquess Branch, Michael B. Frank, and Kenneth M. Sanderson (Berkeley: U of California P, 1988) 174–79.

3. Samuel L. Clemens, *Roughing It*, ed. Paul Baender and Franklin R. Rogers (1872; Berkeley: U of California P, 1972) 146. Subsequent page references to this edition appear in the text.

4. Alonzo Delano, *Pen Knife Sketches; or, Chips Off the Old Block* (Sacramento: Daily Union, 1853) 3.

5. Delano, *Pen Knife Sketches* 13. Twain's narrator in *Roughing It* will take this insight one step further when he discovers that "nothing that glitters is gold" (197).

6. George Horatio Derby [John Phoenix, pseud.], *Phoenixiana* (New York: Appleton, 1855).

7. Edgar Marquess Branch, "'The Babes in the Wood': Artemus Ward's 'Double Health' to Mark Twain," *PMLA* 93 (1978): 959. For a discussion of burlesques by Ward and Orpheus C. Kerr, see Walter Blair, "Burlesques in Nineteenth-Century American Humor," *American Literature* 2 (November 1930): 236–47; for a more general study of burlesque fiction in America and England, see Archibald B. Shepperson, *The Novel in Motley* (Cambridge: Harvard UP, 1936).

8. J. Ross Browne, *Adventures in the Apaché Country: A Tour through Arizona and Sonora* (New York: Harper, 1868) 11.

9. Browne, *Adventures in the Apaché Country* 12.

10. Browne, *Adventures in the Apaché Country* 13; J. Ross Browne, *Yusef; or, The Journey of the Frangi: A Crusade in the East* (New York: Harper, 1853).

11. Clemens, "To Jane and Pamela Clemens," February 1862, *Mark Twain's Letters, 1853–1866* 157; Samuel L. Clemens and Orion Clemens, "Letter from Carson City, May 10, 1862," reprinted in Franklin R. Rogers,

The Pattern for Mark Twain's "Roughing It" (Berkeley: U of California P, 1961) 43–45.

12. J. Ross Browne, *A Peep at Washoe* (1862; Palo Alto: Lewis Osborne, 1968) 122.

13. Clemens, "To Jane and Pamela Clemens," February 1862, *Mark Twain's Letters, 1853–1866* 157.

14. Harold Aspiz and Franklin R. Rogers have made separate cases for Browne's literary influence over Mark Twain's methods as a humorist (Aspiz, "Mark Twain's Reading — A Critical Study," diss., U of California, Los Angeles, 1949, 311; Rogers, *Mark Twain's Burlesque Patterns: As Seen in the Novels and Narratives, 1855–1885* [Dallas: Southern Methodist UP, 1960] 69–70).

15. Albert D. Richardson, *Beyond the Mississippi* (Hartford: American Publishing, 1867).

16. Henry Nash Smith, *Mark Twain: The Development of a Writer* (Cambridge: Harvard UP, 1962) 53.

17. My thesis is aptly summarized in a letter Twain wrote to the New York Society of California Pioneers on October 11, 1869: "Although I am not a pioneer," he wrote, "I have had a sufficiently variegated time of it to enable me to talk pioneer like a native, and feel like a forty-niner." The letter appeared in the New York *Tribune* on October 14, 1869, and was reprinted in the Buffalo *Express* five days later (quoted in Jeffrey Steinbrink, *Getting to Be Mark Twain* [Berkeley: U of California P, 1991] 132).

18. Samuel L. Clemens, *The Autobiography of Mark Twain*, ed. Charles Neider (New York: Harper & Row, 1959) 3.

19. Samuel L. Clemens, *Life on the Mississippi* (1883; New York: Heritage, 1944) 91.

20. Clemens, *Life on the Mississippi* 46.

21. After quoting a description of Lake Gennesaret from a popular guidebook, for example, the narrator of *The Innocents Abroad* comments: "It is an ingeniously written description and well calculated to deceive. . . . [But] no ingenuity could make such a picture beautiful — to one's actual vision" (Samuel L. Clemens, *The Innocents Abroad, or the New Pilgrims Progress* [1868; New York: Signet, 1966] 367).

22. Clemens, *Innocents Abroad* 367.

23. Forrest G. Robinson, "'Seeing the Elephant': Some Perspectives on Mark Twain's *Roughing It*," *American Studies* 21 (1980): 44.

24. Smith, *Mark Twain* 59.

25. James Kirke Paulding, *The Lion of the West*, ed. J. N. Tidwell (1831; Stanford: Stanford UP, 1954) 35–36.

26. James M. Cox, *Mark Twain: The Fate of Humor* (Princeton: Princeton UP, 1966) 87.

27. Rogers, *Mark Twain's Burlesque Patterns* 78.

28. Paul Fatout presents several conflicting firsthand accounts of the history of Virginia City's short-lived *Weekly Occidental* in *Mark Twain in Virginia City* (Bloomington: Indiana UP, 1964) 169–76; other possible versions of the story are presented in Franklin R. Rogers, "Washoe's First Literary Journal," *California Historical Society Quarterly* 36 (December 1957): 365–70; and Eric N. Moody, "Another Last Word on the *Weekly Occidental*," *Mark Twain Journal* 18 (Summer 1977): 11–13.

29. Franklin Walker, *San Francisco's Literary Frontier* (New York: Knopf, 1939) 124.

30. Samuel L. Clemens, "Jim Smiley and His Jumping Frog," *The Works of Mark Twain: Early Tales and Sketches*, 2 vols., ed. E. M. Branch and R. T. Hirst (Berkeley: U of California P, 1979) 2:283.

31. Rogers draws an informative connection between the "narrative plank" that Twain employed in *Roughing It* and his lecture technique (*Mark Twain's Burlesque Patterns*, chap. 3).

32. William Dean Howells, *Atlantic Monthly* 29 (June 1872): 754.

33. Cox, *Mark Twain* 97.

Chapter 5

1. Henry James, *The Art of the Novel* (New York: Scribner, 1909) 4. James referred to *Roderick Hudson* as his first novel, although *Watch and Ward* had actually been serialized in 1871.

2. Samuel L. Clemens, "Old Times on the Mississippi," *Atlantic Monthly* 35 (January–July 1875) 69. Subsequent page references to this edition appear in the text.

3. Samuel L. Clemens, "To Jane Lampton Clemens and Pamela A. Moffett," 20 January 1866, *Mark Twain's Letters, Volume 1: 1853–1866*, ed. Edgar Marquess Branch, Michael B. Frank, and Kenneth M. Sanderson (Berkeley: U of California P, 1988) 329.

4. Samuel L. Clemens, *The Love Letters of Mark Twain*, ed. Dixon Wecter (New York: Harper, 1949) 166.

5. Quoted by Justin Kaplan, *Mr. Clemens and Mark Twain* (New York: Simon and Schuster, 1966) 151.

6. Clemens, *Love Letters of Mark Twain* 178–79.

7. Henry Nash Smith, *Mark Twain: The Development of a Writer* (Cambridge: Harvard UP, 1962) 71.

8. William Dean Howells, "Howells to Clemens," 30 September 1874, *Mark Twain–Howells Letters: The Correspondence of Samuel L. Clemens and William D. Howells, 1872–1910*, 2 vols., ed. Henry Nash Smith and William M. Gibson (Cambridge: Harvard UP, 1960) 1:32.

9. "Clemens to Howells," 2 September 1874, *Mark Twain–Howells Letters* 1:22.

10. "Clemens to Howells," 24 October 1874, *Mark Twain–Howells Letters* 1:33.

11. "Clemens to Howells," 24 October 1874, *Mark Twain–Howells Letters* 1:34.

12. Samuel L. Clemens, *Roughing It*, ed. Paul Baender and Franklin R. Rogers (1872; Berkeley: U of California P, 1972) 191.

13. John C. Gerber, "The Relation between Style and Point of View in the Works of Mark Twain," *Style in Prose Fiction: English Institute Essays, 1958*, ed. Harold Clark Martin (New York: Columbia UP, 1959) 153.

14. Leo Marx is particularly insightful on the two perspectives in "Old Times on the Mississippi" and their relation to Twain's earlier pairings ("The Pilot and the Passenger: Landscape Conventions and the Style of *Huckleberry Finn*," *American Literature* 28 [May 1956]: 131–32).

15. James M. Cox, *Mark Twain: The Fate of Humor* (Princeton: Princeton UP, 1966) 109.

16. Samuel L. Clemens, "Refuge of the Derelicts," *Mark Twain's Fables of Man*, ed. John S. Tuckey (Berkeley: U of California P, 1972) 179.

Chapter 6

1. Samuel L. Clemens, "When a Book Gets Tired," *Mark Twain in Eruption*, ed. Bernard DeVoto (New York: Harper, 1922) 197.

2. "Clemens to Howells," 5 July 1875, *Mark Twain–Howells Letters: The Correspondence of Samuel L. Clemens and William D. Howells, 1872–1910*, 2 vols., ed. Henry Nash Smith and William M. Gibson (Cambridge: Harvard UP, 1960) 1:91. Walter Blair's chapter on *Tom Sawyer* in *Mark Twain and Huck Finn* (Berkeley: U of California P, 1960) thoroughly examines the chronology of the novel's composition, although some minor points of Blair's analysis have been challenged by Charles A. Norton, *Writing Tom Sawyer: The Adventures of a Classic* (Jefferson, N.C.: McFarland, 1983) 8.

3. I use the term "romance" throughout this chapter less as a strict generic category than as a general tag for the large body of fiction that Twain often derisively labelled "romantic." When he used the term to attack writers such as Cooper and Emerson Bennett, Twain had in mind the kind of narrative that makes unreasonably excessive demands on the reader's willingness to suspend disbelief.

4. "Clemens to Howells," 5 July 1875, *Mark Twain–Howells Letters* 1:91.

5. "Howells to Clemens," *Mark Twain–Howells Letters* 1:110–11.

6. Samuel L. Clemens, *The Autobiography of Mark Twain*, ed. Charles Neider (New York: Harper & Row, 1959) 74. M. H. Abrams claims that no author expects or even desires total suspension of disbelief from his or her audience ("Belief and Suspension of Disbelief," *Belief in Literature*, ed. M. H. Abrams [New York: Columbia UP, 1958] 17). My point in this discussion is not to insist on a more radical model of response, but to show that Twain's profound ambivalence toward the interpretive demands that characterize literary romance caused him to modify his narrative strategy in *Tom Sawyer* in several interesting ways.

7. Samuel L. Clemens, *The Adventures of Tom Sawyer*, ed. Paul Baender and John C. Gerber (1876; Berkeley: U of California P, 1980) 239. Subsequent page references to this edition appear in the text.

8. Bernard DeVoto, *Mark Twain at Work* (Cambridge: Harvard UP, 1942) 18–19. Charles Dudley Warner made this observation in a contemporary review of *Tom Sawyer* (Albert E. Stone, Jr., *The Innocent Eye: Childhood in Mark Twain's Imagination* [New Haven: Yale UP, 1961] 60).

9. Forrest G. Robinson, *In Bad Faith: The Dynamics of Deception in Mark Twain's America* (Cambridge: Harvard UP, 1986) 50.

10. Walter Slatoff has argued that a narrator's struggle for consistency, even when it ultimately fails, ought not to be counted automatically as a strike against the work. The confusion that besets the narrator's performance in a poem such as Milton's *Paradise Lost* or in a novel such as Kafka's *The Trial* can enhance the reader's experience, according to Slatoff, by suggesting that a human consciousness is actually struggling with deeply conflicting feelings. He explains that "the contradictory emphases and vague or ambiguous rhetorical fumblings seem not so much flaws as evidences of the severity of the struggle" (Slatoff, *With Respect to Readers: Dimensions of Literary Response* [Ithaca: Cornell UP, 1970] 129–31). I find Slatoff's comments particularly relevant to the incessant discussion of "flaws" in *Tom Sawyer*, not to mention those other hopelessly flawed novels, *Huckleberry Finn* and *Pudd'nhead Wilson*.

11. Quoted in Abrams, "Belief and Suspension of Disbelief" 8.

12. James M. Cox, *Mark Twain: The Fate of Humor* (Princeton: Princeton UP, 1966) 140.

13. Alan Gribben describes Tom's ability to manipulate the materials he extracts from literary romance in "How Tom Sawyer Played Robin Hood 'By the Book,'" *English Language Notes* 13 (March 1976): 201–4.

14. Samuel L. Clemens, *Roughing It*, ed. Paul Baender and Franklin R. Rogers (1872; Berkeley: U of California P, 1972) 325–36.

15. With its rival storytellers competing for narrative authority, *Tom Sawyer* resembles what Katerina Clark and Michael Holquist, in their study of Bakhtin, call a "heteroglot" novel. Borrowing their terminology,

one might explain that Tom's parodic voice constantly destabilizes the narrator's "official" romantic language, and the novel "constitutes itself out of [this] very stratification of discourse" (Clark and Holquist, *Mikhail Bakhtin* [Cambridge: Harvard UP, 1984] 292).

16. Everett Emerson's *The Authentic Mark Twain: A Literary Biography of Samuel L. Clemens* (Philadelphia: U of Pennsylvania P, 1984) is the most recent major study of the "voice" that links Twain's early writings, including the Twain–Brown newspaper correspondence, to his later work as a novelist.

17. What I call a "conditional romance" is really, in Mikhail Bakhtin's parlance, a fictional discourse that makes no effort to conceal its heterogeneity (*The Dialogic Imagination: Four Essays*, ed. Michael Holquist, trans. Caryl Emerson and Michael Holquist [Austin: U of Texas P, 1981] 375–76).

18. The sequel to *Tom Sawyer*, on the other hand, begins with Huckleberry Finn's explicit critique of the earlier narrator's performance (Samuel L. Clemens, *Adventures of Huckleberry Finn*, ed. Walter Blair and Victor Fischer [1885; Berkeley: U of California P, 1985] 1).

19. Judith Fetterley, "The Sanctioned Rebel," *Studies in the Novel* 3 (1971): 293–304.

20. Samuel L. Clemens, "The Chronicle of Young Satan," *Mark Twain's Mysterious Stranger Manuscripts*, ed. William M. Gibson (Berkeley: U of California P, 1969) 165.

21. Robinson, *In Bad Faith* 26.

22. Robinson disagrees emphatically on this point. He writes that "Tom is blind to the blindness he masters; he fails utterly to recognize his own signature on the culturally constructed world in which he plays" (*In Bad Faith* 173). In fact, Robinson grants Tom none of the self-conscious creativity that is essential to my sense of his role as a spokesman for the novel's yarn-spinning community and a rival for narrative authority. For a more extensive consideration of Tom's role as a showman, see Sargent Bush, Jr., "The Showman as Hero in Mark Twain's Fiction," *American Humor: Essays Presented to John C. Gerber*, ed. O. M. Brack (Scottsdale, Ariz.: Arete, 1977) 79–98.

23. Fetterley, "Sanctioned Rebel" 301.

24. Wolfgang Iser, *The Act of Reading: A Theory of Aesthetic Response* (Baltimore: Johns Hopkins UP, 1978) 37. Iser discusses this phenomenon in his section "Readers and the Concept of the Implied Reader," 27–38.

25. Henry Nash Smith, *Mark Twain: The Development of a Writer* (Cambridge: Harvard UP, 1962) 82.

26. Cox, *Mark Twain* 148.

Chapter 7

1. Samuel L. Clemens, *Life on the Mississippi* (1883; New York: Heritage, 1944) 90. Subsequent page references to this edition appear in the text.

2. R. W. B. Lewis, *The American Adam: Innocence, Tragedy and Tradition in the Nineteenth Century* (Chicago: U of Chicago P, 1955) 5.

3. Samuel L. Clemens, *Roughing It*, ed. Paul Baender and Franklin R. Rogers (1872; Berkeley: U of California P, 1972) 189.

4. Samuel L. Clemens, *Mark Twain in Eruption*, ed. Bernard DeVoto (New York: Harper, 1922) 360–61.

5. This explicitly gendered locution is neither accidental nor intended to create offense. Twain did not conceive of women as candidates for the yarn spinner's interpretive inner circle. My sense that the rhetoric of the tall tale served as a paradigm for his efforts in fiction would therefore seem to support Judith Fetterley's point that much American fiction asks women to identify against themselves (*The Resisting Reader: A Feminist Approach to American Fiction* [Bloomington: Indiana UP, 1979]). For an interesting discussion of women's humor in America, including an analysis of gender stereotypes that Mark Twain embraced and perpetuated in his work, see Nancy A. Walker, *A Very Serious Thing: Women's Humor and American Culture* (Minneapolis: U of Minnesota P, 1988).

6. Lionel Trilling, introduction, *Adventures of Huckleberry Finn* (1885; New York: Harper, 1948) ix.

7. Samuel L. Clemens, *Adventures of Huckleberry Finn*, ed. Walter Blair and Victor Fischer (1885; Berkeley: U of California P, 1988) 78. Later in the novel, after Jim had been sold back into slavery, Huck recalls their life together on the raft: "we a floating along, talking, and singing, and laughing" (270). Yet even here, laughter is strangely displaced from the text and from Huck's immediate experience. Subsequent page references to this edition appear in the text.

8. Two of the most eloquent and persuasive voices in Mark Twain criticism interpret this collusive arrangement between the novel's reader and implied author very differently. Both James M. Cox and Forrest G. Robinson argue that what I call the reader's "privileged interpretive posture" amounts to an evasion of moral responsibility, or what Robinson calls "bad faith" (Cox, *Mark Twain: The Fate of Humor* [Princeton: Princeton UP, 1966]; Robinson, *In Bad Faith: The Dynamics of Deception in Mark Twain's America* [Cambridge: Harvard UP, 1986]). Building on Cox's interpretation of the novel's "joke" ending, Robinson maintains that "reader-response to *Huckleberry Finn* recapitulates [the] complex cultural pattern" of evasion that dominates the Bricksville episode (163). As I understand our disagreement, Robinson and I are essentially describing

two sides of the same coin, and describing them very differently. I hear in the reader's collaborative effort an echo of the yarn-spinning community, a faint but distinctly affirmative reminder of the power that Twain associates with tacit interpretive activity, the power of being "always understood." Robinson, on the other hand, describes the same collaborative project as a "reciprocal deception of self and other," a joint effort by Mark Twain and his complicitous reader to "conceal problems of grave importance" (2). We seem to be interested in the same textual features, yet I do not think that our positions leave much room for agreement.

9. Samuel L. Clemens, "How to Tell a Story," *Selected Shorter Writings of Mark Twain*, ed. Walter Blair (Boston: Houghton Mifflin, 1962) 239.

10. Quoted in Fred W. Lorch, *The Trouble Begins at Eight: Mark Twain's Lecture Tours* (Ames: Iowa State UP, 1966) 219, 32.

11. Quoted in Lorch, *Trouble Begins at Eight* 32.

12. Quoted in Lorch, *Trouble Begins at Eight* 226.

13. Artemus Ward visited Virginia City in December 1863. For an account of the event, see Paul Fatout, *Mark Twain in Virginia City* (Bloomington: Indiana UP, 1964) 118–34.

14. Lorch, *Trouble Begins at Eight* 28–29.

15. John C. Gerber, "Mark Twain's Use of the Comic Pose," *PMLA* 77 (1962): 297.

16. Franklin R. Rogers offers the most useful discussion of the Twain–Brown character axis in *Mark Twain's Burlesque Patterns: As Seen in the Novels and Narratives, 1855–1885* (Dallas: Southern Methodist UP, 1960) 26–95.

17. Critics have often referred to Huck as a yarn spinner because he lies skillfully and often. In my view, this confuses an obvious distinction between the lie and the yarn, one of which is told for expediency and the other for entertainment.

18. Henry Nash Smith makes a related point when he explains that by turning the story over to Huck, Twain succeeded in "transforming the vernacular narrator from a mere persona into a character with human depth" (*Mark Twain: The Development of a Writer* [Cambridge: Harvard UP, 1962] 114).

19. Gerber, "Mark Twain's Use of the Comic Pose" 303.

20. Robinson has argued that the figure I call a "cultural insider" is in fact better understood as an accomplice in Mark Twain's ritual deception of self and other (*In Bad Faith* 179–80). He is certainly right to point out that the joint fictive project that interests us involves both embellishment and distortion. I would add only that the tall tale typically distorts reality as a backhanded way of celebrating actual conditions, often very difficult conditions that constitute the group's shared experience. In other words, a

yarn spinner transforms reality less as a way of evading its bitterness than as a way of celebrating the group's perseverance and endurance.

21. Wayne C. Booth, *A Rhetoric of Irony* (Chicago: U of Chicago P, 1974) 141.

22. Cox, *Mark Twain* 168–69.

23. Robert H. Hirst, ed., "Note on the Text," Clemens, *Huckleberry Finn*, ed. Blair and Fischer, 450. I follow Leo Marx in reading Huck's journey as essentially a quest for membership in a special kind of community, albeit a futile quest ("Mr. Eliot, Mr. Trilling, and Huckleberry Finn," *American Scholar* 23 [Autumn 1953]: 423–39). Cox speaks for Robinson and many other readers when he contends that Huck's journey "simply is not at any time a quest. A quest is a positive journey, implying an effort, a struggle to reach a goal. But Huck is escaping. His journey is primarily a negation, a flight *from* tyranny, not a flight toward freedom" (*Mark Twain* 172–73).

24. Kenneth Lynn makes the point that Huck plays a modified version of the role traditionally played by the "Self-controlled Gentleman" of southwestern humor in *Mark Twain and Southwest Humor* (Boston: Little, Brown, 1959) 213.

25. Everett Emerson makes this observation in *The Authentic Mark Twain: A Literary Biography of Samuel L. Clemens* (Philadelphia: U of Pennsylvania P, 1984) 137.

26. George Monteiro, "Narrative Laws and Narrative Lies in *Adventures of Huckleberry Finn*," *Studies in American Fiction* 13 (1985): 235.

27. Walter Blair, "The French Revolution and *Huckleberry Finn*," *Modern Philology* 55 (August 1957): 21–35; Blair, *Mark Twain and Huck Finn* (Berkeley: U of California P, 1960).

28. Harold H. Kolb, Jr., explores Huck's naive performance as a derivative instance of deadpan narration in *The Illusion of Life: American Realism as a Literary Form* (Charlottesville: UP of Virginia, 1969) 73–74. Mary K. Lee also observes a connection between the structure of the tall tale and Twain's method of exposing "societal inconsistencies and contradictions" in *Huckleberry Finn*. She maintains that "of course, the implied author anticipates a sophisticated understanding from his implied readers to judge these contradictions and inconsistencies. This code of operation is similar to that implicit in the tall tale, demanding as it does, vernacular language and a conscious awareness of the participation in a fictive world that recognizes the contradiction and duplicity of men and nature, and exemplifies it in form" (Lee, "The Overt, Unreliable, Naive Narrator in the Tall Tale and *Huckleberry Finn*," *Mark Twain Journal* 21 [1983]: 39).

29. Twain and the reader do conspire to produce what I have called an

unwritten text, but there are points in the novel where the implied author withholds information from his "interpretive cohort." The reader, for example, is as surprised as Huck when the drunken clown turns out to be an actor in Chapter 22. For a similar instance of deception by the implied author, see Keith Kraus's essay on *Huckleberry Finn*: "A Final Irony," *Mark Twain Journal* 14 (Winter 1967–68): 18–19.

30. In his theory of aesthetic response to literary texts, Wolfgang Iser describes the reader's interpretive activity as an effort to fill textual "gaps" and "indeterminacies." Iser's approach to "the phenomenology of reading," according to which "reader involvement coincides with meaning production," suggests a very close parallel with the dynamics of performance and response in the oral tall tale (*The Implied Reader* [Baltimore: Johns Hopkins UP, 1974]; *The Act of Reading: A Theory of Aesthetic Response* [Baltimore: Johns Hopkins UP, 1978]).

31. Twain's waning confidence in the privileged detachment of the yarn-spinning community may bear out Robinson's belief that such detachment is rooted in bad faith. Perhaps Twain eventually came to realize that underlying the dynamics of the tall tale are the inevitable dynamics of evasion and self-deception, a pattern of authorial disillusionment that gets played out, I would argue, in *Pudd'nhead Wilson*. In admitting this much, however, I do not think that we necessarily diminish the importance of the tall tale as a rhetorical structure in *Huckleberry Finn*.

Conclusion

1. Twain's projected outline for *A Connecticut Yankee* appeared in the New York *Sun* on November 12, 1886, and was reprinted in the Hartford *Courant* the next day (quoted in Howard G. Baetzhold, *Mark Twain and John Bull: The British Connection* [Bloomington: Indiana UP, 1970] 106).

2. Samuel L. Clemens, *A Connecticut Yankee in King Arthur's Court*, ed. Bernard L. Stein (1889; Berkeley: U of California P, 1979) 21. Subsequent page references to this edition appear in the text.

3. Howard G. Baetzhold provides the authoritative chronology for the novel's composition in "The Course of Composition of *A Connecticut Yankee*: A Reinterpretation," *American Literature* 33 (May 1961): 195–214.

4. Henry Nash Smith has suggested that Hank's Camelot, with its intellectual apathy and entrenched biases, its blend of cruelty and credulity, and its lazy pastoral landscape, bears a curious resemblance to Huck's Mississippi Valley (*Mark Twain: The Development of a Writer* [Cambridge: Harvard UP, 1962] 156–57).

5. Judith Fetterley, "Yankee Showman and Performer: The Character

of Mark Twain's Hank Morgan," *Texas Studies in Language and Literature* 14 (Winter 1973): 678.

6. Albert Bigelow Paine, *Mark Twain: A Biography*, 4 vols. (New York: Harper, 1912) 2:887–88.

7. Quoted in Louis J. Budd, *Mark Twain: Social Philosopher* (Bloomington: Indiana UP, 1962) 143.

8. Smith, *Mark Twain* 138.

9. Samuel L. Clemens, *Adventures of Huckleberry Finn*, ed. Walter Blair and Victor Fischer (1885; Berkeley: U of California P, 1985) 210.

10. Smith, *Mark Twain* 145.

11. Quoted in Baetzhold, *Mark Twain and John Bull*, 120.

12. Samuel L. Clemens, *Mark Twain's Notebook*, ed. Albert Bigelow Paine (New York: Harper, 1935) 195.

13. Samuel L. Clemens, "Personal Habits of the Siamese Twins," *Sketches Old and New* (Hartford: American Publishing, 1875) 211. Subsequent page references to this edition appear in the text. The history of Mark Twain's composition of *Pudd'nhead Wilson* has been documented in several important studies, none more thorough than Herschel Parker's *Flawed Texts and Verbal Icons: Literary Authority in American Fiction* (Evanston: Northwestern UP, 1984) 119.

14. Samuel L. Clemens, *Pudd'nhead Wilson and Those Extraordinary Twins*, ed. Sidney E. Berger (New York: Norton, 1980) 119. Episodes from the Morgan Manuscript pertaining to the Siamese twins appeared as a separate story in an appendix to the American Publishing Company's first edition of *Pudd'nhead Wilson*, issued on November 14, 1894. The story is reprinted in Berger's edition of the novel. Subsequent page references to the latter edition of both the novel and the story appear in the text.

15. I am not here referring to the celebrated "vestigia" of the Morgan Manuscript — that is, the passages that Twain inadvertently missed when he separated the twins during his final revision. George Feinstein was the first to comment in detail on remnants of the early tall tale that survive conspicuously in the published novel ("Vestigia in *Pudd'nhead Wilson*," *Twainian* [May 1942]: 1–3).

16. Daniel Morley McKeithan, *The Morgan Manuscript of Mark Twain's "Pudd'nhead Wilson"* (Cambridge: Harvard UP, 1961) 40.

17. Review of *Pudd'nhead Wilson* by Samuel L. Clemens, *The Athenaeum*, 19 January 1895, quoted in Frederick Anderson, ed., *Pudd'nhead Wilson/Those Extraordinary Twins* (San Francisco: Chandler, 1968) 7.

18. Evan Carton makes the point that Wilson's remark does more than imply "the interdependency of parts"; it "evidences this interdependency by the very structure of the communicative act that it initiates" ("*Pudd'nhead*

Wilson and the Fiction of Law and Custom," *American Realism: New Essays*, ed. Eric J. Sundquist [Baltimore: Johns Hopkins UP, 1982] 83).

19. James E. Caron observes that Pudd'nhead performs the role of the classical *eiron*, or self-deprecating man, a close relative of the deadpan yarnspinner of tall humor ("Mark Twain and the Tall Tale Imagination in America," diss., U of Oregon, 1983, 318).

20. George E. Toles, "Mark Twain and *Pudd'nhead Wilson*: A House Divided," *Novel* 16 (Fall 1982): 56.

21. Lee Clark Mitchell, "'De Nigger in You': Race or Training in *Pudd'nhead Wilson*?" *Nineteenth-Century Literature* 42 (1987): 312.

22. Toles, "Mark Twain and *Pudd'nhead Wilson*" 56. This general approach to the novel's inconsistencies has been challenged in a collection of recent essays (Susan Gillman and Forrest G. Robinson, eds., *Mark Twain's "Pudd'nhead Wilson": Race, Conflict, and Culture* [Durham: Duke UP, 1990]).

23. Walker Gibson, "Authors, Speakers, Readers, and Mock Readers," *College English* 11 (February 1950): 268.

24. Carton, "*Pudd'nhead Wilson* and the Fiction of Law and Custom" 93.

25. Samuel L. Clemens, *Mark Twain's Autobiography*, 2 vols., ed. Albert Bigelow Paine (New York: Harper, 1924) 1:xv–xvi.

26. James M. Cox, *Mark Twain: The Fate of Humor* (Princeton: Princeton UP, 1966) 265.

27. Samuel L. Clemens, "No. 44, The Mysterious Stranger," *Mark Twain's Mysterious Stranger Manuscripts*, ed. William M. Gibson (Berkeley: U of California P, 1969) 376.

28. Clemens, "No. 44," 273.

29. Samuel L. Clemens, *Personal Recollections of Joan of Arc* (New York: Harper, 1896) 32.

30. Cox, *Mark Twain* 263.

31. Clemens, *Joan of Arc* 461.

32. Clemens, "The Chronicle of Young Satan," *Mark Twain's Mysterious Stranger Manuscripts* 164.

33. Clemens, "Chronicle of Young Satan," 165–66.

34. Cox, *Mark Twain* 286.

Index